1) argument - author's main argument
2) How does slavery
3) How does women's treatment differ from men

Chained in Silence

Chained in Silence

Black Women and Convict Labor in the New South

Talitha L. LeFlouria

The University of North Carolina Press CHAPEL HILL

*Published with the assistance of the William Rand Kenan Jr.
Fund of the University of North Carolina Press.*

© 2015 The University of North Carolina Press
All rights reserved
Set in Espinosa Nova by Westchester Publishing Services
Manufactured in the United States of America

The paper in this book meets the guidelines for permanence and durability
of the Committee on Production Guidelines for Book Longevity of the
Council on Library Resources. The University of North Carolina Press
has been a member of the Green Press Initiative since 2003.

Jacket illustration: African American women prisoners in Georgia carry hampers
of beans. From the *Atlanta Journal-Constitution*, Nov. 3, 1940. © 1940. All rights
reserved. Used by permission of the Atlanta Journal-Constitution.

Complete cataloging information for this title is available from the Library of
Congress.

ISBN 978-1-4696-2247-7 (cloth: alk. paper)
ISBN 978-1-4696-2248-4 (ebook)

Portions of the text were previously published as " 'The Hand That Rocks the
Cradle Cuts Cordwood': Exploring Black Women's Lives and Labor in Georgia's
Convict Camps, 1865–1917," *Labor: Studies in Working-Class History of the Americas* 8,
no. 3 (Fall 2011): 47–63.

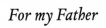

For my Father

Contents

Illustrations and Tables

Acknowledgments

There are not enough words to express my gratitude to those who have played such an instrumental role in the development of this work. My first thanks goes to God for making this book possible and for giving me the strength to persevere. To my editor, Brandon Proia, you embody everything a great editor ought to be: diligent, resourceful, supportive, and honest. Thank you for taking this study to new heights. You are amazing! To the University of North Carolina Press Justice, Power, and Politics series editors, Heather Ann Thompson and Rhonda Y. Williams, thank you for generously endorsing this project and for setting a high standard of excellence for me to aim toward. The two of you exemplify everything I could ever hope to be as a scholar, and I appreciate you more than you know.

I would like to extend major thanks to the two anonymous reviewers who invested so much time and attention into this project. Your insightful suggestions helped shape this book into everything it should be. Equal thanks go to the UNC Press Board of Governors and John Sherer, director of the press. I also thank editorial director Mark Simpson-Vos; Paul Betz, managing editor; Mary Caviness, assistant managing editor; Katherine Fisher, editorial assistant; Vicky Wells, director of contracts and subsidiary rights; Dino Battista, marketing director; Jennifer Hergenroeder, senior publicist; Susan Raines Garrett; and Melody Negron, senior production editor at Westchester Publishing Services. I feel extremely fortunate to have had the opportunity and pleasure to work with such a wonderful team.

Without the generous financial support of the Dorothy F. Schmidt College of Arts and Letters and the Department of History at Florida Atlantic University, this book may have never seen the light of day. Many thanks go to my colleagues in the history department and to the FAU Committee on Research and Other Creative Activity for awarding me a Scholarly and Creative Accomplishment postdoctoral fellowship to help further my research and publishing goals. I would like to also thank the many archivists who have assisted me throughout my research journey.

To Dale Couch, thank you for giving me my first introduction to the records of the Georgia Archives and for teaching me how to "think from the gut." I must admit, when you said this to me ten years ago it sounded a bit strange. But, over the years, I've come to understand what you meant; deep investigation is sometimes built on intuition. The gut is often wiser than the head. To past and present Georgia Archives staff members Anna Appleman, Steve Engerrand, and Amanda Mros, I also thank you for helping me uncover information I never thought to explore and for always lending your services with a smile.

Equal thanks go to several other archivists who have helped me in this process: Lynette Stoudt and Katharine Rapkin, Georgia Historical Society; Luciana Spracher and Virginia Blake, Savannah Municipal Archives; Richard Watson, Harry Ransom Center, the University of Texas at Austin; Meredith McDonough, Alabama Department of Archives and History; Traci JoLeigh Drummond, Southern Labor Archives, Georgia State University; and Ida Jones, Moorland-Spingarn Research Center. A very special thank-you goes to Peggy Galis for making my research trips to Elberton and Athens fruitful ones and for finding ways to get me access to places and records that my professional credentials could not. Also, to my research assistant, Lauren Silk, thank you for graciously rendering your services at a moment's notice and for helping me to get past the finish line.

Without my village of scholar-friends, mentors, and fabulous colleagues, I would be lost. To my sistah-scholars, Kennetta Hammond Perry, Deirdre Cooper Owens, LaShawn Harris, Sowandé Mustakeem, and Sasha Turner Bryson, thank you for your unwavering support and encouragement over the years. I appreciate you for celebrating with me in the high times and for picking me up during the low. I am truly grateful for our bond and for the opportunity to share real-life and professional experiences with you all.

To my professional mentors, role models, and supporters, Edna Greene Medford, Emory Tolbert, Daryl Michael Scott, Selwyn Carrington, Sharon Harley, Derrick White, Mark Rose, Catherine Clinton, Daina Ramey Berry, Kali Gross, Mary Ellen Curtin, Vivien Miller, Douglas Blackmon, Danielle McGuire, John Inscoe, Paul Ortiz, Pero Dagbovie, Cheryl Hicks, Rosalyn Terborg-Penn, Robert Chase, Norwood Andrews, Kristen Block, Evan Bennett, Glenn Eskew, LeeAnn Whites, Josephine Beoku-Betts, Jane Caputi, Cleavis Headley, Marina Banchetti, Sika Dagbovie Mullins, Jelani Favors, Sharita Jacobs, Daniel Broyld, and Regis Mann, I admire and appreciate you so much. Thank you for sharing your intellectual and professional wisdom and resources with me, encouraging me, and helping me to better understand my place in academia.

Quality feedback is crucial yet sometimes difficult to come by. Thank you, Beverly Bond, Kidada Williams, Elizabeth Hayes Turner, Jane Dailey, Janell Hobson, Barbara McCaskill, Freddie L. Parker, Francille Rusan Wilson, Heather Ann Thompson, Rhonda Y. Williams, Mary Ellen Curtin, Alex Lichtenstein, Khalil Muhammad, Donna Murch, Kelly Lytle Hernandez, Pippa Holloway, Robert Perkinson, Vivien Miller, Ethan Blue, David Hernandez, Volker Janssen, Catherine Lavender, Keramet Reiter, and Heather McCarty for reading and commenting on conference papers and/or essays in progress. Huge thanks also go to Douglas Blackmon, Sam Pollard, Daphne McWilliams, Catherine Allan, Sheila Curran Bernard, and Michelle Phillips. Working with you on the *Slavery by Another Name* documentary project was one of the highlights of my life and career. Thank you for inviting me to be a part of such a dynamic work and for giving the women in this study a small role on the main stage.

For all that I've accomplished professionally, I have achieved so much more in my personal relationships. I've been blessed with an amazing family and friends that have always supported and celebrated me. To the Johnson, LeFlouria, Isaac, and Baker clans, thank you for keeping me grounded, cheering me on, and loving me just because. To my mother, you have been an incredible source of strength, inspiration, and support. Thank you for pressing me to be my best self. To my father, thank you for introducing me to African American history and for planting early seeds of knowledge within me. I wish you were alive to see how much your little weed has grown. To Ed, thank you for helping me to see the value in education and for fathering me all of these years. You are my hero.

Ma and Pa Mich, thank you for always believing in me, encouraging me, and setting an example for me to follow. I am so fortunate to be your "Baby Doc." To all of my siblings (including you, Kamal), thank you for making me laugh and for never allowing me to give up. To my "sisters," Shonda, Anika, Alicia, Lea, Heather, Stacey, Ruquayya, Nicole, and Tanisha, and all of my sister-cousins and friends, thank you for praying for me, being an ear to listen, and for daring me to do things I never thought I could. Finally, to all of my nieces and nephews (biological and fictive) and my godbabies, D. J. and Lexi, everything I do is with you in mind. My greatest hope is that you will surpass me someday.

Chained in Silence

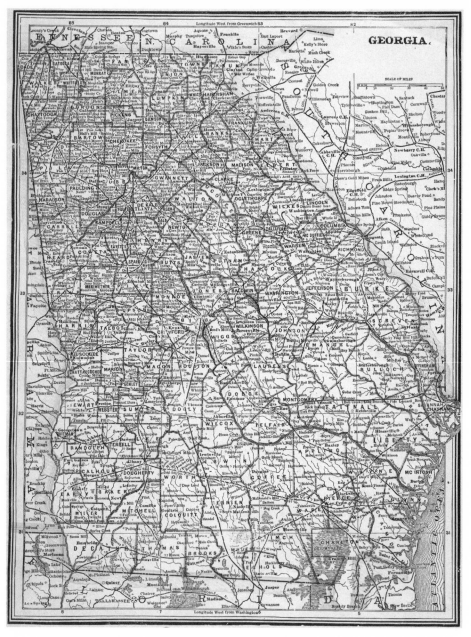

Map of Georgia, 1886. Courtesy of the Georgia Archives,
Vanishing Georgia Collection.

Prologue
Between Sound and Silence

This book is an effort to give voice to a group that has been too long silent. There was no greater inspiration for this effort than memories of my great-grandmother, a woman of quiet dissemblances, meaningful pauses, and reticence when it came to sharing "too much" about *the past*. Born in 1904 in Troup County, Georgia, to a family of sharecroppers, Grandma Leola had a mental strongbox filled with memories. Though occasionally she would unfetter her recollections and reveal the details of her life, there was much about her youth that never left that sacred container.

As a young girl, I spent many Saturday afternoons at my great-grandparents' charming little house on Harvest Lane. I would whiz through the front gate, with my mother trailing behind, and make my way to the front porch, where "Gramma" would be sitting on a sun-bleached wooden bench scouting the "purty cars," "rowdy chilluns," and strangers passing by. Among the neighborhood folks, she was renowned for her ability to wield an axe like a samurai, wring a chicken's neck with half a twist, turn fried meat with her bare hands, and flip blazing-hot cornbread into her leathery palms without scalding her flesh.

Our greeting was always the same: "Hi, Gramma!" "Hi, baby." Next she would bend down to hug me. Her skin looked and felt like chocolate pudding, and her powder-scented dresses gave off a faint scratching sound whenever she moved. Then I would tiptoe past her snuff can and spit bucket and take a seat on the bench. Now and then, Gramma would reach into her heart and offer me a tiny morsel of her life history.

I enjoyed watching the light come into Gramma's eyes as she proudly spoke about "birthin' all thirteen a dem chilluns" or of the days my great-grandfather spent "makin' a fool outta hisself" trying to woo her. She would say, "Yo' grampa was a purty man. All dem gals wanted em, but not me." Then an earthquake of laughter would shake her entire body. But when I would ask what it was like coming of age in Rough Edge—a rural farming town on the outer edge of LaGrange, Georgia—all that joy would vanish. A vulnerability would enter her eyes. She would run her wide fingertips against her wrinkled forehead. In a low, serious tone she would say things like, "Chile, them white folkses was sumthin' else in ma' day . . . Couldn't cross dem tracks after dark . . . Mama, Jessie Lee, Sallie Fannie, and Willie [her older siblings] wukked hard in dem fields cause ma' daddy gone dead . . . Me and Horace got us some schoolin' though . . . I got real good wit' ma' readin and writin.' Then I had to start helpin' out . . . We was real po' . . . But, when we got grown, we got us some famlies and we ain't neva get in no trouble. Naw, suh."

On this subject, Grandma Leola was never quite clear. Her sentences broke off and ran together, forcing me to read between obscure lines to understand her. When she died, at age ninety-five, she left me with more questions than answers. What unnamed indignities had she endured at the hands of southern "white folkses"? Why did she so esteem her reproductive power and find it essential to publicly reinscribe her femininity by conceiving and birthing many "chilluns"? Why, despite the racial and gendered barriers strewn in her path, did she dare to hope literacy would improve her ability to maneuver the rough terrain of poverty and exclusion? Why did she endorse a strict code of respectability almost exclusively steeped in obedience to law and order? And why did the specter of white racial hostility, violence, terror, and legal subjugation bewilder her recollections, causing her to conceal certain segments of *the past*?

In writing this book, I have studied my great-grandmother's pain and come face-to-face with more than a handful of excruciating truths. I found that Troup County, Georgia, the place Grandma Leola called home, was the headquarters for "the worst chain gang in Georgia." It was a place where "fearless, hardened men from other camps who had escaped and were recaptured, and those who were without friends or political aid" were brutalized for not "keeping the lick."[1]

Among these men was Robert Burns, a white northern miscreant whose classic exposé, *I Am a Fugitive from a Georgia Chain Gang*, revealed one part of the human tragedy taking place in Grandma Leola's backyard— but not all of it. The other side of that calamity forms the subject of this book.

In 1932, the year Burns's memoir was published, five black women were sentenced to hard labor on the Troup County chain gang. Nearly two hundred others were forced to toil in labor camps scattered throughout the state of Georgia. For nearly a century, the specter of mass imprisonment haunted black Georgians—women included. "Respectable" ladies like Grandma Leola, as well as the more rebellious echelon of freedom's daughters, were all burdened by southern injustice. They coexisted in a milieu where the threat of incarceration was omnipresent. Thus, *Chained in Silence* is as much an attempt to excavate the memories Grandma Leola dared to forget as it is an opportunity to give voice to the women still waiting to be heard.

Introduction

"Only Woman Blacksmith in America Is a Convict"

In 1896, Mattie Crawford was convicted of murder by a Meriwether County judge and sentenced to life imprisonment in the Georgia state penitentiary. She killed her stepfather, who, reportedly, abused her. One day, "when he came into the house she took up a chair and brained him with it."[1] Shortly after her sentencing, Crawford was transported fifty-five miles north to Atlanta to work in the remote environs of the Chattahoochee brickyard. The brick factory was her first destination in an elaborate sequence of forced migrations across the Georgia countryside. "After being there a while, her great strength and activity caused those in charge of her to plan heavy work for her. She expressed a desire to become a blacksmith and she was taught the trade."[2]

Crawford spent three years at the brickyard before being transferred one hundred miles southeast to the newly constructed state prison farm for women, adolescent boys, and "aged, infirm, and diseased" men in Milledgeville. She was quickly promoted to the rank of "trusty" and made sole blacksmith of the farm. Her privileged position within the penal colony allowed her to delicately tread unfreedom's rocky terrain and to circumvent the highly restrictive categories of "men's" and "women's" work. Crawford outclassed the best ironsmiths in Milledgeville, and she could "shoe a mule quicker than any man in the vicinity."[3] Yet she remained stranded between a free labor market that refused to admit her as a skilled worker and an open system of prison labor that would only allow her to work in chains.

Mattie Crawford's enigmatic presence within Georgia's penal system was made known to public audiences in 1903 after her story was profiled in the *Atlanta Constitution*. Reporter E. C. Bruffey's candid portrayal of his encounter with Crawford was accentuated with a photograph of the bondwoman dressed in men's "knickerbockers," suspenders, and a shirt made of "gray goods." She displayed her blacksmithing kit below a headline that read, "Only Woman Blacksmith in America Is a Convict." Crawford's reputation as a smith brought her attention in post–Civil War Georgia. But there are many less prominent members of the female prison population whose stories have remained untold and whose voices have been left unheard.

Prisoner Mattie Crawford posing with her blacksmithing kit at the Georgia state prison farm. From the *Atlanta Constitution*, August 19, 1903.

Chained in Silence tells the stories of the lived and laboring experiences of Georgia's (and the South's) most inconspicuous workforce—black convict women. This study follows African American female subjects across the matted landscape of New South Georgia, through freedom's sunlight, into the overcast of postemancipation life, and finally into the darkness of the state's convict camps. In doing so, this book chronicles how imprisoned women's lives and labors were ordered within Georgia's carceral polities, and it discloses how the mediums of space and economy influenced the gendered workings of involuntary servitude in the much touted "industrial capital" of the New South.

Within the cavernous hold of Georgia's state penitentiary system, black women's laboring bodies were tossed to and fro. Some landed on the northwest side of the "Empire State of the South" in the Dade coal mines, while others were set adrift in "flying" railroad camps and mobile chain gangs. A sizable cluster was crammed into Atlanta's already overcrowded brickyards, while the remainder soldiered through the sprawling pine forests and cotton fields of the Northeast. Everywhere they landed, terror and violence pursued them. At the same time, public and private acts of resistance helped to sustain them during their journey through unfreedom's wild territory.

By taking on the underexplored subject of black female convict labor in the post–Civil War period, this study addresses important questions about the extent of African American women's contribution to the construction of New South modernity. Though limited in volume, black women prisoners were a fundamental asset in the development of Georgia's postbellum industries. They formed the nucleus of the state's African American female industrial workforce, which, at the present, remains overlooked in the historical literature. This study forces a scholarly reinterpretation of the occupational responsibilities held by southern black women, whose labor has been widely understood in binary terms. Most scholars have contended that the rigorous limitations placed on black women's work forced them into two distinct professional spheres—domestic service and field labor. Yet, within the convict lease and chain gang systems of Georgia, African American women's working roles were much more varied. To better understand black women's occupational strivings in the post–Civil War South, it is critical to include the less familiar narratives of the region's imprisoned female labor force.

This book advances the growing body of scholarship on poor working-class African American women in the postemancipation South. It builds on the works of scholars such as Sharon Harley, Jacqueline Jones, and Tera Hunter, who have made invaluable contributions to the study of wage-earning black women's lives and labors, and it presents new possibilities for interpreting African American women's social, economic, material, and legal status after the Civil War. *Chained in Silence* enriches the existing historiography by redefining the social context of black women's lived and laboring experiences in the First New South (1865–1920) and by incorporating female prisoners into the broader historical dialogue on black women workers in the postbellum period.[4]

In conjunction with existing studies of working-class black women's history, this book analyzes African American women's social and economic position in the postemancipation South as producers and objects of exploitation. But *Chained in Silence* ventures further, looking beyond freedom's fence into the peculiar domain of the convict camp. Although this work is partially centered on the lives and labors of wage-earning poor black women, it is chiefly invested in rebuilding the historical viewpoint of the unwaged, bound black female worker.

While *Chained in Silence* makes a critical intervention in the study of African American women's labor by tracing a clandestine population of black female industrial workers in the postemancipation South, this study also contributes to convict lease studies, where the paucity of scholarship on black female convict labor is most heavily felt. In recent decades, studies of the southern convict lease system have evolved, significantly, from a basic emphasis on the atrocities latent within the system to a more complex discussion of political economy, labor dynamics, and the conscious construction of neo-slavery.[5] The diverse scholarly productions of Matthew Mancini, Alex Lichtenstein, David Oshinsky, Karin Shapiro, Douglas Blackmon, Robert Perkinson, and Paul Ortiz, among others, have been extraordinarily influential in shaping scholars' understanding of the interplay between the social, economic, and political forces undergirding the convict labor systems of the New South. Yet these historians' works elude any in-depth discussion of women's experiences of confinement within the carceral regimes of the postemancipation South.

The lack of attention to black female prisoners and their strivings may stem from their limited numbers and/or overarching perceptions about their reduced profitability when compared with black men or from limitations wrought by the scarcity of historical evidence. Nonetheless, scholars such as Mary Ellen Curtin have found it important to question women's roles in the South's penal regimes. In her pathbreaking study, *Black Prisoners and Their World* (2000), Curtin reframes the historical discourse by exposing scholars, for the first time, to the lived and laboring experiences of black female felons who were forced to dwell among men in convict barracks, forged bonds with male inmates, and frequently resisted contractors who "treated them as servants and subordinates and punished them as brutally as they did men."[6]

Chained in Silence builds on Curtin's scholarship by recalling the terrifying social encounters, demoralizing living conditions, inhumane violence, and astonishing work-related abuses black female convicts endured in the New South. An exploration of women prisoners' vitality, commitment to resistance, and unwillingness to acquiesce to enforced dehumanization is another related focal point of this work. This study makes a stark differentiation between the exclusively domestic vocational roles of Alabama's female inmates and the highly diverse laboring expectations of Georgia's convict women. In Alabama's lease camps, where "gender conventions were respected," women did the cooking, cleaning, and sewing for male convicts in the prison mines and farms throughout the state, and they also labored as the personal servants of male wardens.[7] Conversely, Georgia's black female prisoners were decisively integrated into the male-dominated workforce and became a counterpart in the building of the New South. Whether working together or separately, bondwomen and bondmen assembled railroads, mined clay, fired bricks, chopped down trees, sawed lumber, built roads, plowed fields, and raised crops.

In the same way that this study reaches to the outermost margins of history to salvage the voices of imprisoned African American women, it also carves out new conjectural categories for them. Black bondwomen of the New South were not slaves in the antebellum sense of the term, or free people, but individuals stranded between two selves (one *free(d)* and one bound) and two Souths—one Old and one New. While the Old South model of violence, sexual abuse, overwork, absolute terror, and bondage was reproduced in the New South convict labor regimes, gendered nuances exist that complicate the thesis that convict leasing was simply a return to slavery.

Even though the language of the Thirteenth Amendment to the U.S. Constitution allowed for thousands of "duly convicted" African American men, women, and youth to be subjected to slavery or involuntary servitude "as a punishment for crime,"[8] subtle variances do exist between slavery and convict leasing. Significantly, these differences are firmly connected to black women's procreative engagement in the system. Convict leasing was not a heritable institution of slavery, nor did it rely on natural reproduction to grow its forces. In the production-driven convict lease and chain gang systems of Georgia, maternity was reviled in a way that it hadn't been before emancipation. Whereas in the Old South slavocracy reproduction was the linchpin for slaveholders' success, the New South fiscal model saw pregnancy and childbirth as threats to economic progress and productivity. Lessees relied on the state and counties rather than the women themselves to resupply their labor forces.

By reckoning with African American women's unique experiences of involuntary servitude in the postbellum South, this book encourages scholars to more deeply contemplate whether or not, and to what extent, convict labor was in fact "slavery by another name." It also recovers age-old debates concerning the degree of continuity and discontinuity between the Old and New Souths, and it places this discussion in a gendered framework. By way of their hybridized, agro-industrial laboring identity, which contrasted with the mono-industrial design of imprisoned men's work, black female convicts helped referee the contentious relationship between the Old and New Souths and fostered a contemporary balance between the Old South agrarian model and the New South industrial infrastructure.[9]

The "Empire State" of Georgia furnishes a fertile intellectual space to study female convict labor in the post–Civil War period. In the industrial headquarters of the New South, an extensive range of industries blossomed after the war, which commanded the indiscriminant energies of black prisoners—male and female—to labor in the state's brickyards, mines, sawmills, railroads, and farms. Yet the terms of African American women's labor were more oblique than their male counterparts' were. Black female felons' occupational duties oscillated between manual and skilled trades, alongside domestic and agricultural work. In like manner, misdemeanant women's labor transcended gendered borders.

In the historical colloquy on the "promise" of the New South, where convict lease studies have recently acquired a central voice, the study of black female prison labor adds a new tint to an otherwise achromatic portrait of New South modernity. This monograph situates black women as producers in the South's postwar industrial economy and as modernizing instruments. Besides shoring up monetary gains for lessees, African American women's presence within the industrially driven convict lease and chain gang systems of Georgia helped modernize the postbellum South by creating a new and dynamic set of occupational burdens and competencies for black women that were untested in the free labor market.

In Georgia, New South modernity was reflected not only in the industry that emerged from the state but also in the distinct laboring roles formed for black female prisoners. The barriers that had impeded ex-bondwomen and their daughters from moving beyond the fields and domestic service were unsuitable to Georgia's penal enterprises. Paradoxically, the mutability of Georgia's carceral structure thereby expanded the possibilities of black women's labor in the New South while, simultaneously, immobilizing female detainees.

Nearly from the point of its inception in 1868, Georgia's convict lease system was unisex. Following a decision made by the General Assembly, to decentralize the prison population, "all able-bodied convicts" (women included) were legally parceled out to a series of private industries and farms. Unlike today's brick-and-mortar carceral facilities, Georgia's state penitentiary had no walls. Instead it was composed of independently operated lease camps, governed by a syndicate of private contractors, "whipping bosses," and guards at the behest of the state.

On May 11, 1868, provisional governor Thomas Ruger granted the first lease of convicts to William A. Fort of the Georgia and Alabama Railroad. Despite the subsequent deaths of numerous prisoners, the state government deemed the trial lease a success and, in doing so, sealed the fate of Georgia's future felons. Motivated entrepreneurs such as William Grant and Thomas Alexander wasted no time casting their bids on the state's rentable labor force. In December 1868, the duo procured 113 bodies from the state. Six months later, all 393 felons of the Georgia state penitentiary were "farmed out" to the Grant, Alexander, and Company contracting firm to labor on the Macon & Brunswick Railroad. Thirteen female convicts were included in the roundup and were immediately put to work in the "cuts," where they graded surfaces for railroads, shoveled dirt, and drove carts.[10]

Between 1868 and 1908, the operating years of Georgia's convict lease system, more than two thousand felons cycled in and out of the state's private camps. Lessees exploited the energies of an average of 1,991 prisoners each year, nearly 90 percent of whom were black men. African American women, on the other hand, made up only 3 percent of all leased felons, but they represented more than 98 percent of the female prison population. As shown in Table 1, between 1873 and 1908 (excluding missing years), an average of fifty black female convicts labored annually in Georgia's private lease camps; twice as many labored in its public chain gangs.[11]

More than 90 percent of long-term female felons were convicted of burglary and violent crimes, such as murder, attempted murder, manslaughter, assault, and arson.[12] By the same token, roughly 95 percent of African American male prisoners were sentenced for property- and violence-related offenses, including robbery, burglary, murder, attempted murder, rape, attempted rape, and manslaughter. Comparable sentences were doled out to both groups, whose prison terms were rarely set below five years. In fact, by the fall of 1900, nearly one-fourth of Georgia's black prison population (and more than half of its female population) would be condemned to life imprisonment.

By 1874, several new companies were added to the state's roster of lessees. Among these was Joseph E. Brown's Dade Coal Company. A former governor, ex-senator, and entrepreneur, Brown built his wealth through the production of Georgia coal. More than one hundred convicts (mostly African American men) were placed under his charge and forced to toil within the subterranean world of the Dade mines. Aboveground, a pocket-

TABLE 1 Number of Male and Female Felony Convicts Leased from 1873 to 1908

Date	White Male	White Female	Black Male	Black Female	Total	Percentage of Black Women
1873	89	1	505	19	614	3.19
1874	90	1	805	30	926	3.34
1876	114	0	954	40	1,108	3.74
1879	120	1	1,078	31	1,230	2.58
1880	114	1	1,041	30	1,186	2.59
1882	112	1	1,100	30	1,243	2.47
1884	125	1	1,218	33	1,377	2.45
1886	148	1	1,337	41	1,526	2.76
1888	149	0	1,336	52	1,537	3.5
1890	168	0	1,478	42	1,694	2.54
1892	194	2	1,690	54	1,940	2.86
1893	185	2	1,917	64	2,186	3.0
1894	189	2	2,069	68	2,328	3.0
1895	213	1	2,144	66	2,424	2.79
1896	192	1	2,098	66	2,357	2.88
1897	196	1	1,981	57	2,235	2.61
1898	239	2	1,941	55	2,228	2.53
1899	245	3	1,885	68	2,210	3.6
1900	255	—	1,925	—	2,180	—
1901	252	—	1,908	—	2,160	—
1902	252	—	1,978	—	2,230	—
1904	249	—	1,973	—	2,222	—
1905	284	—	1,908	—	2,192	—
1906	207	—	2,052	—	2,259	—
1907	272	—	2,114	—	2,386	—
1908	315	—	2,175	—	2,490	—

size female workforce was assembled to carry out domestic duties. In Brown's mining camps, the work-related obligations of female prisoners mimicked the professional roles of city-dwelling black women in the free labor market. Yet the application of wholly feminine modes of labor in Georgia's lease camps was more an exception than a norm.

During the 1880s, coal and iron production, railroad construction, and brick manufacturing became the prevailing industries that ordered the greatest use of male and female prison labor. By the 1890s, James W. English, a member of Georgia's political elite, gained a foothold on the state's lucrative bricking industry. At the turn of the twentieth century, the Chattahoochee Brick Company (of which English was a majority stakeholder) controlled more than half of Georgia's leased convicts. Not unlike his peers, the lessee made no explicit distinction between the laboring obligations of male and female convicts. Women prisoners were called on to perform any combination of duties: cooking and cleaning camp kitchens, digging clay, mixing raw materials, firing brick, transferring processed goods to a pallet to be shipped off to waiting patrons, gardening, making brooms, or even blacksmithing.

Within the broader matrix of the state's convict leasing enterprise, contractors subjectively established the terms of women's labor. The work-related needs of individual contractors, and not a collective recognition of gender positions, ultimately influenced the types of occupational duties female prisoners were impressed to perform. Lessees hired out of economic necessity and, when expedient, prescribed labor duties that were often arbitrary and non-gender-exclusive. Such was the case at Camp Heardmont, the first centralized female prison camp in the state of Georgia.

At Camp Heardmont, William H. Mattox employed a three-tiered approach to convict leasing: industrial, agricultural, and domestic. Women prisoners plowed fields, sowed crops, paddled through rivers of cotton, felled trees, sawed lumber, ran gristmills, ginned cotton, forged iron, cooked meals, cleaned camp quarters, and washed their faded stripes. Mattox's prison camp is one of the most lucid examples of how black female convict labor, under the guise of *reform*, was used to promote New South modernity.

Between 1892 and 1899, Camp Heardmont was one of the most prosperous penal farms in Elbert County. Mattox's (artificial) dedication toward reforming women prisoners did not go unnoticed by statewide officials. He was praised for transforming female felons into competent workers and for pounding morality into their "dark" souls. But, in 1899, the state decided to reclaim its valuable female property from the lessee and to transfer its cargo to a newly established prison farm in Milledgeville, the former state capital. It would take all seventy-one hands on deck to build one of Georgia's most profitable public penal settlements.

As if the unremitting slog of hard labor in the state's camps was not unbearable enough, female inmates were tormented by violence. With no protection, these women were left vulnerable to the predations of white whipping bosses (overseers), guards, camp doctors, and lessees who used acts of physical and sexual force to punish, control, and terrorize female victims. Some inmates were flogged in public acts of humiliation and torture, while others were sexually attacked in barns, storehouses, and other secret spaces. *Chained in Silence* stresses the inexorable violence that circumscribed African American women's lives in Georgia's postbellum prison camps, and it pairs this reality with the broader experience of terror that unbound black women were forced to bear.

Recent studies such as Hannah Rosen's *Terror in the Heart of Freedom* (2009), Crystal Feimster's *Southern Horrors* (2009), and Kidada Williams's *They Left Great Marks on Me* (2012) have made important advancements in the historical literature by formulating gender-based conclusions on the hostile suppression of black citizenship rights, as well as the conquest of freedwomen's economic and social mobility on bodily terms. While these explorations are paramount to the study of sexualized violence, lynching, and the intersection of race, class, and gender, they exclude any mention of the South's most defenseless victims—black female convicts. By integrating a discussion on gendered violence in Georgia's convict camps, this study provides scholars with a total understanding of how enmity and terror affected black women's lives in the postemancipation South.

As an extension of the developing discourse on violence and its ineradicable presence in the lives of African American women, *Chained in Silence* also considers, for the first time, how medical terror impacted female inmates in the New South. In Georgia's penal camps, black women prisoners were forcibly subjected to intrusive medical procedures and had their sexuality, as well as their gynecological and obstetric health, displaced into the hands of white southern physicians. Prison camp doctors with mediocre experience were hired to attend to the general medical needs of ailing convicts and to manage the delicate health concerns of female patients. Expounding on historian Marie Jenkins Schwartz's claim that, after emancipation, the withdrawal of white physicians from service to the black community provided freedwomen a chance to gain control over their bodies, and to recoup the ability to manage pregnancy, childbirth, and other health-related issues on their own terms, this study reflects one way in which medical power was restored in the postbellum South.[13]

Distinct continuities exist between the gynocentric medical struggles enslaved and incarcerated black women endured. Like female slaves, women prisoners were powerless against lessees and medical men who made subjective choices about how to address gynecological health matters. Prison camp officials were attuned to antebellum suppositions about bondwomen's reproductive health and its impact on labor productivity and, thereby, sought medical intervention to enhance productiveness—but *not* reproductivity—among female convicts.

In opposition to the rough assaults on their bodies, pride, and personhood, black women prisoners vigorously resisted encroachments on their dignity and pushed back against the systemic forces that threatened to subtract their humanity. Each act of resistance administered by a female captive, whether large or small, individual or collective, was a hopeful gesture toward preserving her self-worth within an inhumane system built on terror and control. Bondwomen set fires, ran away, malingered, disobeyed orders, fought camp guards, cursed their superiors, and destroyed property. In an effort to combat compulsory defeminization, some inmates resorted to burning their stripes. The practice of clothing arson, in particular, represents one of several imperceptible narratives of "everyday resistance" found in this monograph. Drawing on what historian Stephanie Camp views as the "enormous possibilities for understanding the meanings of actions [like burning clothes] that might otherwise appear to be little more than fits of temper,"[14] this study acknowledges, interprets, and appreciates the art of day-to-day resistance crafted by bondwomen in all spatial categories of captivity (plantations, convict lease camps, chain gangs, etc.) and at all levels of unfreedom.

While labor, violence, and resistance are the issues that form the high tide of this study, criminality has an important place in this work. Building on historians Kali Gross's and Cheryl Hicks's formative histories of black female crime and punishment in the urban North, *Chained in Silence* trails the footprints of black female lawbreakers across the southern landscape. By outlining the distinct social variables that impelled black women to commit acts of violence and vice in Georgia, one is better able to determine how white racial hostility, sexual violence, economic oppression, and occupational exclusion, all centered within a polluted legal atmosphere, accelerated the rise of black female crime in the rural and urban centers of the New South.

In the aftermath of the Civil War, African American women were left with few options: work for little or nothing, or endure the harsh legal penalties awaiting black female vagrants. Working-class black women that migrated to southern cities, such as Macon, Atlanta, Savannah, Augusta, and Columbus, to escape white violence and to explore new economic opportunities reluctantly joined the domestic labor force. Unfortunately, household service placed freedwomen proximally closer to white families and replicated the antebellum cycles of racial subordination and exploitation. Servants were reintroduced to job-related abuses, including excessive work hours, unfair wages, and physical and verbal assault. Sexual violence also persisted in white households, deepening freedwomen's contempt for domestic service. While some exercised political agency through the act of quitting, others resorted to petty theft to settle scores with their employers. Black domestics salaried themselves by stealing food, jewelry, cookware, clothing, money or any other commodities that they could use or sell to bolster their fragile incomes, feed their children, and keep their households afloat.

Though the extent of black female crime did not stop at petty theft, nor was it confined to the urban sphere, larceny was the most prevalent offense committed by freedwomen in the postemancipation South. The consequences could vary widely as a result of white employers' and legal officials' divergent interpretations of theft. Taking leftover table scraps, in a practice commonly referred to as "pan-toting," was unlawful in some households and permissible in others. Legal officials uniformly supported and defended white supervisors by convicting, fining, jailing, and placing thousands of black female misdemeanants to work on local chain gangs. Female felons who committed violent crimes, such as assault, attempted manslaughter, or murder, occasioned by self-defense, fatal altercations, and so on, met a much more dismal fate. These women were sentenced to serve lengthy prison terms or condemned to a lifetime of confinement in the state penitentiary system.

Chained in Silence draws on a wide array of sources that, when combined, form an atlas for mapping imprisoned black women's lives and labors across the New South. An amalgam of primary documents, including applications for executive clemency, prison registers, principal keepers' and principal physicians' annual and biennial reports, annual reports of the Georgia Prison Commission, prison camp hospital registers, monthly reports of corporal punishment ("whipping reports"), grand jury presentments, misdemeanor chain gang monthly reports, rare trial transcripts, census records, testimonies of ex-slaves, southern medical journals, and newspaper articles, in addition to an interdisciplinary set of secondary sources, was welded together to form this study. But mining southern black women's voices from below has proven no easy task. Illiterate and semiliterate female convicts left no diaries and very few written records behind.

Official documents, such as prison records, provide the basic quantitative, demographic, and administrative proofs essential to the writing of this history. Annual and biennial reports of the Principal Keeper and Prison Commission, for example, furnish elemental data about incarcerated women: first and last name, race, age, crime and county of conviction, date convicted, length of sentence, and the number of an individual's assigned prison company. Convict registers replicate this function but occasionally inject physical descriptions—weight, height, health status at the point of intake, and identifiable scars or other distinguishable features (e.g., missing teeth), as well as the name of the lessee to whom the female inmate has been rented.

Within the official record, the most revelatory accounts of the management of imprisoned women's bodies are to be found in clemency applications. These sources provide lucid details concerning the arrest, conviction, incarceration, pardoning, and commutation of prison and jail terms for Georgia's felony and misdemeanant offenders. Moreover, these records disclose the injurious impact of convict labor on the black female body. Principal physicians' reports and hospital registers supplement the medically related information found in clemency requests, conveying the overall health conditions found in the state's private lease camps, cataloging the frequency and manner of illnesses detected among felony inmates, and tallying the number of reported deaths.

"Whipping reports" describe an additional administrative instrument that was used to regulate prisoner behavior. They serve to inventory the acts of violence and terror that took place inside Georgia's convict lease camps. Whipping bosses, hired by lessees and endorsed by the state, meticulously notated every "stroke" and "stripe" tendered by the lash, and they cited the name of every wrongdoer and the content of his or her misdeed(s). Bosses also chronicled their use of alternative methods of discipline—the "water cure," sweat box, "blind mule," and so on. Yet, in the process of cataloguing brutality, these "overseers" (as they were also called) unintentionally publicized black female prisoners' resistance.

Though "whipping reports" have been classically read as narratives of cruelty and suffering, these sources actually serve an important additional function. After reassessing the historical record, it becomes clear that resistance is as well documented as violence is. By examining the types of offenses for which bondwomen and girls were punished, as opposed to scrutinizing the processes of punishment alone, one is better able to ascertain the habits of dissent cultivated among female incarcerees while, at the same time, gathering wisdom about the nature of gendered and racialized violence in Georgia's private lease camps.

While official archival prison records furnish the data necessary to pinpoint, catalogue, and synopsize black women's travails within the carceral state, these sources are often fragmented, negligent, and reductive, and they offer no detailed description of events, circumstances, or even verbal expressions made by female captives. In essence, southern black women's voices are muted and their lived and laboring experiences encapsulated inside the official record. Consonant with historian Kali Gross's judgment on the investigative techniques essential to the writing of histories of black female incarceration, this study calls for the application of a "comprehensive methodology" that merges traditional archival research with an "elastic" analytical framework.[15] Newspaper articles are what loosen the otherwise contracted body of available historical evidence.

In spite of the political shortcomings of conservative white newspapers that often hyperbolized and pathologized black female criminality, these articles offer rare clues and testimonies that are often unavailable elsewhere. Unfortunately, the methodological strategies used in studies where there is an abundant pool of evidence to draw from are not as easily applied in the subfields of convict labor studies and working-class African American women's history. In my effort to extract new meaning from the broken body of sources that does exist, I am, as scholar Saidiya Hartman puts it, endeavoring to "embody life in words," while, at the same time, respecting what we cannot know.[16]

In this narrative, I capitalize on urban dailies such as the *Atlanta Constitution*, *Macon Telegraph*, *Columbus Daily Enquirer*, and *Augusta Chronicle* for their evidentiary value, especially when the information aligns with what is presented in the official record. While these sources are in fact "double-edged," they permit access into the interior world of black female prisoners living and laboring in Georgia's convict camps. Plus, the sensationalist and muckraking appeal implicit in these periodicals is beneficial when it comes to exposing the hidden horrors of the state's convict lease and chain gang systems. As a whole, newspaper articles—despite their provenance—fill in the gaps of this splintered history.

In five chapters, *Chained in Silence* unpacks the critical histories of black female convicts in the New South. Chapter 1, "The Gendered Anatomy of 'Negro Crime,'" traces the contours of African American life in post-emancipation Georgia and centers on the convergence of racism, poverty, violence, legal injustice, and social anarchy that exacerbated the "problem" of "Negro crime." In this chapter, I dissect the late nineteenth-century and early twentieth-century pseudoscientific and criminological explanations for black crime, and I examine how scientific racism, notions of sexual deviance, and misconstructions of African American womanhood and manhood helped engineer an imaginary black criminal class.[17]

In chapter 1, the problem of "Negro crime" in the white southern imagination is juxtaposed against the authentic issues that nourished the growth of Georgia's rapidly expanding black criminal population. Legitimate acts of violence and vice among black female lawbreakers are particularly assessed by examining the types of crimes these women committed and the motivations governing expressions of lawlessness among female offenders. This chapter also explores how white Georgians mobilized to curtail black crime and to restrict the social, political, and economic autonomy of freedmen and freedwomen through the inception of a state-sponsored system of convict leasing.

Chapter 2, "Black Women and Convict Leasing in the 'Empire State' of the New South" underscores the centrality of prison labor in fulfilling the postbellum vision of modernization and industrial prosperity. According to Henry Woodfin Grady, a prominent Georgian and proverbial "spokesman" of the New South, industrialization was to benefit whites, exclusively, and industrial progress would hinge on the perpetuation of white supremacy. Consequently, the apparatus of convict leasing was put in place to secure racial hegemony and to dispossess freedwomen and freedmen of their newly acquired liberties. This chapter examines how local and state politicians, as well as southern speculators, communally orchestrated the convict lease system of Georgia, and it unfurls the tightly shrouded existence of black female felons who labored, indiscriminately, within the state's male-dominated private lease camps. Illustrations of violence, rape, disease, and medical exploitation are used to exhibit how these complex variables complicated bondwomen's survival. This chapter also emphasizes the resistance strategies implemented by female convicts, who individually and collectively challenged physical, sexual, and economic exploitation in an act to preserve their humanity and self-respect.

During the 1890s, Georgia industrialists struggled to maintain the vision of New South prosperity while negotiating female felons' place within the state's convict lease system. Southern entrepreneurs were forced to regulate their industrial aspirations to accommodate a growing public and political desire to see black women prisoners moved beyond the bounds of masculine confinement and utilized in more traditional customs of labor (e.g., farming and domestic work). The presence of female convicts in male-dominated prison camps, and the said "immorality" of combining the sexes, influenced the earliest efforts toward penal reform. Chapter 3, "The Hand That Rocks the Cradle Cuts Cordwood: Prison Camps for Women," charts the transition of women prisoners from sexually integrated railroad camps, brickyards, and mines into feminine carceral spaces, and chronicles the life-world of female captives detained within these gender exclusive settlements.

By 1899, Georgia's convict lease system was at the center of local and national debate over the welfare of its inmates, its threat to free labor, and the enduring exploitation of female captives, even in female-centered labor camps. For more than a decade, the condition of women prisoners in the state's private lease camps was a contested public policy issue, which ultimately culminated in the Georgia General Assembly's decision to relocate all female felons to a newly erected state prison farm in Milledgeville. The establishment of the state farm, and not the decentralization of the statewide chain gang system, signified the first major modernizing step toward reforming Georgia's penal enterprises. Thus, the modernization of the state's prison system was partially anchored in the laboring body of African American women prisoners.

Chapter 4, "Sustaining the 'Weak and Feeble': Women Workers and the Georgia State Prison Farm," outlines the development of Georgia's state prison farm, and explores how black female convicts helped transform the public industrial plantation into a "self-sustaining" entity by assuming the burden of fieldwork, effecting skilled trades, and assisting the male inmates, most of whom were "by reason of age, infirmity, or disease, incapable of performing necessary labor," and by supporting the scant population of white women prisoners who were enfeebled by their race. Black female felons were the state farm's most vital asset and its most productive and skilled source of labor. Just as black male captives formed the backbone of the state's industrial penal enterprises, African American women prisoners buttressed the agro-industrial penal complex of the New South.

In the fifth and final chapter, "Broken, Ruined, and Wrecked: Women on the Chain Gang," readers are introduced to Georgia's most bountiful, yet barely discernible, population of black female convicts. Over a period of several decades, thousands of misdemeanant women forcibly expanded the vision of New South modernization by building roads, harvesting turpentine, and laboring in various public works projects. Yet their inner lives remain hidden in the shadows of male convicts. This chapter demystifies the private world of Georgia's female chain gang workers and explores how short-term misdemeanant black women's lives were fashioned within the state's county and municipal labor camps and stockades.

The female misdemeanant experience in New South Georgia has proven that if convict leasing was "worse than slavery," then the chain gang was worse than convict leasing. Like female felons, minor offenders' lives were distinguished by perennial work routines, cosmic exploitation, and neglect. Chain gang operators sought to compress a large quantity of labor into a compact sentence. As a result, female chain gang laborers disproportionately suffered with serious health concerns.

This chapter addresses the "broken, ruined, and wrecked" unprofitable black female body, and it underscores how injury and illness were often persuasive in securing affirmative clemency rulings and medical pardons. The exoneration of feeble, unproductive women workers was, in most cases, steered by the economic infeasibility of maintaining sick laborers, who were incapable of expanding local economies and unable to provide for the state's physical and monetary advancement. Conversely, the demand for a productive, cheap labor force sometimes negated affirmative clemency rulings for able-bodied female convicts. This last chapter encourages scholars to consider both the profitable *and* unprofitable, productive *and* unproductive black female worker in the broader interrogation of the New South convict labor systems.

CHAPTER ONE

The Gendered Anatomy of "Negro Crime"

At the Rising Fawn prison mine, tucked away in the foothills of Dade County, Carrie Massie, "a sixteen-year-old Negro girl," built her home in the depths of despair. The young woman's ordeal began in 1882, when she was convicted of murdering William Evans, a well-known owner of a general store in the town of Summerfield near Macon, Georgia. On the night of the killing, Bill Carstarphen, a black man, heard groans emanating from the shop. He roused the neighborhood and convened a small posse to guard the store. When members of the crowd forced the door open, "a ghastly sight met their view." Mr. Evans was lying on a bed in the rear of the building. His head was "crushed in as if by several blows of an axe, and the bed clothes fearfully saturated with this blood."[1]

The small crowd combed every corner of the store looking for Evans's assailant. Carrie Massie was reportedly discovered "hid away beside a pile of shucks. She was pulled out of her hiding place, and her apron and bonnet were found to be spotted with blood."[2] News of the murder spread swiftly throughout the community. A large mob assembled at the scene of the killing, and a proposition was made to lynch Massie. However, the "calm voice of a minister of the gospel was heard and the mob reluctantly abandoned the project."[3]

Sheriff Wolcott escorted Massie to the county jail, where a reporter was standing by to collect a statement from the sixteen-year-old girl about the murder. "What made you kill him?" asked the journalist. "I didn't kill him. I don't know nothing about it . . . I ain't killed nobody," replied Massie. She went on to explain:

> I went away from Macon last night on the train, and you can ask the conductor if I didn't. I got off there at Summerfield, and I was going to see some people that I knowed. It was so dark and cold that I didn't want to be out there in the woods by myself, so I goes to Mr. Evans' store and knocks. Mr. Evans comes to the door, and I tells him that I want to come in and stay til morning . . . When the train came by [about three o'clock] I saw a man strike a match. I thought he was in the store all the time, and after awhile I heard the

licks on Mr. Evans and heard him say "oh Lord." Then I heard somebody on the outside, and I was so scared I didn't know what to do. When daylight came I heard the crowd outside say they would kill the first person that came out of the store and I hid behind the shucks, and that's all I know about it.[4]

Massie's declaration of innocence fell on deaf ears. Recognizing the hopeless nature of her circumstances, she challenged authorities to "just do what you please with me—I don't care."[5] Notwithstanding the fact that, prior to her indictment, she had never been accused (let alone convicted) of committing or conspiring to commit any act of violence, the young woman was forced to exchange her bloodstained dress for a striped one and to toil in Georgia's ruthless convict lease system.

Carrie Massie's ordeal is part of a larger story of black women's suffering in the post–Civil War South. Freedwomen and their daughters' lives were broadly circumscribed by racial hostility, violence, terror, poverty, and exclusion. The confluence of these menacing social and economic forces, combined with a predatory legal establishment, fostered a fertile environment for notions of black female crime to emerge. During this era, rising criminal delinquency, whether real or imagined, provoked a heightened degree of speculation and anxiety among white sheriffs, magistrates, politicians, anthropologists, criminologists, physicians, and "common folks" eager to diagnose and *treat* the universal cause(s) of Negro criminality.

The body of "Negro crime"—a wicked subcategory of race-based criminality—was first autopsied by white ideologues whose dubious conclusions exposed racial and gendered prejudices and a desire to create causal links between the Negro's moral, mental, sexual, and biological "inferiorities" and his or her "inherent" predisposition toward delinquency. Although rhetorically and literarily centered, racist doctrine played an influential role in feeding white southerners' mounting public obsessions over the proliferation of "Negro crime," and it was a persuasive tool used to promote and rationalize the mass imprisonment of ex-slaves and their progeny after the Civil War.

During the same time that white "truth seekers" picked and probed to discover and authenticate a racialized basis for black criminality, African American social scientists such as W. E. B. Du Bois sliced through thick layers of fabricated data. They found that misdiagnoses of inborn criminal deviance and hereditary debauchery rested beneath what black intellectuals and reformers, including women, considered to be the true causes of Negro criminality: poverty; racism; lack of social, political, and economic opportunity; depraved social surroundings; and the consuming effects of "strong drink." Even so, in the midst of this complex and protracted effort to expose the infectious root of "Negro crime," poor working-class black women in Georgia desperately fought to survive and fashion their lives anew in the "empire state" of the New South.

At Freedom's Gate

When freedom arrived on the front porch of the Turner Plantation in Wilkes County, Georgia, some slaves "rejoiced so they shouted, but some didn't, they was sorry."[6] Adeline Willis personally decided "not to leave my white folks," and, instead, opted to stay on the plantation as a servant. Across the way, in Twiggs County, Frances Willingham rejoiced: "I'se Sho' glad Mr. Lincoln set us free." But her joy soon turned to dismay when she measured the cost of freedom. Instead of striking out to the city and leaving the modest material comforts of the plantation behind, she "stayed on and wukked for Old Marster, cause dere warn't no need to leave and go to no other place. I was raised up for a field hand and I ain't never wukked in no white folks house."[7]

In the aftermath of emancipation, the meanings of freedom held by Georgia's four hundred thousand ex-slaves were multifarious. For some, freedom meant the ability to move about freely without the threat of the lash and the right to define the terms of one's labor. For others, acquiring land, attaining access to education, gaining the privilege of political participation (for black men), exercising religious freedom, and reuniting with loved ones was of paramount importance. Forasmuch as slavery had done to break the physical ties of kinship, the deeper emotional ties formed between bondpeople persevered. Some placed advertisements in black newspapers in hopes of relocating family members. Others relied on word of mouth, or benefited from the compassions of Freedmen's Bureau officials who supported their reunification efforts. But for most, freedom meant stability. The complexities, uncertainties, and expense of relocation acted like quicksand, suctioning freedpeople's feet to southern soil.

During the postemancipation period, approximately 90 percent of African Americans remained in the rural South. Most former slaves worked as sharecroppers and tenant farmers on land owned by ex-planters, and they toiled desperately to eke out a basic living. In the countryside, a substantial number of freedwomen could be found working together with their spouses, digging, hoeing, and chopping in the fields, in addition to performing domestic duties—cooking, tending to children, sewing, laundering, or slaughtering livestock.[8]

Life for ex-slaves residing in rural territories was fraught with challenges. Poverty forced destitute freedmen and freedwomen into contractual agreements with ex-planters, many of whom were their former owners. Sharecropping provided a convenient labor option for landless freedpeople who did not benefit from the federal government's failed plan of land redistribution.[9] Those who opted to remain in the fields were paid in monthly wages or a share of the crop produced, and they were provided with shelter, seeds, tools, and other commodities essential to labor production. While the sharecropping system did not fill the void of independent land ownership, it did create a semblance of normalcy for black families and a basic opportunity for survival.

In Georgia, 80 percent of freedmen and freedwomen inhabited rural counties. Yet, a sizable percentage of married freedwomen that lived in farming communities abandoned fieldwork altogether to focus on the interests of their households, fulfill their maternal duties, and to elude the threat of sexual violence by detaching themselves from the immediate supervision of white men. By 1870, more than 60 percent of African American women residing in Dougherty County stayed at home.[10] While, as a rule, black women in rural Georgia found agricultural work inescapable, some wives (when possible) entrusted their husbands with the business of tilling the fields and reaping a livable wage for their families. One Georgia newspaper reported in 1869, that "the freedmen . . . have almost universally withdrawn their women and children from the fields, putting the first at housework and the latter at school."[11]

In chorus, white southerners aired their grievances over African Americans' desire for family independence, and the tendency among wives and mothers to reject wage labor in favor of attending to their own families. These women were "taken from the field to the shanty, to live the lady,"[12] much to the chagrin of planters, who bemoaned the loss of this valuable labor supply and bewailed the forfeiture of their long-standing authority over African American women's working bodies. When female ex-slaves in Georgia "all but retired from the fields" in the mid-1860s, their withdrawal escalated white landholders' fears about low agricultural productivity and black autonomy.[13]

Female sharecroppers getting their cotton weighed, Cobb County, Georgia, 1900. Courtesy, Georgia Archives, Vanishing Georgia Collection, cob013.

For freedmen and freedwomen who did choose to work the land, the sharecropping system retained the vestiges of slavery and perpetuated a system of racial subordination and forced labor that had existed before the war. The inability of black sharecroppers to meet their expected crop quotas, and satisfy their contractual obligations, resulted in bondage for those who could not leave the land until their debts were settled. To a large extent, the debt peonage system—a type of forced labor—restored hegemonic authority to white planters, giving them the legal power to purchase black farm labor from county courthouses.[14] The policies set forth in the Mississippi Black Code (1865) were implemented in all the southern states, Georgia included. Every civil officer was granted authority to "arrest and carry back to his or her legal employer any freedman, free negro, or mulatto who shall have quit the service of his or her employer before the expiration of his or her term of service without good cause."[15] It was left to the county magistrates to decide whether the "alleged deserter shall be remanded to the alleged employer or otherwise disposed of."[16]

On one plantation in Elbert County, Georgia, a freedman and his wife unknowingly "sold ourselves into slavery."[17] At war's end, the man was asked by his former owner to stay on for one year and work for shares. He consented and was given $3.50 per week and a one-room log cabin on the property. In the same year, he met and married his fiancée, Mandy, who worked as a house-servant for the "Captain" and his family. The couple upgraded to a two-room shack, which made the sharecropper feel like "the biggest man in Georgia." Overcome by his employer's seeming generosity, he renewed his contract consecutively for four more years. By the fifth year, however, his manager had died and left the plantation to a son, "a senator," who persuaded the fieldworker to sign a ten-year contract.

Shortly after signing the long-term contract, the sharecropper noticed that the senator began to assemble a long low-level shanty with rows of frames and stalls running through it. The structure, the man believed, would be utilized for holding horses. However, to his surprise, these were accommodations made for convicts who were hired to work on the farm alongside free laborers. In his words, "Nobody seemed to know what the Senator was fixing for. All doubts were put aside one bright day in April when about forty able-bodied negroes, bound in iron chains, and some of them handcuffed, were brought out to the Senator's farm in three big wagons."[18]

Six months later, a second stockade was erected and "twenty or thirty other convicts were brought to the plantation, among them six or eight women! . . . Most of the time the women who were peons or convicts were compelled to wear men's clothes. Sometimes, when I have seen them dressed like men and plowing or hoeing or hauling logs or working at the blacksmith's trade, just the same as men, my heart would bleed and my blood would boil, but I was powerless to raise a hand,"[19] said the farmhand. He also noticed that "of the first six women brought to the camp, two of them gave birth to children . . . and the babies had white men for their fathers!"[20]

In his ignorance to the letter of the contract, the "Negro peon" consented to a lifetime of indebtedness and bondage. He and his associates gradually learned, "We could not lawfully break our contract for any reason . . . and, more than that, if we got mad and ran away, we could be run down by bloodhounds, arrested without process of law, and be returned to our employer, who, according to the contract might beat us brutally or administer any kind of punishment that he thought proper."[21] On the senator's plantation, free laborers and convicts were expected to toil from daybreak to sunset. But, as the peon recalled it, his wife "fared better than [he] did, as did the wives of some of the other Negroes, because the white men about the camp used these unfortunate creatures as their mistresses . . . When I left the camp my wife had had two children by one of the white bosses, and she was living in fairly good shape in a little house off to herself."[22]

The Bittersweet Taste of Freedom

Freedom came at a heavy price for ex-slaves whose lives were replete with obstacles that extended beyond the deterrents of poverty and exclusion. In the aftershock of emancipation, the meanings of freedom held by the 4 million slaves released from captivity in the American South contrasted with white southerners' violent interpretations of black freedom. Racial violence and extralegal injury spoiled the joy of freedom and, instead, provoked anguish and torment among freedmen and freedwomen who were whipped, maimed, lynched, burned, and raped with impunity.

On a spring afternoon, seventy-year-old Jennie Brantley and two younger women set out for a daylong trek from Gordon to Twiggs County, Georgia. The women attended church services in Twiggs; they had traveled the same route many Saturdays before. On this fateful day, Dallas Dyer happened to be traveling homeward from Gordon in a drunken stupor. A "demon when he drank," Dyer's intoxication and racial antipathy made for an ill-fated encounter with Jennie and her companions. When their paths collided, Dyer first "accosted the old with a proposition to drink, which she declined. He then demanded 'who she belonged to,' and receiving an answer, at which, in his drunken condition, he took offense, and attempted to ride over her. The old woman fended off the horse with her umbrella, and then Dyer, drew a knife and cut her almost into pieces."[23] She died two hours later.

Resistance to the white racial hegemonic order sometimes resulted in lethal consequences for those who dared to defy it. Southern white men were grossly embittered by slavery's end and felt threatened by the social effects freedom produced. Many feared that their "rightful supremacy" had been suddenly stripped away, leaving them unjustly exposed to an inherently inferior race. Having already suffered a calamitous defeat in the war, which produced momentous socioeconomic and political losses, white southerners worried that the emancipation of black slaves, and their endowment with the privileges of citizenship, would compromise whites' racially superior status.[24] The preservation of white supremacy, and the maintenance of the antebellum racial order, was contingent on the subordination of ex-slaves. White southerners relied on terror and violence to reinforce black inferiority and to reverse the course of Reconstruction.

Outrages against women like Jennie Brantley were commonplace in post–Civil War Georgia. Many of the heinous attacks meted out against black womenfolk were performed at the hand of the Ku Klux Klan. Established in 1866, in Pulaski, Tennessee, the Klan quickly became the South's premiere vigilante organization, renowned for brandishing its terror throughout the countryside. Visions of masked men on horses holding torches evoked trepidation among freedpeople who feared for their personal protection and the safety of their families. These anxieties were even greater in the rural landscape, where gendered violence and sexual terror were most profuse. The Klan's exploitation of black women's sexuality had a deleterious impact on individuals, families, and communities, whose lives were turned upside down by the trauma of sexual violence.

Rape, attempted rape, naked whippings, forms of sexual torture, humiliation, and genital mutilation were all forms of sexualized violence wielded against the unfortunate targets of Klan rage.[25] The greatest casualties in the war against sexual abuse were African American women who were overrun by southern white men bent on reasserting their authority over former slaves. Rape was a powerful weapon deployed by white males as a locus of control and a tool of debasement. With the ascendancy of sexual terror in the postwar South, black women were left vulnerable to white men's vexation toward emancipation.

The assault on black women's sexuality in the postemancipation South was bolstered by antebellum exclusions of slave women from the law of rape, and the unwillingness of southern white men to disengage themselves from crude sexual misbehaviors and mythologies formulated in slavery. In freedom, African American women bore the stigma of sexual stereotypes cultivated in the Old South. The "Jezebel" prototype, largely constructed to help justify female enslavement and white men's sexual transgressions, possessed a voracious sexual appetite and invited the illicit overtures of white men.[26] Sexual folklore, as such, produced long-term consequences for black women, who could not evade time-honored mythologies or avoid profligate sexual attacks that persevered in the postbellum South.

In the fall of 1866, Rhoda Ann Childs became a casualty on the battleground of terror. At sundown, she was ambushed by eight Klansmen who invaded a plantation in Henry County, Georgia, where Childs was "under contract with Mrs. Amelia Childs [her former mistress] . . . and worked from Jan. 1, 1866, until the crops were laid by." The vandals seized the defenseless wife and mother, and, in her words, "took me some distance from the house, where they 'bucked' me down across a log, stripped my clothes over my head, one of the men standing astride my neck, and beat me across my posterior."[27] Next, her dirt-caked, half-naked body was pinned to the ground, while "one of the men stood upon my breast, while two others took hold of my feet and stretched my limbs as far apart as they could, while the man standing upon my breast applied the strap to my private parts until fatigued into stopping." Childs was "more dead than alive" after the thrashing, but this did not discourage one of the men from "ravishing" her right before he "ran his pistol into me, and said he had a hell of a mind to pull the trigger."[28] To round off the attack, two of the men overran her cabin, beat her daughters, stole the family's clothing, and then retreated.

While rape was, indisputably, the most overt form of sexual terror used against freedwomen, whippings were highly sexualized rituals that customarily involved forcibly stripping victims before or during a Klan attack. On a quiet Sunday morning in May, Mary Brown was startled by the dreadful sound of the Ku Klux Klan breaking open her doors. Once inside, "They took my mother out first, and asked her where I was; she told them I was in the house. They said: 'Make up a light; we are going to kill her,'" she testified. With her life in peril, Mary said to herself, "I have not done anything; I have not stolen anything, or murdered anybody; so I will not be scared."[29] But she had many reasons to be fearful of the menacing crew. The men had heard rumors of her alleged plan to report their comrades' involvement in the death of Mr. Cason, a white man and a revenue officer.

The Klansmen dragged Mary out the house in her nightclothes, then, as she stated, "threw me down on my face, stripped my clothes up over my head, and gave me about twenty-five licks before they let me up . . . After they got done with me Oakes and two boys, Albert Henderson and Henry Henderson, came up with a rope. They had a chain around my neck, and they drew on it until they choked me so that I fainted."[30] After the men were satisfied with their work, they mounted their horses and rode away. Mary was left lying on the ground, cut "all to pieces."

Expressions of gendered violence and sexual terror in postwar Georgia were not limited to Klan attacks but were also manifested through the act of lynching. Whereas African American men, who were looked on as the archetypal rapists of white women, were lynched as an act of southern chivalry, black women were most commonly hanged for murdering or assaulting a white person, arson, and theft of white property.[31] Others were lynched for issuing verbal threats against white aggressors (male and female), resisting rape, and daring to testify against white male terrorists.

Belle Hathaway of Hamilton, Georgia, was lynched after attempting to defend herself against a sexual attack.[32] In another case, the corpse of Mary

Turner was found dangling from Folsom Bridge in Brooks County, sixteen miles north of Valdosta. She had made "unwise remarks" about the execution of her husband, Hays Turner, who was lynched for his suspected involvement in the murder of Hampton Smith—a white man—and the assault on Smith's wife. As stated by an unnamed reporter for the *Columbus Ledger-Enquirer*, on a Sunday afternoon "the people in their indignant mood took exceptions to her remarks, as well as her attitude, and without waiting for nightfall, took her to the river where she was hanged."[33] As the eight-months-pregnant woman's lifeless body dangled upside down in the air, a spectator "took out a carving knife and cut open her stomach. Her baby fell from her womb and cried. Upon hearing the baby cry, a man from the crowd raised his heel and crushed the baby's head." In a final act of post-mortem torture, "the mob started to burn her and after her clothes were burned off they riddled her with bullets."[34]

Ann Boston, an aged African American woman, was also lynched by a mob of fifty white men after she murdered Mrs. R. E. Jordan, "her mistress of many years associations." Mrs. Jordan was the wife of a prominent planter of Pinehurst in Dooly County. According to one reporter, Ann, "some 60 years old, who has been employed by the Jordans for a number of years, quarreled with Mrs. Jordan in the morning. She left the house in a rage."[35] In the afternoon, she returned to the Jordan plantation and "hid in a clump of bushes at the rear of the house." When Mrs. Jordan appeared, Ann allegedly "attacked her, cutting her throat with a razor from ear to ear."[36] She quickly scurried from the scene of the crime and "went to a field where Mr. Jordan was at work and there informed him that his wife was dead and that she killed her . . . She repeated it over and over again, finally sobbing, apparently regretting her act."[37]

Shortly after the killing, Ann was taken into custody. Sheriff Bennett took the woman to Cordele late that night and locked her up in the Crisp County jail for "safe keeping." Around 10:20 P.M., she was "hurried away by a mob of more than fifty men in automobiles . . . A large posse from Dooly County followed the fugitives and took the woman from the jail to rush her back to Pinehurst and lynch her among her own people and associations." By midnight, the corpse of Ann Boston was discovered "swaying from a tree riddled with bullets in the heart of the negro section of the same little town."[38]

In response to this epidemic of unchecked violence and terror, a small population of Georgia's freedwomen deserted the countryside and fled to the city in hopes of securing greater economic opportunities and protection from the persisting dangers of racial hostility. In June 1871, Hannah Flournoy took flight from Columbus to Atlanta, leaving behind "all my property and bedding," after witnessing the murder of a white Republican Party leader at her boardinghouse. In her words, she had been "working honorably for my living . . . washing and cooking for anybody that wanted me to do it."[39] In Atlanta, Flournoy quickly immersed herself in the city's expanding population of black domestic workers.

Some of Us Are Brave

When she arrived in Atlanta, Hannah Flournoy beheld a city on the brink of modernization. The railroad system, which was a symbol of industrialization throughout the nation, buttressed Atlanta's growing economy. Yet the physical condition of city life was rugged and unsavory. Unpaved roads were customary. Faulty drainage and sewer systems left private wells and springs open to contamination. Foul-smelling waste and other forms of unsanitary debris emanating from pigpens, butcheries, and guano plants, as well as household waste and dead animals discarded in streets and gullies, were normal.[40] However, for black migrants traveling from rural vicinities, Atlanta's aesthetic limitations were hardly a deterrent. The desire for social and economic freedom overpowered the unpleasant sights and smells of this rising metropolis.

Black denizens congregated in segregated districts, filling up row houses, tenements, and shanties, some barely fit for human habitation. With their "freedom bags" in tow, African American women migrants flooded Atlanta's black neighborhoods at Shermantown and Jenningstown, making up the majority of the black residents and representing more than half of the wage-earning population.[41] For new arrivals, domestic service was the most tenable employment option. More than 90 percent of female wage earners in Atlanta engaged in some form of household work, either as cooks, washerwomen, maids, or nurses for white children. In the face of their occupational limitations, black women still fared better than their unskilled male counterparts, who found minimal success in the paid workforce, did. Hence, the restrictions on black men's labor helped foster the expansion of female-headed households in the urban South.[42]

The choices African American women made about wage labor were directly influenced by their age, marital status, and childbirth. Younger and unmarried women tended to occupy white households, "living in" as general housemaids and child nurses.[43] Georgia Telfair "wuz 'bout fo'teen years old" when she was hired to "do washin', ironin', an' cleanin up" for Jack Weir's family. Per her recollection, she "wukked for 'em 'til i married. Day lemme eat all I wanted dere at the house an' paid me in old clo'es, middlin' meat, sirup, 'tatoes, an' wheat flour, but i never did git no money nor pay. Not nary a cent."[44] On the contrary, married women opted to perform day service or worked as laundresses, "living out" and maintaining the lion's share of responsibility when it came to sustaining their families.[45]

Washerwomen were the nucleus of Atlanta's black labor force. Weekly, scores of "washing amazons" filed through the streets, "carrying enormous bundles of soiled clothes upon their heads" from the homes of white clients to their own quarters.[46] Black laundresses usually worked from home, setting their own hours and wages and maintaining autonomy over their domestic lives. When whites contested their occupational independence, washerwomen collectively threatened the labor market by withdrawing their services or commanding higher wages, much to the vexation of white patrons. The Atlanta washerwomen's strike of 1881 demonstrated that black laundresses were politically awake and ready to defend the autonomy of their trade.[47] Yet their agitation was not enough to shrug off the badge of servitude that linked slavery and domestic service.

Atlanta's cooks, maids, and child nurses could expect to work seven days a week, at least twelve to fourteen hours a day, for "the pitiful sum of ten dollars a month!"[48] One "Negro nurse" found her condition to be "as bad as, if not worse than, it was during the days of slavery . . . It's 'Mammy, do this,' or 'Mammy, do that . . . it is not strange to see 'Mammy' watering the lawn with the garden hose, sweeping the sidewalk, mopping the porch and halls, helping the cook, or darning the stockings . . . I am the slave, body and soul, of this family."[49]

Domestic service placed African American women in close proximity to white families and perpetuated the antebellum master–slave relationship. Locked out of the industrial labor market and consigned to vocations that kept them bound in subservient roles, these "beasts of burden" were forced to suffer such work-related abuses as excessive hours, unfair wages, and physical and verbal assault in the pursuit of economic survival. Others preferred to work for nickels and dimes rather than face the cruel punishment awaiting female vagrants. As stated by the "Negro nurse," in Georgia, idle "negresses" could expect to be "arrested, tried, and dispatched to the 'State Farm [or chain gang],' where we would surely have to work for nothing or be beaten with many stripes!"[50]

Occupational hazards, such as sexual abuse, further imperiled black female domestics living in white households. One Georgia woman lost her job because, in her words, "I refused to let the madam's husband kiss me." She concluded that the man's sexual advances *must* have sprung from an "undue familiarity with his servants . . . because without any love-making at all, soon after I was installed as cook, he walked up to me, threw his arms around me, and was in the act of kissing me, when I demanded to know what he meant, and shoved him away."[51] When the newlywed reported the incident to her husband, he immediately confronted the man. The woman's supervisor, in turn, "cursed" her spouse, "slapped him, and—had him arrested."[52] Although innocent, the man was fined $25 by the court.

To Make My Livin'

In the cities of Atlanta, Macon, Savannah, Columbus, and Augusta, black household workers routinely faced off against their supervisors, whose (legitimate and nonlegitimate) accusations of theft landed many in jail and taxed with heavy fines. In Georgia, more African American women were arrested for larceny and "disorderly conduct" than for any other crime. "Larceny from the house" was an all-encompassing offense that promised stiff penalties for servants who rifled through their employer's belongings, stealing clothing, jewelry, cooking utensils, food, and money.

Annie Toasten, a "Negro cook" from Macon, was "dressed in her gladdest spring rags . . . to pay a visit to friends in Fort Valley" when she was apprehended for stealing. One newspaper columnist noted, "She [was] about to leave home without saying good-bye to her employer" when a policeman showed up and "cancelled the date."[53] Annie's boss, Mrs. J. W. Nichols, had alerted authorities when she'd discovered six dollars missing from a trunk in her bedroom. Detective Tom Jones "lost no time in getting to the house and, suspecting the cook who was the only one who could have gotten into the room, found Annie arrayed in her finest and about to use the six dollars on a trip to Fort Valley . . . The money was found on her and she was locked up."[54]

One hundred miles west of Macon, Georgia Alexander was also apprehended by police on charges of larceny after she took two twenty-dollar bills from her employer, Mrs. Reese. After dinner, Reese discovered the money missing and immediately suspected her cook since she was supposedly "the only one in the house besides the family when the money was taken."[55] According to authorities, Georgia "stoutly maintained her innocence for several hours, but finally told the officers they would find a piece of paper beneath one of the windows on the ground." The arresting officer "returned to the house, looked where the negro said and found the missing money wrapped in a piece of newspaper."[56] In a similar case, Mary Lou Shelton was held over in the city court of Columbus to respond to charges of "larceny from the house" after she stole twenty dollars from the purse of her employer's overnight guest. Her supervisor, Will Crow, reported Mary Lou to authorities, who hurriedly "went to work on the case, and found where she had spent most of the money. Five dollars of the money was recovered, but the balance was gone to buy things the woman needed."[57]

Mary Lou Shelton was a member of a growing cohort of servant thieves. A broad range of impulses drove black domestics, like Mary Lou, to steal— poverty, survival, occupational exclusion, greed, and so on.[58] The preponderance of southern black women who risked embezzling from white employers did so out of economic necessity, or as an indignant response to being cheated out of their wages. Household workers used stolen goods to supplement their meager incomes, and they often compensated themselves by stealing table scraps and other "unwanted" morsels from the kitchens of their white employers. "Pan-toting" was expected and allowed in various white households. In the words of one domestic, "White folks expect their cooks to avail themselves of these perquisites." She carefully admitted that "the cooks find opportunity to hide away at times, along with the cold 'grub,' a little sugar, a little flour, a little meal, or a little piece of soap; but I indignantly deny that we are thieves. We don't steal; we just 'take' things."[59]

Most servants who stole did not regard themselves as "thieves." The vast majority of these women were amateur larcenists, not professional burglars. Yet a smaller population of black women masqueraded as servants for the sole purpose of ripping off white patrons. One woman, operating under the alias of "Mary Williams," hired herself to five white women within two days. "Wary Mary," as she was dubbed by her accusers, extended her services as a "good cook." She held each job just long enough to raid her clients' pantries and iceboxes. Mrs. Edward Shaw was the first to come forward and report Mary to the police after she discovered "a lot of foodstuff" missing from her ice chest. By the time the missing goods were detected, Mary had moved on to the home of Mrs. C. Hollorman. After she gathered a dozen eggs and a large ham from Mrs. Hollorman's refrigerator, she continued her exploits in another section of Macon. The eggs, ham, and "Mary" were never recovered.[60]

In another part of Macon, Susie Williams presented herself as a "Negro washerwoman," and garnered the trust of J. H. Brown, who hired her to do his laundry. Six weeks later, the "washerwoman" and the clothing remained at large. Brown informed authorities about the missing subjects— his clothing and laundress—but the investigation revealed that "Susie Williams" was an "unknown quantity" on Reynolds Avenue.[61] Both "Mary" and "Susie" represent extreme, yet telling, examples of the ways African American women responded to economic deprivation and vocational limitations. These two women opted not to enter into the coffers of domestic service where they could be subjected to work-related abuses and, instead, adopted theft as an alternative profession.

Some found success in the informal economy. Black female sex workers, bootleggers, and gamblers economically sustained themselves by engaging in criminal enterprises. Poverty and occupational exclusion compelled otherwise law-abiding black women to take legal risks to secure a basic living.[62] Barred from the industrial and professional labor force, outside of domestic service, underground work was one of the only economic means of support that city-dwelling African American women had. By engaging in illegal professions, southern black women could control their wages and terms of service, and they could guarantee payment for their labor. The informal economy also provided these women with a supplementary source of income to enrich their scrawny earnings.[63]

Dollie Gallimore, a cook, set up a liquor dispensary in the home of her employer, Margaret Flahive. On Sunday afternoons, black patrons could be seen taking flasks from a hole in the wall and, in return, handing cash to a woman on the inside. Unbeknownst to Gallimore, Flahive's home was under surveillance by Macon authorities. On Sunday, June 5, 1912, two officers reportedly "gave a negro, Charles Gray, 50 cents and told him to go to the hole in Mrs. Flahive's wall and buy a pint." A few minutes later, "Gray returned with a bottle of 'Old Joe' and 25 cents in cash. The officers told him to return and buy another bottle."[64] After the second transaction was complete, Gray confirmed for the detectives that Dollie Gallimore sold him the whiskey. She was arrested and fined one hundred dollars.

White Georgians were especially sensitive to the maneuverings of black bootleggers. During the late nineteenth and early twentieth centuries, temperance reformers appealed to the Georgia state government to implement anti-liquor legislation. In 1885, a local option law was put in place, authorizing voters to impose prohibition in their respective counties. By 1907, most constituents had voted their counties dry, but the principal cities of the state, Atlanta, Savannah, Augusta, Macon, and Columbus, stayed wet. The following year, Georgia became the first dry state in the South after its legislature enacted a mandatory statewide prohibition law, which illegalized the sale and consumption of "all spirituous and malt liquors."[65]

The race question was one of the most potent causes of prohibition legislation in Georgia. White Georgians frequently bemoaned the dangerous effects of intoxicating liquor on the Negro, whom they deemed to be "temperamentally given to the use of alcoholic stimulants."[66] Reverend Lovick P. Winter said it best: "The very worst traits of human nature, and of negro nature especially, are brought out by whisky. It is whisky which makes of the negro a criminal, a pauper, a vagrant and a menace to the homes of country people."[67]

Strict disciplinary action was reserved for African American men and women who violated Georgia's statewide prohibition laws. Liquor dealers like Eliza Franklin, a black shopkeeper, were considered enablers to "Negro trifles." The bootlegger was fined one hundred dollars for having thirty gallons of whisky in her establishment.[68] Both Franklin's and Gallimore's penalties set a precedent among blacks in Macon: defying the prohibition laws of Georgia was a dangerous business.

Besides illegal liquor distribution, African American women found other ways to engage in the underground economy. Underemployed or out-of-work black women used prostitution as one way to ease their economic burdens. Records that account for the numbers of black female sex workers are scarce in the metropolises of post–Civil War Georgia, and what data exist indicate relatively few sex workers compared with those at work in the urban cities of Philadelphia, Chicago, and New York. Still, the impetus behind joining the sex trade was fundamentally universal. Prostitution provided a modest degree of economic provision and an outlet for survival while, at the same time, allowing black women to reinforce their bodily autonomy.[69]

Enterprising southern black women like Queen Fleming operated moderately successful "lewd houses" where customers could cozily indulge in disreputable pastimes, such as drinking and gambling, and where black women could sell sex for profit. Fleming's brothel was a main attraction in the Bridwell's Bottom section of Augusta. Among the city's black neighborhoods, the "Bottom" was a notorious setting for domestic squabbles and knife fights. Police officers were frequently dispatched to the area to settle disputes and run down suspected offenders, drawing unwanted visibility to Fleming's brothel. On the night of October 11, 1917, Queen was swept up during a raid on the "Bottom." She was arrested and charged with "running a lewd house."[70]

For authorities in Georgia, prostitution was a clear "social evil." In Macon, lewd houses bred miscegenation, provoking outrage among white citizens who condemned race mixing. Police officials used a dragnet routine to apprehend violators of the city's anti-vice laws and, more importantly, its fixed racial code. When police officers raided the homes of Delia Bowden, Ellen Gilbert, and Minnie Stewart, they found white men "under such circumstances as to warrant the conclusion that fornication or adultery had been committed." The defendants were charged with operating lewd houses, while their rumored "clients" were indicted for "disorderly conduct."[71] The judge's final ruling against these subjects is left absent in the historical record. Yet when Carrie Hollis faced her day in court for "running a lewd house," Judge Hodges gave her a clear set of options; pay a fine of seventy dollars or serve seven months on the county chain gang.[72]

Cunning Cruelty

While some working-class African American women resorted to acts of vice—theft, prostitution, and illegal liquor distribution—to assuage their socioeconomic pressures, others opted to vent their frustrations through acts of violence. Roughly 18 percent of all black female arrests in Georgia were for violent crimes, including murder, manslaughter, infanticide, attempted murder, poisoning, arson, and assault. The majority of culpable (and guiltless) offenders were first-time felons with no traceable record of illegal activity.

The motives that shaped African American women's decisions to commit violent crime were far-reaching. Some used violent behaviors, such as shooting, stabbing, and fire starting, to defend themselves against abusive spouses, fathers, brothers, or lovers. For others, violence emanated from jealousy, fear, rage, or socioeconomic pressures, or from a hypersensitive reaction to disrespect. According to historian Kali Gross, African American women emerged from slavery with a "fragile notion of womanhood" and a resolution to fight back against any further abuse or incivility. In the absence of "standard female protections," freedwomen (and their daughters) relied on violence as "an instrument of power and vengeance, often supplanting the protection and justice that continued to remain elusive."[73]

Ruby Jones, "a young negro woman," and Gus Allen were sashaying on the dance floor at Langley's hall in Augusta when she pulled out her blade and stabbed him in the chest. Earlier at the party, the two had engaged in a heated fuss. Gus got the best of Ruby and "accidentally cut her on the hand." But her deepest injury came from the embarrassment of being "whooped" in public. No amount of salve or bandages could soothe Ruby's rage or rebuild her fractured ego. The only way to pay Gus back was to take his life.

Ruby quietly nursed her stinging wound while plotting her revenge. She even pretended to make good with Gus and consented to another dance. Around 11:30 P.M., as the couple slow dragged, "apparently having settled their differences," Ruby made her move on Gus and pierced him in the heart. Consistent with one reporter's observation, Officer Anderson, "who walks the beat out on Twiggs Street, where Langley's hall is located, was summoned and the couple were placed under arrest. They were carried to the call box, about a block distant, followed by a large crowd."[74] The policeman, Ruby, and Gus conversed for approximately ten minutes; then the wounded man "slipped from the officer's grasp and fell to the ground. He evidently realized that he was dying, for he stated that Ruby Jones had stabbed him. Those were his last words."[75]

In Macon, Miner Armstrong also shot and killed her lover, Joe Simpson, while he was in the act of beating her in the street. She hurriedly raced from the scene, but she was tracked by dogs one mile away where she hid in a swamp.[76] In a similar instance, Sallie Brewington murdered her abusive husband with an axe while he was asleep. She purportedly "drove the full blade of the axe into her victim's head just behind his left ear, literally splitting it open, and then placed the body on fire, burning all the murdered man's clothes off and his face almost beyond recognition."[77]

Like domestic abuse, intraracial and intergendered tensions also impelled some black women to kill in an effort to abate their frustrations, refurbish their shattered pride, or outright dispose of their husbands' and lovers' mistresses or wives. Fatal and nonfatal "scraps" and knife fights arose over infidelity, jealousy, stolen cash, unkind remarks, and so on. These contests were waged on the streets, in living rooms, front yards, bedrooms, juke joints, and other public and private spaces where black women lived, labored, and socialized.

In Bridwell's Bottom, Mabel Johnson and her neighbor, Susie, had a nondeadly street "scrap" after Susie cooked breakfast for Mabel's husband. In her testimony before the city court, Mabel told Judge Foley, "Naw, sir, judge dat black 'oman she cant cook for mah husband, en den laff at me erbout it. Dat man neber ax me to do dat cookin' he jest simple went to her, and she did hit."[78] Mabel prided herself on being a good wife, reassuring the judge that "I goes on, and dose mah bizness, and looks after mah husband when he axes me to." However, "Sunday morning dat nigger come home with some packages for me to cook, I guess, but den he went on down to Susie's and she done cook it, and when I ax her about it she done told me dat she puts her 'lobing arms' round dat man's neck, and so she guesses she can cook for him."[79] Deeply vexed by Susie's audacious behavior, Mabel confessed, "Now, jedge, dat was too much and so I draws a line in the road and axes her if she would step ober it. I had a pair of bricks and a poker, and she wouldn't come so I lit into cussing her."[80] Within a short moment, both women proceeded to exchange blows. No serious injuries resulted from the fight, and the incident was written off as a "little dispute." Yet Mabel was still required to pay a five-dollar fine as punishment for her "crime."

Although fuming spouses were the common aggressors in infidelity-related squabbles, mistresses sometimes upset the status quo by violently pursuing their lovers' wives. In Macon, Cressy Scoggins, the "deserted wife" of George Scoggins, was left "sleeping in the silent stars with an ugly gash just above the right breast and several others about her head and arms"[81] when Anna Walker, George's mistress, knifed her to death in a fit of jealousy. On a Saturday night, Cressy got dressed in her finest rags and set out to Manson Mason's juke house in Macon, where she was one of the first to arrive on the scene. As she scouted the room for familiar faces, her eyes settled on George and Anna. According to witnesses, Cressy "called George off and began telling him how badly their children were needing clothes and begged him to return to her and the children."[82] In the middle of her plea, Anna, "who had become infatuated over George's great qualities," became enraged with jealousy. She drew her knife and began "cutting right and left," until a fatal wound landed just below the right side of Cressy's neck. The wounded wife collapsed to the ground and died twenty minutes later. Anna fled the scene, but the arresting officers were convinced that there would be "little trouble in effecting her capture."[83]

Similar to domestic confrontations, nondomestic conflicts transpired between female rivals over money, personal belongings, verbal insults, colorism, and beauty politics. On a hot summer day in Augusta, Martha Hewitt, a tall, full-bodied, dark-skinned washerwoman and former slave, gave Susan Brown, "a woman of mulatto persuasion," an "unmerciful pounding after throwing her upon the floor and jamming her head between a couple of washtubs" for stealing her hard-earned money. Martha's attack on Susan obviously owed a great deal to the theft of her cash. But the "opprobrious words used to and concerning her charcoal dignity" are what sent her over the edge.[84]

On the surface, it appears as though stolen currency and sniping remarks independently precipitated the fuss between Martha Hewitt and Susan Brown. But a deeper testing of the facts reveals a more complex understanding of the ways in which color consciousness operated amid the black female working class, and it provides a set of elemental clues that can be used to explore the less obvious grounds of opposition between women rivals. Although scarcely documented among the working poor, colorism—a system of intraracial discrimination used to reinforce difference on the basis of skin tone, privileging the lighter-skinned persons within a community of color—had its presence in all spatial and "experiential" communities of African American women before, during, and after the Civil War.[85] Among the "elevated classes," where color consciousness, social privilege, education, wealth, class, and invented notions of intelligence and beauty were most extant, the economy of color was a solidly profitable system with stable perks. For the black masses, however, colorism was a precariously ordered practice with unpredictable results.

Conflicts and divisions forged between working-class black women on the grounds of color were two-toned disputes. Women like Susan Brown internalized public attitudes and temperaments about light-skinned blacks' professedly superior beauty and intelligence, and they invoked racialized terminologies to insult and degrade darkly complexioned black women who already faced a "problematic fate." In contrast, women like Martha Hewitt used their physical force and strength to, literally and figuratively, assail negative ideas about black female inferiority, unattractiveness, unintelligence, and masculinity, and to trounce a fair-skinned "proxy" of the white race. For both groups of poor black women, the economy of color generated no tangible assets and seldom afforded social capital and peer privilege. In the end, poverty and exclusion reduced fair and dark-skinned African American women to the same debased social, economic, occupational, and political level. Even the courts refused to summons the politics of difference in its rulings. In Georgia's penal system, "black," "brown," and "yellow" (mulatto) female offenders were appraised and exploited just the same.

While the motives behind black female criminality were usually perceptible, nondomestic disputes among African American women sometimes sprang from unintelligible causes and escalated from minor skirmishes into lethal altercations. For instance, Ella Horne, a Macon native, was assaulted by a small mob of women in a fracas for no apparent reason. While several accomplices held Horne down, Lucinda Williams allegedly bit Horne's finger off. Within two to three days, the victim's wound became infected. In keeping with one reporter's observation, as "the pain increased the arm began to swell, and now the woman is raving, according to the physicians, with an aggravated case of hydrophobia [rabies]. She will die."[86] All parties involved in the case were arrested, and Williams stood trial as a "murderess."

Extraordinary Wickedness

On occasion, socioeconomic pressures drove black women to perpetrate exceptionally "vile and unnatural" acts of violence. Infanticide cases, although rarely recorded, reflect black women's desperate response to economic deprivation. With limited employment opportunities and an absence of orphanages or maternity homes servicing black patrons, some indigent mothers (and grandmothers) resorted to infanticide rather than risk losing valuable employment or tipping their families over the brink of poverty.[87]

On February 20, 1914, Lena Fry, "an unlettered and poor" African American woman, was convicted of infanticide in the Superior Court of Bibb County and sentenced to life imprisonment. In a letter from the solicitor general of the Macon County Judicial Court, the details of Fry's actions were described as follows: "Lena killed her baby very soon after she gave birth to it, probably within a half hour. She had recently come from Jones County where she did farm work and where she left two or three children, to whom she had given birth, with her mother."[88] Fry had recently secured a position in Macon as a cook at a private residence and, according to the legal officer, "had no means of living except by her work, and with the encumbrance of the baby she could not have continued her work as a cook. It seems that such must have been her thought that she killed the child not from any ill will towards the infant . . . but merely to rid herself of the burden she felt unable to carry."[89]

In Jasper County, one unnamed adolescent was forced, by her mother, to kill her newborn baby. Upon her mother's command, the young woman allegedly "took the infant and attempted to drown it in a tub of water. Fearing its cries and struggles would expose her infamous conduct, she wrapped the child up in bedclothes and threw it under the bed, where it soon suffocated."[90] The deed was discovered soon after, and both mother and daughter were arrested. In a similar case, Rachel Stallworth, a sharecropper, was accused of murdering her four-day-old grandchild by "taking it from the bed of the mother and deliberately breaking its neck." She was subsequently arrested after an autopsy on the baby's body revealed that it had been killed. In each of the abovementioned cases, economic pressures led women to commit or endorse infanticide. But, in rare instances, moments of mental instability alone gave rise to child murder.

For first-time mothers like Fannie Paten, childbirth ushered in a mixed range of emotions: joy, anticipation, fear, and anxiety. During her pregnancy, the twenty-one-year-old newlywed leaned on the support of friends like Lucy Williams—a co-laborer and confidant on the Reid plantation in Jasper County, while her husband worked at a nearby depot in the tiny community of Machen. One summer morning, during the "first part of cotton chopping time," Lucy observed her pregnant friend in a "helpless condition." She complained of being "sore" and "stiff" the day before, so Lucy found no cause for panic when Fannie left the fields early to return home.

As she sat in her cabin on the edge of her bed, Fannie's discomfort began to escalate. She sent her stepdaughter into the fields to get Lucy, requesting that she "carry something to rub her with. She said she was sick and felt bad all over."[91] Consistent with Lucy's testimony, when she showed up "there was another woman in there, and she says they sent after the Doctor. I says if you have, I won't rub her and have anything to do with her . . . I says, I hav'nt got time to fool with Fannie, I have got too many clothes to iron."[92] Two hours later, Lucy went back to her friend's shack to assess her situation. When she arrived, Fannie was all alone, rocking on the edge of her bed.

Lucy spoke to Fannie: "I says, good gracious poor woman, you here by yourself, she says, yes, and then I walked a little further and I saw the afterbirth. I says, how come that, Fannie? She says that is all that come. I says, no it isn't. I got a stick and opened the after-birth and saw a child had come out of it, and I was looking all about for the baby, and I says how come that baby s—t down there. She said that is all that come."[93] Lucy continued her pursuit for the newborn. She finally discovered the child laying in an ash pile. The baby had been "wrapped up in a coarse under-skirt, and put out there in the ash pile head-foremost." The discovery scared Lucy "nearly to death." But she was relieved to see the baby girl "alive and kicking."[94]

In March of 1899, Fannie Paten was arrested and indicted for "assault with intent to murder." She was found guilty of the crime and freighted to the state prison farm in Milledgeville to serve out her two-year sentence. While the motive for Fannie Paten's attempted infanticide remains undisclosed in the historical record, a wide range of explanations can be drawn from this case. It is highly plausible that Paten's crime was not merely a deviant response to socioeconomic pressure, but the by-product of childbirth-induced psychological trauma.

Fannie Paten's abnormal psychosomatic response to childbirth could have been brought on by several variables: intense pain, fear, feelings of powerlessness, and a lack of social support. Her condition likely escaped the purview of nineteenth-century medical professionals, whose sophomoric knowledge of mental illness declassified childbirth-related "madness" as a category of lunacy. Yet modern scientific research has revealed causal links between childbirth and post-traumatic stress disorder, especially among poor minority women. In accordance with psychologists Johanna Soet, Gregory Brack, and Colleen Dilorio's findings on this subject, the experience of childbirth has been proven to have a negative effect on a mother's psychological functioning and postpartum adjustment.[95] Nevertheless, these scholars have concurred that childbirth satisfaction outcomes are improved when a female support person and a companion are present. However, when a partner is absent and support is lacking, post-traumatic stress disorder symptoms are likely to appear.[96]

Although one must be cautious not to project twenty-first-century knowledge onto a nineteenth-century historical situation, modern research does provide new understanding of the expectations some African American women may have had of childbirth, and the mixed emotional responses that impelled them to murder. For women like Paten, an unsupervised birth encouraged feelings of fear, danger, and helplessness. Psychological trauma was even further exacerbated by extreme physical pain and a lack of social support. Moreover, the delivery of an ill or stillborn infant compounded a woman's emotional stress—especially if legal repercussions were likely to ensue. Whether or not Paten's infant demonstrated signs of life at its time of birth will never be known. But the traumatizing circumstances of her labor and delivery, and her unusual response, reveal credible signs of psychological unrest. A close evaluation of Paten's mental condition allows scholars to broadly diagnose the root of postbellum infanticide cases. Though economic vulnerability was a chief motivating factor for child murder, mental and emotional disturbances also influenced some mothers to kill.

While infanticide has been most commonly read as a crime involving mothers, grandmothers, and other female guardians, men also murdered their offspring and forced their daughters and stepdaughters to censor such acts of "extraordinary wickedness." This was particularly so in the case of incest births. When an infant born of forced sexual contact between a male and female of biological or near-biological relation (father–daughter, stepfather–stepdaughter) was killed by a man, it was normally done to conceal the crimes of rape and incest and to escape public ridicule and community ostracism. If girls and young women conspired with kindred rapists, it was done for a number of reasons: fear of physical violence, to avoid the social and economic ramifications of unwed mothering, to envelop their nonconsensual incestuous relationships from public view in an effort to "save their character," and to carry out a personal desire to terminate their assailant's seed.

In 1890, Jasper Williams's "horrible lust" was publicly exposed when he was arrested for drowning his newborn infant in a tub of water. Estella, "a fine looking girl of seventeen," and Williams's only daughter, was the mother of the dead baby. The father–daughter pair was well known in Upatoie, a small farming village eighteen miles outside Columbus. Williams, a "negro blacksmith aged about forty-seven," was seen as a respectable member of the community. But when news of the nonconsensual incestuous relationship existing between him and his daughter was exposed, the townspeople "looked with disfavor upon the intimacy" and repudiated Jasper Williams as a "beast in human form."[97]

In Upatoie, and in communities throughout the postbellum South, child murder was recognized as a reprehensible and highly immoral act. The "crackdown" on infanticide that ensued after slavery resulted from the changing social mores among black southerners, particularly the middle class and conservative working class. The reputations and character of African Americans—women especially—took on a new level of importance, as black women strived to disengage themselves and the race from prominent sexual and criminal stereotypes. For this reason, certain community members had a vested interested in controlling and suppressing infanticide among black women (and men), even if it meant sending them to prison.[98] On account of this rising intolerance, Williams and Estella were exposed. Williams stood trial for the "dreadful crime" of infanticide, while Estella walked away from the ordeal unscathed by the law. Nevertheless, both parties were convicted in the court of public opinion for having violated the standards of black "middle-class morality."

The Criminal Negro

As escalations in black female criminality proliferated during the post-emancipation era, innocent and guilty bands of poor working-class African American women found themselves trapped in a deluge of pseudo-scientific and civilian ideologies used to publicly malign their gendered, racial, and sexual identity. Racial radicals roused public fears by invoking violent and nonviolent criminal cases and behaviors, and they reinforced a theoretical premise that distinguished the Negro woman as a criminal by genetic design—a "true monster" prone to commit barbaric acts of cruelty.[99] The quasi-scientific narrative that emerged to explain the *problem* of black female criminality (and "Negro crime" as a whole) refused socioeconomic or even psychological duress as a credible factor in eliciting violent and nonviolent criminal behaviors. Instead, black (female) crime was cast as an irredeemable race trait.

Famous Italian criminal anthropologist Cesare Lombroso laid one of the first philosophical stones to be used toward constructing an exclusively "scientific" image of the black female offender, which reduced her to a savage beast or, in an ideal circumstance, a prostitute. *Criminal Woman* (1893), Lombroso's tour de force, invented a new index in the study of female crime. A pioneer of criminal anthropology—the scientific approach to examining the physical characteristics, mental traits, and instincts of the "born" criminal—the theorist claimed to have identified a new variety of inherent criminals in the female form. By classifying women offenders in distinct racial, biological, physiological, and behavioral categories, he authenticated new claims of racial and biological inferiority and further retarded the image of black female criminals in the United States. By the time an English-translated version of Lombroso's text reached American bookshelves in 1895, long-standing assumptions about black lawbreakers, female and male, were firmly entrenched. Yet, by corroborating African American female criminal deviancy in purely "scientific" terms, he established a new praxis by which black women's criminality could be measured.[100]

"It is sad but true: among brutes, savages, and primitive people, the female is more cruel than compassionate, although she is not as cruel as the male," declared Lombroso. But "there is a small subgroup whose criminal propensities are more intense and perverse than even those of their male counterparts. These are the female born criminals, whose evil is inversely proportionate to their numbers. Woman is rarely wicked, but when she is, she is worse than a man." Although intelligence supposedly improved a woman's ability to accomplish calculated acts of malice, such as poisoning, "to kill in a bestial rage requires no more than the mind of a Hottentot."[101]

Lombroso viewed female born criminals as "anomalous and rare . . . exhibiting more extreme wickedness than male criminals and a masculine character," with the "Negro Venus" (the most "inferior" female of all races) bearing the closest anatomical resemblance to a man. He found it "difficult to believe that these are really women, so huge are their jaws and cheekbones, so hard are their features."[102] By and large, Lombroso's suppositions about black female "born criminals" helped canonize black female criminality, which was cached under the parasol of "Negro crime."

The criminalization of southern African American women occurred in tandem with the criminalizing of the black race throughout the country. During the late nineteenth and early twentieth centuries, pseudoscientific and criminological explanations for "Negro crime" set the criterion by which black criminality (as a whole) would be ranked. White criminologists relied on biological determinism to explain the underlying causes of black lawlessness. Yet gendered and racialized presuppositions about blacks' penchant for crime were largely derived from cherished notions about the innate proclivity of African Americans, female and male, to commit acts of violence and vice.

The scientific roots of black criminal deviance can be most easily traced to the antebellum period, when notions of Negro inferiority and degeneracy were in vogue. The paternalist ethos of southern slaveholders was largely supported by the scientific "fact" of hereditary Negro incompetence. The slave's biological, psychological, moral, and intellectual deformity was regarded as a derivative of his or her African ancestry. West Africans' physical and psychical "characteristics"—superstition, vanity, "animal sexuality," "moral insensibility," "callousness to the suffering of others," inability to resist disease, "improvidence," deception, and "lack of inhibitive power," made them "instinctive and habitual criminal[s]."[103] African Americans supposedly inherited these degenerative traits.

During the pre–Civil War era, early American anthropologists theorized about the origins of human species and the Negro's place in the order of civilization. Polygenist thinkers proclaimed that blacks were a separate species, incapable of change over time. Samuel Morton, a physician and "dean" of the polygenesis school of thought, helped galvanize the intellectual movement by furnishing material proof of the Negro's "true position as an inferior race." He paraded his prized collection of human skulls among his peers, and he marketed the notion that the degree of moral and intellectual facility among the races could be determined by the size of their cranial measurements. Predictably, the "large-brained Caucasoid" was seated at the tip of the ancestral pyramid.[104]

While polygenists were a minority voice in the nineteenth-century origins debate, their opinions were paramount in justifying the continued enslavement of African Americans. Respected theorists like Josiah Nott, an Alabama physician and protégé of Samuel Morton, championed the belief that blacks were an infantilized and separate species. Like his contemporaries, Nott considered bondmen and bondwomen to be childlike, lacking the ability to self-govern or implement discipline in their daily lives. White southerners acknowledged that slavery had taught "absolute savages" to be skilled agriculturalists, domestics, and, to some extent, skilled mechanics and industrial workers, but presumed that these advances were made only because they transpired in a state of slavery or quasi slavery.[105]

In the years following the Civil War, white social scientists stayed faithful to earlier scientific pledges regarding Negro "indolence" and ineligibility for freedom. They expanded their crude and highly speculative knowledge base to incorporate sophisticated statistical data to explain the rapid increase in black crime.[106] These "experts" rationalized that the *gift* of personal autonomy excited the dormant criminal sensibilities of the Negro, which were kept intact by slavery. All at once, panic-stricken white southerners clung to the idea that emancipation was a dangerous alleyway that guided blacks toward becoming "vicious vagabonds, whom the states would have to maintain in poorhouses and jails until they perished under their vices or were expelled back to Africa."[107]

During the late nineteenth century, black crime was placed under a national microscope as social scientists sought to understand the causes of Negro criminality. In urban cities—north and south—such as Philadelphia, Chicago, New York, Atlanta, and Charleston, crime was rife. Moderate backers of scientific criminology in the North maintained that excessive criminal activity among blacks in the inner city stemmed from an assortment of issues: unemployment, economic distress, social decomposition, "low morals," and inborn criminal deviance. White southerners, on the other hand, unswervingly diagnosed the problem of "Negro crime" as an incurable race trait.[108]

As historian Khalil Muhammad observes in his analysis of race and crime in modern urban America, the 1890 census and the publication of German-born scholar Frederick Hoffman's *Race Traits and Tendencies of the American Negro* (1896) raised both white northerners' and southerners' ability to quantify black criminal "pathology" through statistical evidence and to display, in concrete terms, the long-term effects of emancipation on the Negro—retrogression and inevitable destruction.[109] "It is not in the *conditions of life*, but in the *race traits and tendencies* that we find the causes of the excessive mortality," asserted Hoffman. "So long as these tendencies are persisted in, so long as immorality and vice are a habit of life of the vast majority of the colored population, the effect will be to increase the mortality by hereditary transmission of weak constitutions, and to lower still further the rate of natural increase, until the births fall below the deaths, and gradual extinction results."[110] In sum, immorality, disease, and vice constituted the triple inheritance of emancipation. These pernicious "race traits" were generously conferred on freedpeople, whose "weak constitutions" and susceptibility to physical, mental, and moral infirmities, as well as criminality, made them suitable heirs.

Weak Constitutions and Diseased Bodies

The interlocking variables of race, crime, and disease made African Americans a threefold menace to white southern society. Like criminality, disease was considered a distinctive race trait of the Negro. The same factors that inclined black southerners to commit acts of violence and vice were deemed the fundamental causes of contagion and exposure: heredity, biological inferiority, immorality, "shiftlessness, ignorance, carelessness, and poverty."[111] Like the black crime "epidemic," disease was also a key aspect of the "race problem" and the "white man's burden." On the word of Georgia ex-governor William J. Northen, emancipation bred a "new made criminal character . . . loaded with infections and contagions and crimes that appall the nation," and "the white man is to be blamed." He has "left the Negro to himself to desolate the land with his wickedness, scattering death by his diseases and blood by his crimes and laying waste all along the tracks of his miserable going."[112]

Criminality and disease were troublesome "plagues" that threatened to destabilize white southern communities. Although African American women and men were believed to be predisposed to contract and transmit a broad range of infectious illnesses, like smallpox, yellow fever, diphtheria, pneumonia, typhoid, dysentery, and syphilis, the abundance of tuberculosis (consumption) cases, in particular, was a great source of panic for white Atlantans, many of whom were in daily contact with "contaminated Negroes." Cooks, laundresses, child nurses, office boys, coachmen, and draymen [wagon drivers] were seen as a "frightful menace" to southern communities, "carrying disease and death at every turn."[113] Remarking on the city's Negro "problem," Northen complained, "The diseased ones know little and care less about the harm they are doing the community by infection. They spit where they please; sleep with those who are not diseased; breed flies by the millions; know nothing of disinfectants and would hardly use them if they did."[114] Disease breeding among "Negro criminals," who, in his opinion, possessed acutely "weak and defective physical constitutions," "smaller respiratory power," and an overarching predisposition to "consumption and bronchial infections," posed an even deeper threat to the security and welfare of white Georgians.

Just as tuberculosis was racialized, and its victims criminalized, black sufferers of sexually transmitted diseases were likewise branded as sexual outlaws. White southern physicians, such as Dr. J. Madison Taylor, construed the spread of syphilis and gonorrhea by working-class African American men and women as a form of "sexual lawlessness." He brusquely conveyed his race-based thoughts on the medicolegal ramifications of venereal disease, asserting that the African American man "is nearly always infected with gonorrhea . . . When chronic prostatic irritation ensues . . . sexual impulses frequently become overmastering. Hence, the first female he meets he is tempted to assault."[115] More subtle, yet equally derisive terms were used to connect black female "lasciviousness" with the "criminal" spread of syphilis.

The black female prostitute, servant, and wage worker were the principal "culprits" in advancing the syphilis epidemic. Syphilitic African American women were named the incubators and transmitters of this blight, scarcely outnumbering their male peers in the infection totals. For the medical experts of this time, this "social menace" threatened the future of the black race. Dr. H. L. Sutherland was persuaded that "the Negro will disappear from the South, as a race, but it will be caused by decimation and disease, and the sterility of its females."[116] Drs. Kenneth M. Lynch, Kater

McInnes, and G. Fleming McInnes expanded on Sutherland's conclusions, citing that the prevalence of syphilis in black women was borne out of "sexual indulgence from practically all of the unmarried women . . . virginity is rare among the poor members of their race . . . until some curb is placed upon this promiscuous sexual communication in this class of these people, or until proper therapeutic measures are forced upon them, syphilis will run rife among them and threaten those of us with whom they come in contact."[117]

These fears of venereal disease did not ultimately drive public policy in the way that the antituberculosis crusade did, but they nevertheless remained a vital aspect of southern public health concerns. Because sexually transmitted diseases were localized in black bodies, and mitigated by the racial and sexual mores that limited intimate contact between black and white, the exchange of syphilis and gonorrhea posed less of a threat to white southern communities than tuberculosis did. Nonetheless, venereal disease was a lateral component of the "white man's burden."

Sexual Savagery

Physical freedom and sexual independence licensed black southerners to select their intimate partners, create their own body politics, and to engage, freely, in the sexual behaviors of their choice—married sex, fornication, adultery, prostitution, and so on. Despite calculated attempts to patrol the sexual behaviors of freedmen and freedwomen, African Americans developed their own sexual identities and formulated independent choices about how to use their bodies. In response, white southerners fancied notions of black sexual immorality to besmirch the character of freedpeople, criminalize the black body, and to stimulate fear of the sexually ravenous black male and the undomesticated syphilis-bearing black woman.

Race-based scientific theories that evolved in the post–Civil War South placed a flagrant emphasis on the anatomical structure of black female and male sexual organs—the source from which venereal disease, reputedly, flourished. Although the black body was, for generations, an object of scientific curiosity, the threat of miscegenation, widespread disease, and sex crimes (e.g., rape and prostitution) provoked a renewed interest in "genital peculiarities." African American women's "animallike" genitalia was a topic of enduring fascination in southern medical journals. Doctors vividly described so-called abnormalities in black female sex organs: "the labia are much flattened and thinned, approaching in type that offered by the female anthropoid ape, hepale, lemur and other pithecoid animals."[118] Also typical were physicians' descriptions of black men's "virile organs" that supposedly reached "massive proportions . . . To offset this penile excess, the testicles are, as a rule, smaller than among white men; the scrotum is also shorter and less voluminous and is frequently retracted after the manner of a dog's,"[119] wrote one physician.

Sexual differentiations made to exist between the races furnished additional "proof" of the Negro's inferiority, solidifying his or her place at the base in the sequence of humanity or placing him or her in a separate category of species altogether. Exaggerations in the size, position, and shape of black genitalia reinforced the idea that African Americans were biologically, sexually, and morally deviant and unprincipled. Gross accusations that black men and women possessed enlarged or malformed sex organs and a heightened "sexual potency" gave new life to preexisting racialized assumptions about black sexuality. Like so, "inbred carnality," sexual impropriety, and criminality became interlaced with anatomical difference.

In the postemancipation South, race-based and hereditary "sexual savagery" were used to explain the black man's purported "bestial yearning" to rape white women and the ensuing escalation in sex crimes. It was widely argued that the Negro male's "stallion-like passion and entire willingness to run any risk and brave any peril for the gratification of his frenetic lust" made him a "menace to the Caucasian race."[120] For those African American men who transgressed racial boundaries and engaged in sexual activities with white women—consensual or nonconsensual—lynching was usually the end result.[121] When the criminal justice system prevailed over the more powerful lynch mobs, black men were imprisoned for life. But this was not the case for African American women. Black female prostitutes who engaged in illegal sex for profit were provided more relaxed sentences—a jail fine or three to six months' service on a county chain gang.

The difference in the rendering of punishment for African American men and women convicted of sex crimes reflects the varying degrees of severity relevant to the offenses allegedly committed, but it also discloses white southerners' static ideological association with black female "licentiousness." Fixed beliefs about black female promiscuity in the South made unsullied African American women and prostitutes nearly indistinguishable. According to one southern physician, black women as a whole suffered from an "utter contempt and cynical disbelief in the existence of chastity."[122]

Lifting as We Climb

The spread of this malignant discourse, with regard to black female eroticism, depravity, and criminality, aggrieved middle-class black women who were struggling to improve the image of black womanhood in the white mind. One anonymous "colored woman, wife and mother" spoke for the "the best class of negroes in the South," saying that "a colored woman, however respectable, is lower than the white prostitute." She continued by stating, "Whenever a crime is committed in the South the policemen look for the negro in the case . . . If one low, ignorant black wretch commits a crime . . . all of us must bear his [or her] guilt."[123] In an effort to neutralize fixed ideas about black female hypersexuality and criminality, elite club women of the National Association of Colored Women (NACW) steered a campaign to reclaim the "lowly, illiterate, and even the vicious" members of their race and sex.[124]

Established in 1896, the NACW emerged from the consolidation of two black women's clubs—the National Colored Women's League and the National Federation of Afro-American Women. The social, political, and economic problems that presaged the development of this dynamic organization were multifarious: the legalization of segregation in the South; ensuing white racial violence and lynchings; the suppression of African American's social, political, and economic mobility; the rise of debt peonage and convict leasing; and the nationwide forswearing of suffrage for women. In general, it was the demand for justice, for the race and for themselves (black women), that sculpted the NACW's organizational attitude.[125]

"Lifting as we Climb," the NACW's mantra, defined the expressed purpose of black women's reform—to elevate the underprivileged members of the race and sex, to alleviate lingering patterns of "ignorance" and poverty inherited through slavery, and to impart respectability to their "benighted sisters." In essence, African American women reformers saw the black female masses as the "black woman's burden." As founding NACW member Fannie Barrier Williams put it, "Among colored women the club is the effort of a few competent in behalf of the many incompetent . . . Among white women the club is the onward movement of the already uplifted."[126]

Educator, reformer, suffragist, and first president of the NACW, Mary Church Terrell,[127] and Olivia Davidson, cofounder of Tuskegee Institute and the first wife of Booker T. Washington, were two of the most energetic black female progressives who worked separately to fulfill a unified goal: to spread reform to "lower-class" black women whose image threatened to further endorse disparaging ideas regarding black womanhood, and to, as Davidson put it, "make the women of the race, physically, morally, and intellectually stronger."[128] This was to be accomplished by creating tangible connections with the underserved populations of African American women and children. "Homes, more homes, better homes, purer homes," was the expressed desire of Terrell, Davidson, and the "colored women" who worked tirelessly to give their "unfortunate sisters" opportunities for improvement and education.[129]

In a speech delivered before the Alabama Teacher's Association in 1886, Olivia Davidson encouraged the organization's members to "go into the miserable shanties and hovels in town or country" where their less fortunate sisters resided and spread the light of knowledge and the gospel of cleanliness. "Someone has said, 'cleanliness is next to Godliness,' but I would say cleanliness is godliness," exhorted Davidson. "No soul can be a godly one that . . . inhabits an unclean body or submits to unclean surroundings . . . By your own example in dress and daily habits as well as by precepts show them how to clothe and care for themselves according to the hygiene laws."[130] Taking up Mrs. Booker T. Washington's charge, black female teachers visited the homes of their lowly peers and, in her words, "organized them into self and home improvement clubs, got them to give up taking snuff, to lay aside the old white cotton wraps and arrange their hair neatly, to wear collars, cuffs, and aprons to school, encouraged them to plant flowers in their yards . . . and so appealed to their pride, and modesty, and self-respect."[131]

Besides tidying their appearances and smartening up their ramshackle living quarters, poverty-stricken black women were coached in the art of child rearing. The proper care of youth was a fundamental lesson that middle-class African American women felt compelled to share with their underprivileged peers. In an effort to dissuade poor working-class mothers from taking Saturday night strolls into town to "stand on the streets or in stores and saloons, dip snuff, beg for treats, gossip, and listen to, and pass jokes,"[132] and to rebuff the "carelessness" and "ignorance" with which they reared their young, club women established mothers' clubs.

In 1898, Terrell reported on the "progress of colored women" in an address commemorating the fiftieth anniversary of the National American Woman Suffrage Association. "Through mother's meetings, which are a special feature of the work planned by the Association, much useful information in everything pertaining to the home will be disseminated," she pledged. "We would have heart-to-heart talks with our women, that we may strike at the root of evils, many of which lie, alas, at the fireside."[133]

Fearful of the generational transmission of vice, Terrell and Davidson strove to decrease the spread of criminal tendencies and "evil habits" to black youth by inculcating "women who are daily brought before the police courts in our large cities" and "illiterate Negroes, who are the only ones contributing largely to the criminal class," with middle-class values.[134] "Make a tour of the settlements of colored people, who in many [southern] cities are relegated to the most noisome sections permitted by the municipal government, and behold the mites of humanity that infest them," Terrell warned. "Here are our little ones, the future representatives of the race, fairly drinking in the pernicious example of their elders, coming in contact with nothing but ignorance and vice, till at the age of six, evil habits are formed which no amount of civilizing or Christianizing can ever completely break."[135] In a similar tone, Davidson remarked that "the seeds of disease and suffering are sown in infancy, childhood and girlhood by mothers, at first, through ignorance of proper methods of caring for their little ones from their birth."[136] Thus, Terrell, Davidson, and middle-class African American women (and men), en masse, made it their mission to inoculate Negro youth from the scourge of criminality, negative influences, and low moral standards by depositing spores of reform among them.

W. E. B. Du Bois and the Problem of Negro Crime

By the turn of the twentieth century, preeminent scholar, historian, sociologist, activist, and criminologist W. E. B. Du Bois began to register his thoughts on the subject of "Negro crime."[137] He made particularly impressive strides in the study of black criminality in the South, and he produced scholarship that challenged white southerners to eliminate convict leasing altogether. Du Bois placed a distinct emphasis on the sociological rather than the biological variables used to explain the problem of "Negro crime." He consciously rejected the notion that criminality was an innate racial characteristic and, instead, fostered a counter discourse centering on the depressed social, material, and economic circumstances of black life in the nation's urban spaces—North and South.

Racism, prejudice, unfair sentencing criteria for black offenders, poverty, economic exclusion, and the psychological impact of migration from

South to North, and countryside to city, were all cited by Du Bois as potent causes of black crime. In his opinion, the Negro's "peculiar environment," in conjunction with the "influence of homes badly situated and badly managed, with parents untrained for their responsibilities," as well as the "influence of social surroundings which by poor laws and inefficient administration leave the bad to be made worse," promoted a fecund atmosphere for the production of black crime.[138]

The same social and economic forces that seemingly aggravated the rise of black crime in the North existed in the South: poverty, racism, prejudice, economic immobility, "displacement and strain" brought on by migration to southern cities, and "moral debasement" produced by slavery. However, the added burden of ubiquitous violence and terror and the southern convict lease system made black southerners, whether innocent or guilty, excessively vulnerable to calculated forms of legal and extralegal exploitation. Du Bois criticized the South's determination to maintain slavery, firmly contending that with the advent of the convict lease system "a new slavery and slave-trade was established."[139]

The corrupt collaboration of politicians, courts, legal officials, and industrialists had resulted in the rise of convict leasing. The system restored the fragile economies of the southern states after the Civil War, but it also preserved "the worst aspects of slavery." As Du Bois bluntly articulated, "The innocent, the guilty, and the depraved were herded together, children and adults, men and women, given into the complete control of practically irresponsible men, whose sole object was to make the most money possible. The innocent were made bad, the bad worse; women were outraged and children tainted; whipping and torture were in vogue, and the death-rate from cruelty, exposure, and overwork rose to large percentages."[140]

Between 1897 and 1910, while serving as a faculty member in the department of sociology at Atlanta University, Du Bois pinpointed the brutality and abuses inherent within Georgia's convict lease system. "The Spawn of Slavery" (1901) and *Some Notes on Negro Crime* (1904) furnished two of the earliest scholarly treatments of convict leasing. The latter study was most essential as a sociological survey of black criminality in the South. The cities of Atlanta, Savannah, Columbus, and Macon were rife with lawlessness, and rural communities did not fare much better. Acutely aware of the statewide problem of "Negro crime," Du Bois ventured to study and trace the origins of violence and vice among black Georgians. He broadly concluded that white oppression and the legacy of slavery—"immorality, crime, and laziness"—were to blame.

While Du Bois's position on the problem of "Negro crime" was, to a large extent, in disagreement with the perspective of most of his white contemporaries, his conservative stance on the quandary of black criminality was laced with class biases and tensions that, inadvertently, buttressed allegations made by racial radicals against African American offenders—the "scourge" of southern communities and the black race. He contended that "to the minds of many," the problem of black criminality "is the real Negro problem."[141] To address this dilemma, Du Bois called upon a small legion of race leaders, the "talented tenth," to lift the demoralized Negro from the muck and mire of slavery's past; to train the black masses in middle-class civility, morals, and manners; and to indoctrinate them with the bourgeois credo of "respectability." Steeped in moral turpitude, the "lowest class of criminals, prostitutes, and loafers; the submerged tenth" would prove the most difficult to reform.[142]

The "white man's burden" was a shared affliction of the black middle class. The upper crust of the Negro race saw their advancement in society to be inextricably joined to the progress of the black masses. Degenerate social activities like gambling, drinking, fornication, loitering, and carousing the night away in smoke-filled juke joints cast a foggy shadow over the race as a whole. The black masses and the elite would be forced to collectively carry the weight of racism and prejudice and would struggle to divide themselves from the fixed stereotypes that disfigured their racial identity. Race men and women were compelled by a sense of righteous indignation to civilize the "lower classes" and to promote sexual purity and abstinence from illegal and disreputable pastimes. While the black elite did not wholly replicate the forms of hostile paternalism exercised by white southerners, subtle rhetorical overlaps reveal strong biases against poor blacks and criminals—the greatest threat to African American progress.

Everyday Crusade against Black Idleness

White southerners' solution to the problem of "Negro idleness" counteracted the remedy afforded by the black middle class. Unconvinced of freedpeople's ability to reform, racial radicals doggedly averred that without the institution of slavery or a fixed system of forced labor to regulate the deep-rooted psychological, biological, sexual, and moral deficiencies of the Negro, the ex-slave would surely revert to his or her listless, profligate, and criminal ancestral "self." Scientific racism tacitly and overtly reassured white southerners in their attack against the social and economic free will of former slaves, whose productivity rested on the discipline of the "dominate" race. Without white supervision and the persuasion of the whip, black southerners threatened to idle away precious hours in lewd houses, saloons, pool rooms, railway stations, and on street corners at a time when, according to Charles H. McCord, "business, manufacturing, and farming interests are suffering for lack of labor," which "exasperates the more ambitious white man, and especially so since he knows he is supporting these same worthless loafers anyhow."[143] The national government was fiercely criticized for encouraging black idleness and debauchery, and the Freedmen's Bureau—the nation's first social welfare agency—was perceived as a great enabler of Negro apathy.

At the close of the Civil War in 1865, the Bureau of Refugees, Freedmen, and Abandoned Lands, also known as the Freedmen's Bureau, was created by the federal government to assist ex-slaves in making the transition from slavery to freedom. Field agents, officers, clerks, and medical personnel descended on the South to carry out the orders of bureau commanders: to provide economic relief to ex-slaves, foster educational opportunities, offer medical support, and regulate labor.[144] By intervening in contract negotiations, bureau agents functioned as intermediaries between white planters in search of cheap black labor and ex-slaves in pursuit of economic opportunity.

The written labor agreement became an essential tool of conciliation and a critical element in the long-term goals of Reconstruction. Contracts allowed bureau officials to reassure untrustworthy white employers and skeptical black employees that free labor agriculture would succeed.[145] Affixed to the northern-based free labor ideology was the optimism that contractual arrangements would solidify a system of labor fairness in the South, where the rights and obligations of planters and ex-slaves would be recognized and mutually respected. Yet, for all that the Freedmen's Bureau did to facilitate work agreements, it did little to protect illiterate and semiliterate black workers from miscalculating the value of their hire or subjecting themselves to the exploitation of cotton lords.

Labor negotiations routinely tipped in favor of white planters, leaving freedpeople vulnerable to the predations of their former owners and the highly corrupt legal systems of the South. Even if bureau officials were cognizant of the extent to which white Georgians upheld the South's code of racial injustice, they consistently supported policies that denied federal relief to able-bodied freedmen and freedwomen.[146] Sympathetic bureau authorities classified some unemployed freedwomen as dependents worthy of assistance, while the remaining unwaged "idlers, loafers, gamblers . . . drunks, disorderlies, and flimflammers" were left to fend for themselves.[147] Acting as a buffer between legal authorities and ex-slaves, agency representatives in Georgia maneuvered to cajole freedpeople back into the fields, rather than see them imprisoned for vagrancy.

On March 12, 1866, the Georgia General Assembly approved the state's first vagrancy law, ushering in a state-sponsored crusade against black "idleness." Under the law, vagrants were defined, in part, as "all persons leading an idle, immoral, or profligate life, who have no property to support them, and are able to work and do not work." Landless blacks with "no visible and known means of a fair, honest, and reputable livelihood," or "who live by stealing or by trading in, bartering for, or buying stolen property [and gambling],"[148] were susceptible to harsh legal penalties.

Black Codes—a set of laws and statutes put in place to define and limit the rights of ex-slaves after the Civil War—were passed in all the southern states, and each polity adopted its own vagrancy laws. Although the Black Codes were prohibited by the federal government by 1868, loosely defined laws pertaining to vagrancy and loitering lingered on the books for several decades. White southern authorities exploited abstractions in the law to substantiate the illegitimate arrest of black men, women, and teenagers for negligible offenses.

Small towns and urban metropolises alike commissioned wholesale arrests of black vagrants. In south Georgia, Dougherty County sheriff Edwards wasted no time assembling a posse to raid black barrooms and dives in the districts of Smoky Row and Sandy Bottom. One news writer claimed that the first raid "netted twelve vagabonds and all during the afternoon and night the jail has been filling up . . . When the news of the raid spread, dozens of negroes could be seen sprinting for the city limits through alleys and side streets."[149] Some fled north to the cities of Macon and Atlanta, but they were quickly disillusioned to find police squads waiting for them at the city gates. In Macon, Chief Butner's regiment strategically invaded black hangouts, including "Heifer Pen," one of the "toughest negro dives in the city."[150] Police authorities in Atlanta shared similar success, but found it difficult to manage its vastly swollen vagrant population. Atlanta's jails were too small to hold the mass of new arrivals, which numbered in the thousands. Hundreds of unemployed black migrants were siphoned off to the Fulton County chain gang, while others were confined in local jails.

The vagrancy statutes of Georgia left all unemployed and propertyless freedmen and freedwomen, throughout the state, at deep risk of "lawful arrest," fine, imprisonment, or a sentence to "work on the public works or roads for no longer than a year," or, at the discretion of the court, to be "bound to some person for a time not longer than one year."[151] Despite the Freedmen's Bureau's efforts to promote industry among ex-slaves, white Georgians firmly contended that the federal government helped turn the Negro into a "miserable object of charity." Northern radical Republicans, carpetbaggers, and educational and religious optimists were accused of furthering the damage by promoting social, economic, and political equality, and by giving the Negro "a consciousness of being unharnessed, unhitched, unbridled, and unrestrained."[152]

A Critical Remedy to a Bleak Diagnosis

To eradicate the highly contagious disease of black criminality, white Georgians decided to quarantine African American men and women in state-sanctioned convict lease and chain gang camps. Scientific notions of black criminal deviancy, from the antebellum period to the turn of the twentieth century, played a considerable role in shaping white southerners' preoccupation with black crime and the decision to institute a system of convict leasing largely based on the plantation design. Remote settings, the presence of whipping bosses, long work hours, brutal floggings, poor diet, threadbare clothing, dilapidated housing, comingling of female and male captives, arbitrary labor expectations for men and women, and unprovoked sexual assaults against black female victims were the core ingredients used to formulate this toxic penal establishment.

It is clear that lessees' quest for profit and white southerners' paranoid fixation with the overthrow of freedpeople's social, political, and economic liberties had a critical impact on the expansion of Georgia's carceral infrastructure. However, scientific racism and prevailing race-based assumptions about how to settle the problem of "Negro crime," "idleness," disease, and sexual "impropriety" also helped instigate and validate the forcible use of black convict labor. Scholars should not dismiss the outsize influence this pseudoscientific discourse had among white southerners, who yearned to return blacks to a model of slavery where they once "thrived" and had their hereditary impulses toward immorality, violence, and vice regulated. Indeed, this racially inspired body of thought was crucial to the assembly and operation of involuntary penal servitude. By employing a racialized and gendered approach to the study of "Negro crime," one is better able to assess how the aforementioned social, economic, and legal struggles collectively and comparatively imperiled the lives of black female and male subjects. Moreover, this type of analysis allows for a deeper perusal of some of the most critical, yet neglected, issues that helped facilitate black women's introduction to the powerful convict labor regimes of the New South.

CHAPTER TWO

Black Women and Convict Leasing in the "Empire State" of the New South

On the afternoon of October 24, 1884, Ella Gamble sat stock-still in the Hamilton County courthouse while an all-white male jury deliberated her fate. The twenty-two-year-old pregnant newlywed and domestic worker had been nearing the end of her first trimester when she was charged with the murder of Pink Buchanan, her employer. Gamble was accused of poisoning the man by putting "Rough on Rats"—a popular form of rodenticide—in a tub of meal consumed by the deceased. Although the evidence against her was "circumstantial," it took the panel merely two hours to return a verdict of "guilty with recommendation to imprisonment for life."[1]

Twenty years later, Gamble was granted executive clemency. From the point of her incarceration in 1884 until the date of her release, she was a productive asset to Georgia's penitentiary system. Under the sting of the lash, she superintended the cook squad at the B. G. Lockett brickyard, hauled slabs at the Chattahoochee brick plant, stitched brooms at the Bolton broom factory, and tilled the fields of Camp Heardmont and the state prison farm. Albeit by force, Gamble established a laboring repertoire that was elastic and complex, embodying the flexible nature of convict leasing in the New South's industrial capital.

After experiencing two long decades of labor, Gamble's body was left "in terrible condition, liable to die at anytime from sudden hemorrhage."[2] Her womb, bladder, and rectum had been eaten away by cancer, making her unprofitable for future use. She was declared by authorities as, simply, "a woman now in poor health on account of the heavy work she has been compelled to do since her confinement in the penitentiary."[3] Yet the full historical record contradicts this uneven rendering of Gamble's circumstances. Certainly, "heavy work" was the principal contributor in the deterioration of her physical state. However, merciless floggings, sexual abuse, injurious childbirths, and medical neglect all contributed to laying waste her health.

Ella Gamble's case spotlights the quintessential features of imprisoned black women's lives and laboring experiences in post–Civil War Georgia, and it animates the suffering many female felons endured within the state's private lease camps. Her example also shows the intractable optimism some women possessed, even in the face of death. As Gamble's melanoma-ravaged body was being handed over to the custody of her brother, the petitioner in her case delicately "explained to her the possibility of her trip causing her death by hemorrhage." The dying woman insisted that she "wanted to be sent home with her brother so that she could find a cure."[4]

This chapter places female prisoners at the center of a historical narrative that recognizes and interprets African American women's roles within the convict lease system of Georgia, the "Empire State" of the New South. Black female felons played an important part in the development of Georgia's postbellum industries and constituted a fraction of the state's black female industrial population; chain gang women made up the rest. Women and girl prisoners toiled in brickyards, coal and iron foundries, sawmills, railroad camps, kitchens, and washhouses, while confronting the ever-present threat of physical and sexualized violence. Although overlooked by scholars, and excluded from historical conversations, black female convict labor was, in effect, an important mechanism used in the construction of New South modernity.

Black Women Workers and the New South Promise

As the South rose out of the ashes of the Civil War, southern entrepreneurs began contemplating the direction the region should take in restoring its economic fortunes. New South advocates encouraged white southerners to relinquish their dependence on agriculture and to engage in the Industrial Revolution by redirecting their focus toward developing a new system of factories, businesses, and railroads. These visionaries concluded that, in order for the South to become an essential part of the nation's economy after the war, it would have to incorporate a newly diversified financial system. With its heterogeneous economy of mixed agriculture, factories, railroads, and mines, Georgia became the benchmark of industrial progress in the New South.

Henry Woodfin Grady, a distinguished orator, entrepreneur, journalist, managing editor of the *Atlanta Constitution* newspaper, and proclaimed representative of the New South creed, was the leading voice for Georgia's aspiring postwar industrialists.[5] During the 1880s, he used the *Constitution* as a public platform to express his enduring optimism in Georgia's ability to lead the South in the Industrial Revolution. In his famous "New South" speech of 1886, Grady opined that the Old South lifestyle "rested everything on slavery and agriculture, unconscious that these could neither give nor maintain healthy growth." But the New South promised "a diversified industry that meets the complex needs of this complex age."[6]

Georgia's most "brave and beautiful" city, Atlanta, quickly rose to prominence as the jewel of the New South. Once the town resurfaced after Sherman's raid, it took on a new identity. The city was given several aliases—"a town of giants," "the Chicago of the South," and "the offspring of the railroads." Each appellation described a city on the brink of modernization and industrial progress. The railroad, the universal emblem of nineteenth-century industrialization, was at the center of Atlanta's growing economy. Male newcomers, black and white, flocked to the "Gate City" to hunt for transportation jobs, while others sought employment in Atlanta's steel mills and manufacturing plants. Women of both races searched for employment in the city's textile mills and clothing factories, but black women found little success entering the industrial labor market.[7]

On August 4, 1897, twenty black women clocked in for their first day of work at the Fulton Bag and Cotton Mills. The company's owner, Jacob Elsas, recruited these women to sort and fold bags—a significant departure from otherwise menial categories of labor black women were usually hired to perform (e.g., sweeping and cleaning). After multiple failed attempts to hire white women for these jobs, Elsas upset the status quo by hiring across racial lines. The newly minted black female operatives were swept away to a separate corner of the factory and kept at a respectable distance from white employees. But the sheer presence of "nasty, black, stinkin' nigger wimmin" at the factory, and the fear of "wholesale replacement of white labor by blacks," was too much to bear. Jacob Elsas's labor experiment was brought down by approximately fifteen hundred white strikers, and his black female employees were promptly dismissed.[8]

From 1879 to the turn of the twentieth century, two separate female labor forces were formed in Atlanta; the first being composed of blue-collar white women and girls that manned the city's manufactories, and the other being composed of working-class African American women who ran laundry services or conducted domestic work. Atlanta's working women were separated by a rigid color line that enforced artificial barriers between black and white. The universal category of woman did little to dissolve the calcified racial borders that prohibited black and white women from sharing occupational space.

From the 1880s through the early decades of the twentieth century, Atlanta's female factory workforce was almost entirely white. White women and young girls migrated from mill villages in the Georgia countryside to occupy vacancies in the city's thriving industrial sector. Upon arrival in the "Gate City," these emigrants settled into work in Atlanta's clothing factories, textile mills, sack- and box-making plants, cracker factories, and confectionaries. By the 1920s, new factories modeled on the practices used by employers in Atlanta were exported to the country towns of Macon, Columbus, Roswell, Winder, Rome, and Savannah. Box plants, overalls factories, shoe manufactories, and cigar plants, among others, supplied employment alternatives to cotton textile mills for females in pursuit of industrial jobs.[9]

During the postemancipation period, freedwomen desperately sought professional options that would release them from domestic service and fieldwork. However, "cotton lords" in the Deep South were unwilling to hire black women as mill operators or as menial laborers on a prolonged basis. According to historian Jacqueline Jones, as late as 1910, only 883 (most were scrub women) out of a total of 728,309 southern black women engaged in nonagricultural pursuits. The majority of these women were employed in tobacco plants in the Upper South.[10]

In her survey of occupational distribution among African American and white women in seven southern cities (including Atlanta) during the post–Civil War period, Claudia Goldin contends that between 1870 and 1880 only 0.1 percent of black women were classified as semiskilled "manufacturing workers," and 0.4 percent were skilled laborers ("including apprentices, painters, and bookbinders").[11] While the presence of African American women in Atlanta's manufacturing plants is fully demarcated in Goldin's study, the specific function of their labor is less clearly defined. Most scholars have asserted that black women's work in the city's factories did not extend beyond cleaning, sweeping, ironing, and scrubbing floors.[12]

As black women's industrial labor force participation perked up in parts of the North during World War I, the extent of southern black women's industrial labor force participation stagnated. This was certainly the case in Georgia's manufactories, where African American women remained grossly underrepresented in the industrial workforce. Even so, their numbers become augmented when combined with the population of black female misdemeanant and felony convicts whose labor remains unaccounted for in the historical literature. Considering the centrality of convict leasing and chain gang labor to the building of the New South, and its ineradicable impact on the modernization of the region, black women's position in the penal industrial labor market must be clarified. In the subsequent pages of this narrative, readers will be able to gauge the full sum of Georgia's postbellum industrial workforce, convict and free.

The Origins of Convict Leasing in the Empire State

In the fast-growing economic frontier of the New South, convict labor became a critical element in the restoration of the region's war-torn economy. Throughout the southern states, industrialists prudently and predatorily stalked prison workers. Amid the swift race toward fiscal regeneration and modernization, felons were herded, by the thousands, into privately operated convict camps. In Georgia, the epicenter of industrial progress, lessees fabricated one of the most prosperous and lucrative systems of forced prison labor in the region. In the decades following the Civil War, the "Empire State" garnered an uncontested reputation for its magnitude of new industries and became a synonym for New South prosperity.

The convict lease system of Georgia evolved out of a ruthless tradition of punishment introduced during the colonial period. In 1732, the first system of convict labor was imported into the colony. Thousands of petty criminals and debtors were packed into English vessels and forcibly migrated across the Atlantic Ocean until they reached the North American mainland. Once they arrived in Georgia, British convicts were auctioned off to plantation owners to work as indentured servants. By the onset of the American Revolution, this primitive system of convict leasing had disappeared. But by the late nineteenth century, the system rematerialized in a bigger, bolder, and more sinister form.

Until 1812, the English system of penal law was still being exercised in Georgia. Convicts were punished by public hanging, branding in the hand with a hot iron, public whipping, ear cropping, banishment, fines, and imprisonment in the stocks, pillory, or common jails.[13] When the state's penal code was modified in 1812, felonies became punishable by "confinement and hard labor." Plans were approved by the Georgia legislature to erect a three-story granite penitentiary in the old capital city of Milledgeville. On May 10, 1817, the facility opened its doors to receive its first prisoner.[14]

By the 1820s, one hundred inmates occupied the state penitentiary. During the same period, several prison workshops were established and populated with male convicts who built wagons, sculpted saddles, stitched shoes, tailored clothing, and executed blacksmith work. Goods were sold on the open market, which triggered much consternation on behalf of

Milledgeville's artisans, who were forced to compete with convict labor.[15] The economic inefficacy of operating prison workshops made prison-based manufacturing in Milledgeville a short-lived experiment. Yet this trial initiated an early "prison for profit" ethos, which was intensely vital to the implementation of Georgia's system of convict leasing.

Georgia played a leading role in the southern convict lease system. While the state of Alabama held the prize for operating the longest-running and most profitable system of forced prison labor in the South, Georgia's leasing enterprise was the most economically diverse, and it boasted the widest variation of industries in the region. To add to its repertoire, Georgia's lessees imposed the most arbitrary use of its black convict population. Its deep reliance on the energies of both female and male prisoners alike makes the state of Georgia iconic in its relationship to the southern enterprise of convict leasing.

By the late 1870s, Georgia's convict lease system evolved into a sustained source of wealth for the state government and lessees. Penal labor was as much a product of entrepreneurial ingenuity as it was a source of economic relief. Inspired by the New South doctrine and emboldened by the Thirteenth Amendment, which permitted slavery or involuntary servitude as punishment for crime, southern industrialists capitalized on the expanding pool of prison "slaves" that could produce "twice the work of free labor." New South prosperity was inextricably linked to the use of convict labor, which bridged the gap between an agriculturally based slave economy and a society in the beginning stages of industrial development.[16]

While convict leasing held no corrective influence on its victims, white southerners believed in the system's ability to expunge blacks' "fondness" for criminal behavior and languor. Prison officials promoted convict leasing as a reprieve from black "idleness" and as an institutional custodian of white supremacy. John W. Nelms, principal keeper of the Georgia Penitentiary (1877–85), spoke for himself and his peers when he professed the following: "If we look into the history of those brought to the penitentiary, we will find that a large proportion are persons who have never formed habits of industry; they know not what systematic labor is, either from a want of early training, or from a constitutional dislike for it. They look in every other direction for the means of subsistence rather than to earn it by hard labor. Such persons are but a step removed from the commission of crime."[17] Hence, the only way to teach these missing "habits of industry" to the Negro was to place him or her under the pitiless tutelage of prison contractors, whipping bosses, and guards to be ruled with a heavy hand until their "lawless tendencies" were crushed or, at the very least, exhausted.

The convict lease system was altogether adopted in the southern states soon after the close of the Civil War, and it served a series of vital functions. Foremost, convict leasing furnished a practical resolution to the South's postwar fiscal crisis while, at the same time, effectively minimizing the social, economic, and political freedoms of former slaves and their offspring. Furthermore, it released the southern states of the financial burden of building and maintaining prison facilities to warehouse its deeply engorged prison population. By siphoning off its excess inmate populations, southern governments reduced prison-related costs while simultaneously increasing state treasures. Between 1872 and 1886, Georgia lessees paid more than $250,000 into the state's reserve.

In Georgia, as was the case in other southern states, emancipation coincided with the immense, calculated overgrowth of the state's prison population. Rather than construct a new penitentiary to detain future inmates, the Georgia General Assembly provided authorization to disaggregate the convict population and create a string of privately operated prison camps. The revised penal code required that "all able-bodied convicts," including women, be rented out to an expanding conglomeration of independent industries. On May 11, 1868, provisional governor Thomas Ruger tested out the new mandate by surrendering one hundred "healthy Negro convicts" to William A. Fort, for one year, to labor on the Georgia and Alabama Railroad. Fort paid $2,500 per month to rent the state's felons. Although dozens of prisoners died in his custody, the Georgia state government labeled the lease a success and expressed great confidence in the future perpetuation of the system.

RAILROADS

Workin' on the Rails

Thomas Ruger's experiment in convict leasing facilitated a vicious trend that would become more robust under future leadership. In 1868, Rufus Bullock became Georgia's first Republican governor. Even though he was not the most auspicious candidate among southern Democrats, his business connections in the Northeast, and commitment to the New South vision of economic progress and prosperity, placated his political dissenters for a short time.[18] Bullock drew investment dollars to the state of Georgia through the incorporation of railroads, and made preliminary steps toward transforming Atlanta into a "Yankee City." When he moved the state capital from Milledgeville to Atlanta, he predicted that the city would become the nerve center of the South. Yet the "prophecy" of the New South presented an ominous revelation to the ex-slaves Bullock claimed to support; Georgia's industry and commerce would develop, principally, at the expense of black convict labor.

While Rufus Bullock was carving out his economic plan for Atlanta, Thomas A. Scott was devising a grandiose strategy to erect a national railway system. Scott's line would stretch from Washington, D.C., to New York, then west to Seattle. Next, it would make its way around the Appalachian Mountains, up the foothills of the upcountry, and enter the towns of Gastonia, Spartanburg, and Atlanta.[19] In Georgia, Scott found an ally in Bullock, who, in his younger years, served as a telegrapher for several of Scott's close affiliates. A willing accomplice and supporter of Scott's initiative to tie Georgia to the rest of the South, Bullock consented to contract the state's prisoners to Grant, Alexander, and Company—the contracting firm hired by Scott to build the Georgia segment of his Air-Line.[20]

In December 1868, the contracting firm of William Grant and Thomas Alexander acquired 113 convicts from the penitentiary to help build the Macon & Brunswick Railroad. By June 1869, all 393 inmates of the state prison were leased to Grant, Alexander, and Company for a two-year term "to be held, used, and controlled by them for their own use and benefit."[21] Company agents reprieved the state of its fiscal obligation to provide for the rapidly increasing prison population. With its postwar economy already overburdened, the Georgia legislature consented to release all privileges to the Grant and Alexander firm, whose sole responsibility was to clothe, feed, transport, and guard prisoners; provide medical attention to sick laborers; and pay all expenses, "free of charge to the state, excepting the salary of the Principal Keeper of the penitentiary."[22]

Until June 1869, all female felons (thirteen in total) were detained at the prison "walls" in Milledgeville, where they worked as washerwomen and seamstresses. Healthy male convicts labored in the prison's blacksmith and wagon shop, shoe tannery, and harness shop, and performed carpentry work, while "invalids," "cripples," and those afflicted with old age and "bodily infirmities" languished, "unable to do a sufficiency of labor to earn their subsistence."[23]

At the "walls," black female convicts labored within a system that upheld a strict separation of the sexes and a rigid adherence to prescribed gender roles. These women were given duties of the "most servile kind."

But once they were hurled beyond the margins of the penitentiary into the state's railroad camps, female felons worked without discrimination with male prisoners.

The precarious work arrangements that evolved in the postwar prison camps were a partial derivative of the Old South plantation regime. In the antebellum period, planters established a promiscuous pattern of utilizing female slaves in masculine modes of labor (excluding skilled trades). Bondwomen and bondmen worked side by side, plowing fields, hoeing weeds, sprinkling seeds, picking, ginning, sorting, and moting cotton.[24] The most "athletic" members of the female sex were sometimes forced to dig ditches, cut trees, and haul lumber. Although the convict-leasing paradigm embodied some tenuous aspects of plantation slavery, including the ungendering of bondwomen's labor to satisfy fluctuating pecuniary and work-related needs, lessees decisively prioritized heavy manual work as the status quo, not the exception. Furthermore, unlike slavery, the obligatory demands placed on black female convicts to enact "men's work" also included the perpetration of male-oriented skilled labor.

The first generation of female captives (1868–80) confined in Georgia's prison camps followed a similar demographic pattern. Each was born into slavery, and the vast majority were arrested in the counties of their birth. Nearly all were between the ages of eighteen and twenty-five years old. Yet numerous girls and elderly women also passed through the state's camps. Most lived in the Georgia countryside and worked as farm laborers. Others resided in urban areas, working as cooks, housekeepers, and washerwomen. The convict lease system disrupted antebellum labor practices and ushered in a new definition of African American women's work.

Georgia's railroad system was the first industry to experiment with the use of black female prison labor. Less than one year after assuming sole proprietorship over Georgia's felons, the Atlanta-based contracting firm of Grant, Alexander, and Company had in its possession seventeen female convicts, all of whom were former slaves. Born into bondage, Mary Brooks enjoyed three years of freedom before she was restored to a lifetime of servitude. In March 1868, at the tender age of sixteen, she was convicted of murder by a Bartow County judge and sentenced to "natural life" in the "walls" of the state penitentiary. One year later, Brooks and twelve other female convicts traded in their sewing machines, cooking utensils, and washtubs for pickaxes, carts, and shovels. By 1874, roughly thirty-two women had been "farmed out" to the Macon & Augusta, Brunswick & Albany, and Air-Line Railroads.

Railroad construction, even in its crudest form, required a complicated level of technical and organizational skill. Work squads were separated into several divisions and given specific tasks to fulfill in a precise order. First, grading crews leveled the grade with shovels and pickaxes to prepare the ground for tie-layers. Cart drivers moved the drift from the "cuts" to the fills, which consisted of large rock heaps. "Tie hacks" cut trees and shaped them by hand, then passed them off to tie-layers, who hand-carried the wooden railroad ties and hammers to the worksite. Behind the tie-layers came "rust eaters," who installed the massive rails. Four strapping laborers lugged one rail at a time until they reached the grated runway. Once the heavy steel was positioned on the gravel bed, a team of spike drivers commenced to hammer large iron spears into the rails to secure the ties.

In the railroad camps operated by William Grant and Thomas Alexander, female convicts did the same kind of work as men did in the "cuts," where they graded surfaces for railroads, drove carts, and shoveled dirt.[25] In the absence of modern technology, the work had to be done by hand in a time-consuming process that required strength and dexterity. Graders milled miles of terrain, while cart drivers helped load large pieces of rock and debris in a wheelbarrow, then rolled it up the dirt rock heap of the "cuts." The tough grind of railroad construction lasted from sunup to sundown, leaving some female prisoners desperately exhausted and unable to churn out more labor. Consequently, "weak," unproductive workers were flogged and sometimes "bucked" and hit with rocks that would "knock them speechless."[26]

Violence was used to extricate the maximum labor possible and to terrorize black victims into submission. Camp officials insisted that corporal abuse was the only way to enforce discipline among inmates; they responded to the whip when everything else failed. Therefore, whipping bosses were appointed to inflict punishment on any prisoner that lagged in his or her work assignments, quarreled with other convicts, physically or verbally challenged camp authorities, or dared transgress against the rigid code of white supremacy.

In 1870, reports of misconduct in the state's private camps prompted the first of several investigations. Members of a special joint committee were assembled to collect testimonies from lessees, ex-inmates, and whipping bosses. In his statement before the committee, Jesse DeVaney, a whipping boss for Grant, Alexander, and Company, owned up to beating female railroad workers (all of whom were former slaves) for "disobeying orders, not working, impudence, running away or plotting to run away, for fighting, for stealing from each other, and for abusing stock."[27] DeVaney's testimony is clearly beneficial in showing how bosses went about inflicting punishment on women prisoners, but it is just as useful in showing the different resistance strategies used by female railroad workers.

While evidence of female defiance is uneasily located in the records of the Grant, Alexander, and Company, it is apparent that some inmates fought, defied directives, attempted to escape, malingered, and took special pleasure in mistreating livestock (e.g., mules) by striking them with rocks or bludgeoning them with sticks. Like other forms of labor-related sabotage, harming work animals was a significant way of interfering with the economic productivity of the carceral establishment. Injured mules could not effectively transport tools, building materials, or other implements down the gravel beds of the "flying" railroad camps. From a psychological angle, however, abusing the stock allowed bondwomen to overcome feelings of powerlessness; what they were incapable of achieving against their armed white male antagonists was easily executed against defenseless beasts. Nonetheless, wounding profit-bearing chattels was risky business. If one was caught, a whipping was sure to follow.

The strap—an instrument of torture first used to punish the enslaved— was reintroduced in Georgia's prison camps. The whipping bosses for the Grant and Alexander firm utilized both a single and double strap to discipline female captives. As described by Hubbard Cureton, a former convict, the double strap was made of a "piece of leather about as thick as my shoe sole, with holes in it, about two feet long, with a wooden handle, 1 ½ feet long. They had one doubled and fastened together with brass rivets; another was single."[28]

In traveling railroad camps, naked and seminude floggings were unleashed as a public display of the camp overseer's superlative authority.[29] During these sexualized attacks that, in many ways, animated white men's perceptions about black female licentiousness, women prisoners were ordered to strip (usually from the waist down), while others were whipped "stark naked." With their bosoms, buttocks, and vaginas exposed, captives were beaten, mercilessly, in the presence of their jailed counterparts—male and female. Some whipping bosses also resorted to the practice of "bucking," a remnant of antebellum days where a victim, often completely or partially nude, was forced to lay bound across a log where she was brutally flogged.[30]

In one such instance, a prisoner had her clothes pulled over her head, with "the overseer standing on them, with her head between his knees, and he was whipping her on her naked butt."[31] Others were "whipped on the shoulders and on the rump, getting from one to fifteen lashes: clothing dropped to the waist and whipping over thin underclothes."[32] At the Macon & Brunswick Railroad camp, ex-inmate James Maxwell stood witness as women were, in his words, "whipped on the bare skin, and in the same way the men were . . . when they refused to keep themselves in position, men were made to hold them; the clothes were pulled over their heads; they were whipped in the presence of men. I have seen them get from 15 to 50 lashes—15 was the lowest."[33]

Although rarely documented, male convicts were sometimes forced to assist in acts of violence against female prisoners. These beatings were public performances staged in the presence of other inmates, male and female, to humiliate, demoralize, and terrorize abuse victims and frightened onlookers. Certain whipping bosses relied on the tool of communal violence to instigate feelings of intraracial and intergendered discord and suspicion among black detainees and to emasculate and disempower African American men. Although the effectiveness of this disciplinary strategy is uneasily verified, the initiative behind the action gives a sense of the ways in which violence was used to oppress black detainees—whether they were on the receiving end or not.

Amid wanton physical and sexualized violence, and the psychological turmoil it engendered, female convicts still somehow found a way to accomplish the sophisticated and intensive duties associated with railroad construction. Albeit by force, they co-assembled Thomas Scott's Air-Line Railroad fifty-five miles north of Atlanta through the hill country of north-central Georgia. More than one hundred thousand ties were laid, several thousand rails aligned, and more than four hundred thousand spikes were driven to build the Georgia portion of the Air-Line.[34] Although convict leasing did not necessarily produce a throng of skilled workers who could expect to use their training in the free labor market, it did generate a highly experienced population of black tradeswomen and tradesmen after the Civil War. Thus, it is important that prisoners' work routines are not underplayed as mere exhibitions of untrained manual labor, but understood according to the complexity required to fulfill such tasks.

Joe Brown's Mines

During the mid-1870s, as the industrial economy accelerated its activity, Georgia's reliance on convict leasing escalated. In 1874, Governor James

Milton Smith broke the Grant, Alexander, and Company's monopoly on convict labor, and instituted a five-year lease with several new individuals and corporations: John T. and William D. Grant, T. J. Smith and H. Taylor, Henry Stevens, Northeastern Railroad, Wallis, Haley & Company, George D. Harris, and Dade Coal Company.[35] Two years later, the Georgia General Assembly took an unprecedented leap by authorizing Governor Smith to issue a new lease for a minimum of twenty years, to be divided among three prison companies that were respectively known as Penitentiary Companies Nos. 1, 2, and 3. As specified in the *Second Annual Report* of the Prison Commission, "No. 1 was composed of Joseph E. Brown, Julius L. Brown, John T. & William D. Grant, and Jacob W. Seaver; No. 2, B. G. Lockett, John B. Gordon, L. A. Jordan, and W. B. Lowe; and No. 3, William D. Grant, John W. Murphy, W. W. Simpson, Thomas Alexander, and John W. Renfroe. The price to be paid was $25,000 per annum, irrespective of the number of convicts."[36]

By the 1880s, a new congregation of long-term lessees was united in the temple of New South prosperity. Henry Grady, an exhorter of the New South gospel, found an eager following in Georgia's aspiring industrialists. With the railroad business in full bloom, he led his flock down a new commercial pathway that he considered "the base of all industrial progress"—coal and iron manufacturing. Tennessee, Georgia, and Alabama, the South's greatest producers of coal and iron, were the projected frontrunners in the race to control the nation's iron market. Because ore could be produced in these states at almost half the cost of the North, there was ample cause to side with Grady's predictions.

During the late nineteenth century, the growth of the coal and iron industry in the South outpaced the industrial growth in the North during the same period.[37] Coal and iron production drew substantial assets to the region during the Gilded Age and became a pillar of modern industrial economic progress. Yet the development of coal and iron industries in Georgia, Alabama, and Tennessee was largely contingent on the use of convict workers, who were more "reliable" and "productive" than free laborers. The profitability of convict labor exceeded that of free labor. Prisoners could be impressed to conduct labor tasks that were either too dangerous or undesirable for free laborers, particularly mining. By using cheap convict labor in coal and iron production, southern industrialists could sell these commodities at a discounted rate.

By the turn of the twentieth century, Georgia, Alabama, and Tennessee produced 6 percent of the United States' bituminous coal, 13 percent of its coke, and 11 percent of its pig iron. But the height of this production took place in the 1890s. In 1896, these three states combined generated 19 percent of the nation's pig iron.[38] The state of Alabama was especially successful in instituting a financially prosperous lease system through iron and coal production, and it maintained the longest-running operation in the South (1866–1928).

The mining states of Alabama and Tennessee drew the most profit from their use of convict labor. By 1886, each state amassed close to $100,000 per year, which was equivalent to one-tenth of the states' combined revenue. Georgia, Mississippi, Arkansas, North Carolina, and Kentucky also drew substantial earnings from leasing prisoners, ranging from $25,000 to $50,000 annually. On a national level, all penal systems that did not utilize convict leasing recovered a mere 32 percent (or less) of their total operating costs, while those that did capitalize on prison labor earned an unprecedented 267 percent.[39]

In Georgia, Joseph E. Brown's coal mines were the bedrock of one of the South's biggest fortunes. Brown, an ex-governor, former senator, and enterprising industrialist, built his wealth through the acquisition of the state-owned Western & Atlantic Railroad and as founder of the Dade Coal Company. While both corporations were lucrative for Brown, he gained his greatest earnings through the manufacture of Georgia coal. A clever businessman, he purchased his property and materials during Reconstruction, when prices were low, manned his mines with cheap convict labor, and shipped his coal and ore over the W & A Railroad.[40] Brown's ingenuity set him apart from his competitors and situated him as Georgia's leading contender in the coal and iron industry.

In the spring of 1874, Dade Coal Company was awarded the lease of ninety-one prisoners to work in the Raccoon Mountain mines. At the end of that year, sixty additional convicts were shipped off to Joe Brown's colliery. It did not take long for the lessee to gain a return on his investment. By 1888, Dade Coal secured a profit base of $100,000 per year. With the financial proceeds, Brown purchased additional holdings, including Walker, Rising Fawn, Chattanooga Iron, and Rogers Railroad & Ore Banks.[41] He also acquired more convicts to activate his newly acquired businesses. By 1900, more than three hundred convicts disappeared into the hollow of Joseph Brown's northwest Georgia coal fields.

At the Dade quarries, convicts worked side by side with free laborers. Low-ranking miners accrued fifty cents per shift, while supervisors earned almost four times as much. William Thomas Dickson, a foreman at the

Raccoon Mountain mines, was paid $1.75, per shift, to supervise the work of convicts. Dickson implemented a task system of labor at the mines, doling out monetary incentives (twenty-five cents per load) to prisoners that loaded more than their required freight for the day. Although tasking reflected a departure from the gang labor system used to construct Georgia's railroads, it did not reduce the volume of work or eliminate the supreme risk of death lingering in the coal mines of southern Appalachia.

Found in the coalfields of West Virginia and northeastern Pennsylvania, anthracite ("hard coal") was the preferred fuel in cities, substituting wood. But, by 1870, a cheaper grade of bituminous or "soft coal" (manufactured in the South) became the ideal source of energy to power steam engines and locomotives and to make coke for steel. In the southern Appalachian coal mines, convicts refined primitive technologies and improvised a methodical system of mining that could, by contemporary standards, equate with professional engineering.

In the absence of bulldozers, drills, trucks, and modern explosives, convict coal miners used picks, axes, and shovels to dig tunnels. Miners were lowered down the shaft of hand-dug burrows in a metal cage. A long cable cord supported the lift as it descended into the deep, dark pit of the mine. Small oil lamps that produced dense clouds of smoke barely illuminated the chasm. Prison work gangs labored from dawn until dusk, driving their picks and shovels into the walls of the mine, breaking away chunks of coal and iron ore. In the subterranean hold of the prison mine, convicts tackled the hot, dusty, and wet conditions. Steam pumps worked overtime drawing water out of the mines, while furnaces ventilated the shaft. Injury and death were all too common.

Nestled away in the foothills of Dade County were several of the worst prison mines in the South. Convicts and free laborers alike could relate to the words of the popular African American folksong "Beat It on Down the Line": "This job I got is a little too hard / Dangerous money, little pay / Gonna wake up in the mornin' and pack my case / Beat it on down the line . . . / I'll be waiting at the station / When the train come along / Scamperin' on down the line / Lord I'm goin' back from where I used to be/ Down in Joe Brown's coal mine."[42] For convict workers, who couldn't "scamper on down the line," the prison camp was the place where they lived, suffered, died, and were buried.

As stated in the Georgia House Journal (1890), at Joe Brown's mines, prisoners labored "in such places as rendered it necessary for them to lie on their stomachs while at work, often in mud and water with bad ventilation, in order to get out the daily amount of coal that would save them from the punishment to be inflicted by the whipping boss."[43] Some were severely injured by falling rocks and explosions, and more than one dozen others died in "unexplained" accidents. Those who made it out of the mine alive returned to their quarters to rest on filthy bedding "infested with body lice. Window glass was broken, the barracks roof leaked, and the floor was too loose to keep an offensive odor from rising up through it."[44]

At the Dade coal mines, women prisoners found their labor assignments less injurious than their male counterparts did. In 1874, Henrietta Greene, Amanda Riggins, and Elizabeth Sciplin were all sent to Dade Coal to serve as washerwomen, cooks, and seamstresses.[45] Greene spent three years laboring on the Air-Line Railroad before she was transferred to the mines. Her sentence of "natural life" made her susceptible to multiple migrations that would carry her far from her roots in Bibb County to the remote hinterland of Dade County. Her labor responsibilities in the state's camps followed an equally unpredictable course.

The profit-driven economy of convict leasing left little room for an austere devotion to gender subjectivity. Although the available body of evidence reflects an absence of female miners in Joseph Brown's camps, it is not inconceivable that Brown seldom disrespected gender conventions and, intermittently, reserved female convicts for "rough work." Women like Henrietta Greene, who were already indoctrinated into masculine work routines, supplied well-matched surrogates for incapacitated or deceased male workers. Thus, women's occupational roles in the Dade mines may have been more irresolute than what is depicted in the historical record.

While ambiguities persist over the total function of black women's labor in the Dade prison mines, the effect of gendered violence and terror on female victims is less questionable. No uncertainties disorder the fact that Joseph Brown ruled his prison workers with an iron fist and gave whipping bosses the green light to thrash insubordinate or "lazy" convicts, regardless of gender. He affirmed that in the discipline of convicts "you have no other alternative but the strap. As there is no other way to enforce discipline with more humanity, you are obliged, when the necessity arises, to do so by whipping."[46]

Lessees viewed corporal punishment as the most effective elixir used to cure "work-shy" convicts and reprimand those that challenged white male authority. At the Dade prison mines, Joseph Brown publicly endorsed the whip but privately sanctioned the use of other methods of torture.[47]

One prisoner, Carrie Massie, was barely settled in at the Rising Fawn furnace before she was forced to ride the "blind mule." After disobeying the whipping boss, a rope was tied around the girl's wrists, then threaded into a pulley. Next she was hoisted into the air until her toes barely touched the ground, with the weight of her sagging body bearing down on her wrists. For six hours she remained in the same position.[48] By means of the strap, "water cure," sweat box, and "blind mule," Brown's whipping bosses restored time-honored methods of physical violence, while also arousing the vicious trend of sexual assault. During her years of confinement, Massie (among others) was incessantly tormented by physical violence and rape.

In 1882, Massie was condemned to serve a life term in the Georgia state penitentiary, where she spent the first years of her sentence trapped in the washhouse of the Rising Fawn prison mine. From daybreak to day's end, she scoured ore-caked uniforms and hung acres of laundry out to dry. At nightfall, the teenage girl retreated to the women's barrack. Therein, she draped her cotton-and-husk-filled mattress with her wilted body and nursed her sore knuckles. Narrowly chambered by the splintered walls and ceiling of the wooden stockade, she was unguarded against blustery winds, oozing rainfall, and sexual predators that sometimes invaded the women's quarters.

At the prison mine, Massie suffered multiple fiendish sexual attacks. Although Joseph Brown made it a strict policy to divide female and male convicts in separate stockades to, in his words, prevent "consequences which shock the moral sense," women were still victimized by white guards and overseers. Per the observation of one eyewitness, "The senator has built a house entirely outside the stockade for the women. They are not allowed to enter the stockade, except to do washing under the watchful eyes of a guard, and a guard house stands outside where another guard can always see the door which leads into the women's department."[49] The observer also noticed "two scantily-clad pickaninnies of varying color and sizes playing about the door of the women's department." One of these children belonged to Carrie Massie.

Sexual violence against black female convicts was buttressed by the pejorative racial and sexual attitudes that existed toward African American women, in bondage and freedom. Preconceived ideas about black female promiscuity justified the abuse of detainees, who were frequently blamed for the cruelty meted out against them. In Georgia's convict camps, acts of sexual hostility served as an overt display of camp authorities' "economic mastery" and power over black women's bodies. Camp bosses owned the labor of female convicts, if only temporarily, and attempted to exercise control over these bondwomen through sexual and physical assault. Not unlike their slaveholding forbears, camp officials likely felt that they, too, "owned" the right of sexual access to black female "property."[50]

Rape, as it applied to African American women under slavery, was viewed as a crime of property. In assessing the law and its impact on the enslaved, historian Darlene Clark Hine asserts that, under English law, the offended party was the individual who " 'owned' the right to sexual access to a woman's body . . . If everything about a woman belonged to the slaveholder, then obviously the right of sexual access would be included in that."[51] Female slaves were, therefore, rendered "unrapeable." These same antebellum assumptions about the unrapeability of African American women were superimposed onto the postbellum social and legal landscape, allowing southern white men to sexually terrorize black women with impunity. Convict camp officials profited from the wider societal exclusion of white men from the law of rape as it pertained to African American women and—like slaveholders—were exempted from legal punishment for raping black women prisoners. To date, no example of an authority being prosecuted for violating a female captive has surfaced in the historical record.

Wounded Spirits

The imprisoned black female body was a tableau of violence, accentuated with cuts, scrapes, scratches, broken bones, black eyes, bruises, and scabs left by the whip.[52] Like physical scars, emotional injuries caused by sexual assault left a permanent impression on the psyche of female victims. Rape survivors were, more likely than not, plagued by a host of psychological issues that are best understood in contemporary terms. By drawing on modern-day clinical research, one can better account for the ways in which sexual violence affected African American women prisoners. In doing so, scholars can begin to assemble a story from what Saidiya Hartman calls "the locus of impossible speech," and move beyond the epistemological boundaries that have held historians back from imagining what cannot be verified.[53]

It is reasonable to conclude that the emotional impact of sexual violence on black female prisoners was immense. Wounds of the spirit, like physical ones, cut deeply and manifest in a series of symptoms: anxiety, depression, fear, nervousness, disturbed sleep patterns, recurring recollections of the event, low self-esteem, feelings of guilt and worthlessness, suicidal thoughts, self-blame, fatigue, crying spells, and social withdrawal.[54] In extreme cases, sufferers may have experienced long-term sexual dysfunction, including the avoidance of intercourse or a complete loss of sexual satisfaction. This was certainly the case with ex-slave Rose Williams after she was forced to concede to the sexual whims of her "master" and made to breed with a male slave, Rufus. Citing the devastation of being sexually violated, Williams declared, "I never marries, 'cause one 'sperience am 'nough for this nigger. After what I does for the massa, I's never wants to truck with any man."[55] It is highly plausible that some former convict women responded similarly, forgoing marriage or intimate relations with the opposite sex.

Beyond the aforementioned mental and emotional afflictions and sexual dysfunction caused by rape, other physical and psychological reactions likely surfaced in women's attempt to process the pain of sexual violence. Some victims may have shrouded their inner turmoil from public view, electing not to share their feelings with outsiders. These women may have mastered what Darlene Clark Hine calls the art of dissemblance: the shifting of one's behavior and attitudes to create an appearance of "openness and disclosure" while, at the same time, shielding the truth of one's inner life and self from her oppressor(s).[56] Others may have practiced denial, blocking out the traumatizing episode(s) in order to keep their sanity and to survive the remaining years of their terms—which often lasted a lifetime. On the opposite end of the spectrum, some victims may have opted to cope by disclosing the painful events to a trusted party, in hopes of gaining emotional support from other female captives. Regrettably, scholars may never be able to exactly pinpoint how and to what extent African American women prisoners coped with their post-assault anguish and recuperation. Even so, it is important to begin raising critical questions around these issues, and to disassemble historical silences whenever possible.

Bartow Iron Works

In the spring of 1874, George D. Harris was granted a modest lease of prisoners to produce iron ore for Bartow Iron Works in Bartow County, Georgia. The rising entrepreneur paid twenty dollars apiece for his fifty-person labor force. His roundup included forty-nine hale and hearty men and one youthful, robust teenager—Sarah Autry. On April 20, 1871, Autry was convicted of murder by a Lumpkin County judge and sentenced to life imprisonment. At sixteen years old, she was handed over to the Grant and

Alexander firm to labor on the Air-Line Railroad.[57] There, she was joined by one hundred men and fifteen women. In the "flying camp," Autry was in the company of other women who fought, cried, laughed, and collectively salvaged what was left of their blighted lives. But at George Harris's Bartow Iron Works, she found herself shipwrecked in a sea of men.[58]

In the winter of 1875, John T. Brown, principal keeper of the Georgia penitentiary (1872–77), made a routine visit to Harris's convict camp where Sarah Autry was a resident. There he found the convicts in a "deplorable" state. "Scurvy and other diseases were prevailing with the entire force," charged Harris.[59] The lessee was sustaining his laborers on a skimpy diet of corn bread, salt pork, and molasses, which was served up in shovels or "scoops" by the camp trusty. The convicts' clothing was tattered, with holes exposing their bodies to the winter chill. Some of their shoes were worn to the soles, and their toes blackened by a wave of frostbite that had swept through the camp. In the rain, inmates worked without the shelter of a "slicker" or rubber coat. Rainwater, mud, and iron ore residue remained caked on their uniforms for days until they were able to cleanse themselves. But amid the innumerable abuses found at Harris's camp, Autry's pitiful spectacle was perhaps the deepest violation of human decency.

Unlike the Dade coal mines, where female energies were reserved for domestic duties, Autry was hired to "raise iron ore." During John Brown's visit to Harris's camp, he found that the bondwoman and her coworkers "had been at work raising iron ore all the week." As to the physical condition of the convicts, he held that they were "no more dirty than any laboring man would have been after working all the week at the work they were employed at. Raising iron ore is very rough work and the prisoners often tear their clothes during the week," but "as to the woman Sarah Autry . . . She is a person of dirty habits, perfectly indifferent to her personal appearance, and of the lowest order of humanity."[60]

Autry's alleged indifference to her personal appearance made her a "disgusting" vision to Brown and, possibly, the men around her. While it is unclear whether or not the teenage girl had any control over the cleanliness of her garments, or if her grubby appearance was a sign of negligence on the part of the lessee, her unkempt, unattractive, and malodorous presentation (or caricature) raises a critical question: Why was Autry's condition so exaggeratedly appalling?

On one level, the principal keeper's contemptuous remarks about Sarah Autry, drawn from his personal revulsion toward observing what he characterized as an intrinsically depraved and grotesque black woman clad in men's stripes executing masculine labor, may simply reflect his racial and gender-biased opinion about Autry and the broader community of female felons she was seen to represent. However, a deeper reading opens up alternative possibilities that may explain the bondwoman's perspective without privileging Brown's jaundiced outlook. As previously noted, whether or not Autry had any personal autonomy over her appearance or access to clean clothes is unknown. Even so, it is possible to detect an incentive that might motivate a female captive to exhibit poor personal hygiene. Being the only woman imprisoned at Bartow Iron Works, Autry's "dirty habits" may have been independently applied to ward off sexual predators, black and white, free and bound. While no examples of rape initiated by male inmates have surfaced in Georgia's historical reports, it is neither strange nor far-fetched to envision that such attacks could have occurred.

In the absence of a feminine presence, mixed with the emotional anxiety induced by fixed captivity, forced migration, and isolation, Autry's confinement in Harris's camp symbolized a form of "social death." The framework established by historian Orlando Patterson's *Slavery and Social Death* (1982) has allowed scholars to better understand the sociological impact of slavery, as well as other forms of forced captivity (e.g., convict leasing) on its victims. Like the enslaved, lifelong felons were rendered "socially dead" partially formed people who could never belong to the societies in which they lived.

The convict lease system reproduced slavery's murderous effect on the personhood of its victims. Building on what historian Vincent Brown has stated about the role slaveholders played in the "social death" of the enslaved, one could easily argue that lessee's, too, helped "annihilate people by removing them from meaningful relationships that defined personal status and belonging, communal memory, and collective aspiration," and then integrating these "socially dead" persons into their commercial world.[61] Considering the high ratio of black female and male felons serving life terms in Georgia's penitentiary system, with miniature prospects of being released, "social death" was bound to be among the consequences of perpetual captivity. Yet, for Sarah Autry, "social death" had the added effect of being separated from the community of female inmates she once belonged to and being deserted in an all-male prison camp.

Throughout the duration of her life sentence, Sarah Autry shouldered the burden of "social death." When George Harris's lease was suspended in May 10, 1875, following claims that he ineffectively managed the state's prisoners, the bondwoman and her male co-laborers were re-leased to John Howard at three times the rate paid by Harris. Howard paid sixty dollars, per capita, to rent forty-one healthy convicts (Autry included) to "cut turnpike roads and make brick." But his "utter incompetency" to control convict labor cost him the contract. Within six months of placing ownership on Harris's defunct charter, Howard was pressured to turn over his labor force. The convicts were immediately traded to A. Smith Barnwell of McIntosh County, and displaced more than four hundred miles from Bartow. The prisoners' journey finally ceased at Champney Island, "in the Altamaha River."[62]

Chattahoochee Brick Company

By the 1880s, Georgia's catalog of industries expanded, and so did its reliance on convict labor. During the 1870s, mining and railroad construction were the predominant industries that required the greatest application of prison labor. Within a decade, the brick-making business outpaced earlier manufacturing interests. James W. English, an ex-Confederate, former mayor, and onetime police commissioner of Atlanta, secured a tight grasp on Georgia's bricking industry and the state's felons.

English's empire was built through the integration of several companies—Durham Coal and Coke, Iron Belt Railroad & Mining, Georgia Pacific Railroad, and Chattahoochee Brick. By 1886, he became a majority stockholder in the Chattahoochee Brick Company (CBC), and assumed control of Penitentiary Company No. 3. After the company's restructuring that year, English was able to re-lease the company's prisoners to the CBC, gaining an annual return of 380 percent in leasing fees.[63]

During the late 1890s, the CBC managed more than 1,200 of Georgia's 2,881 leased prisoners. At the turn of the twentieth century, convicts at the Chattahoochee brickyard produced close to 33 million bricks in twelve months ending in May 1907, generating sales of $239,402—or nearly $5.2 million today.[64] English's factory was the largest brick producer in the state of Georgia and the South. The best part of his convict labor force was detained at the Chattahoochee camp, while hundreds of others labored in sawmills, mines, railroad camps, and turpentine farms scattered throughout the state.

The Chattahoochee brick plant was strategically located on the east bank of the Chattahoochee River, near the outer reaches of northwest Atlanta. The location was just right for the production and sale of top-quality red

clay brick. The fertile banks of the Chattahoochee fostered an endless supply of clay-rich soil, while the commercial axis of the "Gate City" was only
a stone's throw from the brickyard. The manufacture and sale of Chattahoochee brick became essential to the growth of Atlanta's economy and
physical infrastructure. Even in the twenty-first century, millions of
convict-processed bricks still adorn city buildings and line the through-
fares of what was once the "Chicago of the South." Relics of English's empire can also be found in the midwestern United States, New England,
parts of the southeast, and Europe.[65]

During its heyday, the CBC worked an average of 175 prisoners, each
month, at the brick factory. From sunrise until sunset, a team of twenty
to thirty convicts mined the riverbanks for the finest clay made of "an al-
luvial soil, the deposit of ages . . . Indeed, so fine is this clay that when it
is crumbled between the thumb and finger it goes into dust, and if damp,
smoothes out a surface as slick as glass," shared one observer.[66] Human digging machines pressed deep into the clay bed with picks and shovels to extract the bounty. With each stroke, the clay was heaved into a mule driven
"dump car" then transferred to the processing plant.

As soon as the dump car was emptied, several workers proceeded to break
up the clay, then combined it with "ground schist"—a crystalline form of
metamorphic rock—to make it fitting for the production of conventional
building brick. Water was added to the muddy mixture, which was then
placed in a grinder. Once the brew was thoroughly refined, it was deposited into several brick-making machines. The devices forced the clay through
dies that molded and cut the mud into bricks. The next step involved the
task of drying the miniature slabs.[67]

The uncooked bricks marinated in the sun for three days. Once cured,
hundreds of thousands of these 2½-by-4½-inch rectangles were carried
to the drying kilns, where they bathed in waste heat in preparation to be
burned. The dried bricks were then carried at a rapid pace by two dozen
workers to one of nearly twelve coal-fired kilns, also referred to as "clamps."
At each kiln, one laborer was required to stoop on top of a barrel, throwing the bricks into the top of the ten-foot-high oven.[68] The stove consisted
of two-foot-thick wall enclosures that could swallow up to three hundred
thousand bricks at a time. According to one eyewitness, at full blast, "Hades
or an iron furnace cannot be much hotter than one of these kilns . . . it takes
forty tons of coal to burn one kiln, besides thirty cords of wood and several tons of coke."[69] Convicts barely escaped the violent fires without scorching their skin or collapsing from heat exhaustion. In a final movement, a

Black Women and Convict Leasing   83

"brick gang" hurriedly assembled the bricks onto railroad cars, scarcely avoiding Casey's whip.

Despite claims that black prisoners were "only capable of the simplest and roughest kind of work," the Chattahoochee brickyard was known to supply the "best brick ever put on the market."[70] One onlooker attested to the deftness with which convicts engaged in the brick-manufacturing procedure, stating, "The process of making these fine pressed bricks is quite an interesting study, and I hung around the machines and yard for over six hours, never once tiring at the beautiful work seen on every hand. The whole thing is the most thoroughly systemized work I have ever seen. Indeed, it is so much like a machine, from beginning to end, that if the chain of labor is broken at any point the whole line stops until all are ready again . . . The hand pressed bricks are as perfect as science could make any line."[71]

While brick making was the most integral part of the convicts' laboring lives at the Chattahoochee camp, prisoners also grew their own food, cooked their own meals, stitched their own clothing, and ran the blacksmith and machine shops.[72] No labor was wasted at the brick factory. Injured and feeble male convicts who could not satisfy the rigorous demands of brick production were effective as cooks, washermen, and gardeners. In the same way, sturdily built women were useful in masculine modes of manual labor and skilled trades.

In the brick-manufacturing industries of the "Empire State," the vocational responsibilities of female convicts were kaleidoscopic, shifting back and forth between domestic, manual, and skilled chores. When Ella Gamble was first convicted in 1884, she was sent to the brickyard of B. G. Lockett (a business affiliate of James English and a minority partner in the CBC). Three months' pregnant at the time, her "delicate condition" limited her ability to engage in arduous labor. For a brief period, she was granted amnesty from brickwork. Her days were spent in the kitchen utilizing her skills as a cook—a profession she'd held before her conviction.[73] But, by the summer of 1885, when Gamble was transferred to the Chattahoochee brickyard, her reprieve expired. The twenty-one-year-old, five-six, 140-pound woman was impetuously driven into "heavy work." In like manner, Mattie Crawford's "enormous strength" made her an exploitable figure at the Chattahoochee brickyard. Similar to Gamble, she was given "heavy work"—a general phrase used to describe the onerous labor assignments certain female convicts were expected to fulfill. Crawford's "great strength and activity" were exploited by camp officials, who tested her physical power on the clay banks, in the brick plant, and in the blacksmith shop.

As she excelled in her ability to forge, hammer, bend, and cut iron, Crawford began to take pride in her ability to perform skilled labor, which was used as a measurement of her own womanhood. As historian Laura Edwards notes, in the free world African American women habitually "worked like men, but they insisted that this did not exclude them from the category 'woman.' "[74] The same is true of black female convicts like Mattie Crawford, who waged a formidable struggle to resist compulsory defeminization and to retain their femininity while practicing masculine labor. At the Chattahoochee brickyard, the "only woman blacksmith" physically resisted the whipping bosses' violent imposition on her womanhood. She was flogged repeatedly by an overseer who "forced her to put on trousers" because her skirts were "getting in the way ... Several whippings were necessary to make her consent to this."[75] This same vindictive method of undoing black womanhood was applied to other bondwomen at the Chattahoochee camp and conjoined with vintage forms of maltreatment.

Rawhide Whips and Resistance

For many Americans, Independence Day of 1884 was an occasion for merriment. Sunrise gun salutes, picnics, orations, wheelbarrow races, greased-pig-catching contests, and pulsating fireworks that blistered the sky were popular scenes implanted in America's nineteenth-century viewfinder. But for fourteen-year-old Mollie White, July 4, 1884, signified the closing of her innocence and the suspension of her liberty and bodily sovereignty; it was the day that marked her dreadful passage into Georgia's itinerant state penitentiary system. Convicted of larceny, White was leased to the B. G. Lockett brickyard to serve out a two-year sentence. Upon entry, her pubescent five-foot, 100-pound body was inspected by a camp authority who decided that, based on her frail physique, she would be most useful as a cook and gardener.

At the B. G. Lockett brickyard, Mollie White prepared meals, dished up prisoners' feed, and cleaned the soiled shovels and buckets used to serve the nauseating fodder. One year into her sentence, she was moved from the Lockett camp to the Chattahoochee brick plant, where she served out the remainder of her term as a cook. Even supposing the youngster's work assignments were less rigorous when compared with other female inmates', youth or labor leniency had little effect on her susceptibility to violence. Mollie White recouped in the area of physical cruelty what she was spared in hard labor.

The Chattahoochee brickyard hosted a series of violent episodes starring "Captain" James T. Casey, overseer for the brick plant. The whipping boss excelled in his role as a disciplinarian and enforcer of white supremacy. He practiced his part by beating fifteen to twenty convicts, daily, often until they "begged and screamed," fell dead on the ground, or toppled over from exhaustion, heatstroke, of the effects of fiendish brutality. Casey was loyal to the antebellum ethos of plantation management, and he replicated the processes of terror and brutality perfected by slave drivers who used excessive violence to intimidate black captives. He supplemented the old formula with fresh rage, exercising immense cruelty to extract as much labor as possible and to create a docile workforce.

When it came to black female convicts, the whip was Casey's preferred instrument of torture. An assiduous note taker, the "boss" documented his volatile rage in a series of monthly "whipping reports." On November 3, 1885, Kate Clarke and Susan Hill experienced one of Casey's fits. Both women were given twenty-five lashes apiece for "fighting."[76] Whether Clarke and Hill quarreled with one another or formed a joint attack against Casey is unspecified. Yet, given the collective nature of resistance that sometimes surfaced among female offenders, in addition to Casey's heavy-handed response to these prisoners' indiscipline, it is conceivable that this incident involved direct action against the temperamental whipping boss.

Like violence, resistance was a universal outcome of captivity. Female convicts actively competed in the contest waged between themselves and their oppressors. In Georgia's prison camps, bondwomen set fires, escaped, destroyed property, malingered, violated orders, and cursed their superiors. Even with limited victories, female inmates fought persistently to preserve their human dignity and to frustrate the state-certified onslaught on their self-worth.

The methods of opposition utilized by women prisoners are, predictably, akin to the resistance tactics implemented by female slaves. Formerly enslaved women and second-generation captives (1881–1910) shared space at the Chattahoochee brick plant, where ideas were imported that influenced black women's ability to oppose their white captors. But the plantation was not the only inspirational ground where bondwomen learned how to challenge (or accept) white male authority. Within the grotto of the private lease camp, female convicts constructed their own individual and collective survival methodologies.

At the Chattahoochee brickyard, several women tested Casey's authority: Emma Clark, Ella Gamble, Kate Clarke, Susan Hill, Mollie White, Minnie

Ward, Leila Burgess, and Nora Daniel—one of the most defiant of the bunch. Born a slave on a Baldwin County plantation in 1861, she inherited the gene of dissent. At twenty years old, Daniel was convicted of larceny and sentenced to ten years "hard labor" in the Georgia state penitentiary. Her ordeal commenced in the "cuts" of the Marietta & North Georgia Railroad, where, for four years, she graded miles of terrain on which the tracks were laid and carted debris to the mountainous heaps where it was dumped. The remainder of her ten-year term was spent dueling with "Captain" Casey at the Chattahoochee camp.

At the brickyard, Daniel and Casey regularly crossed swords. The whipping boss quickly became fatigued behind the bondwoman's shenanigans, which included "disobedience," stealing, "cursing," and fighting. On October 3, 1885, Daniel was flogged three times in one day; "5 strokes" for fighting the first time, "10 strokes" for fighting a second time, and "10 strokes" for stealing.[77] In less than one year's time, she accumulated fifty-eight scores from the strap.

Theft among imprisoned women was a private method of "everyday resistance," a phrase used by historian Stephanie Camp to describe the "hidden or indirect expressions of dissent" and discreet ways of reclaiming a degree of control over goods, time, or parts of one's life.[78] Within postbellum prison camps, bondwomen applied "everyday resistance" in the ongoing battle against their oppressors. Power and control were at the heart of these struggles. Even though they were bound to remain captive, black female convicts still sought opportunities to outwit their antagonists and to celebrate silent victories. Getting away with theft, or even simply frustrating one's aggressor at the knowledge she broke the rules, was an important token.

Incarcerated women drew vital psychological satisfaction from stealing food, or other resources, and applied it to make up for the lack of power they otherwise suffered in everyday life. These tendencies were sculpted in slavery and later put on display by underpaid, overworked domestic servants who boosted supplies as a way of remunerating their missing or paltry salaries. But the legitimate act of "taking" from whites was distinguished from the objectionable practice of "stealing" from co-laborers. Oppressed women workers, bound and free, abided by an informal ethical code that permitted theft on the basis of entitlement. At the Chattahoochee camp, female convicts turned a blind eye when a coworker availed herself to the lessee's goods. Yet thievery among co-captives was considered inexcusable. From time to time, upsets in the "moral economy" ensued, fostering bickering and fighting among female inmates.[79]

At the brick plant, resistance was not always conveyed on private terms, but frequently involved the intersection of both the public and "hidden transcripts" of black female defiance. The term "hidden transcript," a phrase first introduced by social scientist James C. Scott, broadly defines the ideological resistance and "secret discourses of domination" forged among subordinate classes—slaves, serfs, peasants, and laborers—in response to the exploitations rendered by large-scale structures of domination.[80] Yet this terminology can be just as easily applied to incarcerated women, who also forged a unique culture of dissent in response to the power structure of the southern penal system and, like other subordinate groups, made use of private and public techniques of subversion.

Within the confines of the Chattahoochee brickyard, the duality of bondwomen's dissent was made most visible through the act of burning uniforms. The burning of clothing allowed some female convicts to openly express their inner discontents and to resist what I call "social rape"; a term that can be used to describe a unique form of physical and psychological oppression experienced by African American women who were forcibly defeminized and masculinized in private lease camps and on public chain gangs and stripped of their choice and *right* to be socially recognized as women. For many black female convicts in Georgia, forced cross-dressing and defeminizing labor symbolized the dispossession of their basic rights to womanhood and the cruel subtraction of their femininity. Drawing on criminologists Kurt Weis and Sandra S. Borges's classic definition of rape, I would argue that social rape, like sexual violence, functioned as a "total attack against the whole person, affecting the victim's physical, psychological, and social identity."[81] The act produced a total loss of control or power on the part of the victim, through the use or threat of violence, and involved a calculated effort on the part of the assailant to oppress, disempower, terrorize, humiliate, and "bodily disfigure" the victim.[82] This is most vividly depicted in the case of Mattie Crawford, mentioned above, who was beaten out of her skirts and into men's trousers by a whipping boss.

My use of the term "social rape" marks an attempt to expand the conceptual framework by which imprisoned women's gender identity can be understood. Unlike the concept of gender erasure, it aims to preserve the psychological aspects of black women's self-definition. I would posit that, for female convicts, gender identity was as much psychical as it was physical and could never be entirely erased. Forcibly dressing a woman in men's clothing did not nullify one's feminine identity; it merely altered it from a somatic, rather than a psychological, standpoint. Thus, black female captives' gender was not excised but temporarily disembodied. With these ideas in mind, it is easier to understand how the practice of burning masculine garments had a deeper symbolic and private meaning among black women than the public performance suggests.

In slavery and unfreedom, African American women assigned political value to their bodies and engaged in contests over their femininity. These scuffles to defend their feminine identity were commonly fought on the grounds of dress. The roots of black women's resistance against the disenfranchisement of their body politics were first planted in slavery, where the body—as stated by Stephanie Camp—"provided a 'basic political resource' in struggles between dominant and subordinate classes . . . Enslaved people's everyday battles for 'regaining' a measure of 'control' took place on very personal terrain: their bodies."[83]

In 1938, the year she was interviewed by a writer for the Federal Writers' Project of the Works Progress Administration,[84] Georgia ex-slave Adeline Willis could still recall the day the slave seamstresses "took a notion to give us striped dresses . . . we sho' was dressed up. I will never forget long as I live, a hickory stripe dress they made me, it had brass buttons at the wrist bands. I was so proud of that dress and felt so dressed up in it I jest strutted er round with it on."[85] On the Wright plantation in Oglethorpe County, she was taught by her mother and other enslaved sewing women and dyers how to transform plain, straight-cut, crude, raggedy dresses into stylish, colorful attires. After the Civil War, Willis and countless other ex-bondwomen throughout the South transported their feminine identity out of slavery into freedom.

For Georgia's freedwomen, dress was an important sociopolitical marker of a woman's transition from slavery to freedom and a symbolic recognition of her femininity. Whether the social function of their dress was occupational, fashionable, or cultural, ex-bondwomen and their daughters appropriated feminine norms into their grooming rituals. Some women bedecked themselves in "outer pigeon bodices and long skirts." Child nurses, cooks, and maids sported mob caps and aprons to work, while field-workers, unemployed, and underemployed black women wore what they had, whether ragged, patched, or out of style.[86] No matter how they looked, feminine garments affirmed African American women's postwar gender politics. But these expressions of muliebrity provoked wrathful indignation among whites. White southerners glowered at the sight of black women wearing "spruced-up modest attire," women who refused to stoop or yield to their will.[87]

Prevailing notions of femininity and of the security that "proper women" deserved were intertwined with whiteness and generally denied to women of color.[88] Freedwomen (imprisoned and unbound), who represented the underside of "true womanhood," were cast as impure, impious, unsubmissive, unfeminine, and lacking domestic habits. To borrow from historian Deborah Gray White's turn of phrase, "'ladydom' was the reserve of white women alone; black women were mere parodies . . . White women were paragons of femininity and domesticity; black women were Amazons and Sapphires."[89] This public affront to black womanhood was reified in private lease camps, as female roles and identities were violently unraveled by camp officials who forced women prisoners to wear men's striped shirts, trousers, and brogans, and to perform mannish labor. While this was done, in part, as a practical way to enhance labor productivity, the practice itself involved a tangible execution of the broader societal exclusion of black women from the "Cult of True Womanhood."[90]

The demeaning assault on black femininity, through dress and labor, was one of many methodologies used to punish female captives, reinforce racial subordination and gendered inferiority, and to offset the strides black women made to have their womanhood acknowledged after the Civil War. Thus, the burning of clothes became a way in which some African American women reclaimed their bodily integrity and attempted to burn away their convict identity. While careful not to make gendered assumptions, or to dismiss any notion that some bondwomen expressively benefited from wearing masculine garb, it is important to note that male attire did not make a female prisoner impervious to sexual assault. Hence, a bondwoman's action of burning men's clothes was one way of affirming her own feminist politics—the right or choice to be represented as a woman without having one's female identity violently extorted or exchanged for a male one when convenient to her oppressor.

While acts of incendiarism by bonded persons have been classically portrayed as a method of property destruction involving buildings and crops, fire starting had more complex implications among female inmates in the New South. The influx of social rape changed the topography of black women's resistance and engendered new forms of protest, including clothing arson. The practice of destroying garments was as much an expression of a bondwoman's dissatisfaction toward ritual abuse and defeminization as it was a way to undercut the lessee's assets and one's personal productivity.

Weighed down by imprisonment and all its masculine accessories, Mollie White and Nora Daniel were among those who exhibited their frustrations by setting their garments ablaze at the Chattahoochee camp. Casey punished the young women on two separate occasions, rendering them ten lashes apiece in each instance for "burning shirts" and "burning clothes."[91] Understanding their material value to the lessee, and the intricate connection between uniforms and the production of labor, these female convicts were symbolically destroying the lessees' property to undermine orderly attempts toward negating their humanity and reducing them into objects of profit, and to satisfy an internal desire to have their femininity recognized.[92]

For the sake of comparison, in other New South localities—such as the mining state of Alabama—incarcerated women also wrestled to preserve their feminine identity. Historian Mary Ellen Curtin has asserted, "Black women prisoners often showed an even greater tendency toward self-assertion than their male counterparts. They especially resented attempts to force them to wear prison clothing."[93] Not unlike bondwomen in Georgia, these captives' yearning for womanly expression was intensified by freedom. Yet female prisoners in Alabama developed an even more profound intolerance for defeminization—or the mere intimation of it—than their neighboring peers did. For them, a striped dress was as much a badge of degradation as a pair of trousers. In essence, the stripes alone were a transposable symbol of criminality and masculinity. To separate themselves from this interchangeable identity, and to inhibit the depreciation of their ladyhood and general self-worth, female felons refused to wear prison garb altogether and, instead, strived to claim, animate, politicize, personalize, and enjoy their bodies.[94]

On account of the institutional differences and contrasts in labor demands imposed on women prisoners in Georgia and Alabama, female convicts detained in Alabama's coal mines were able to more fluidly express themselves. Because, as a rule, female inmates did not mine coal or engage in "men's work," they were often hired out to local residents as cooks and house servants. Thanks to their abbreviated prison terms (stemming from their reduced worth to mining contractors), freedom of movement, and partnership with other women, black bondservants in Alabama fashioned a style of resistance distinct from that of female captives in Georgia.[95]

At the Coalburg mine, female convicts flaunted their temerity by refusing to wear prison-issued costumes and failing to stay put in their employers' homes after hours. Penitentiary inspector Albert Henley grew perturbed by the inmates' unauthorized departure and outright refusal to adhere to the dress code, complaining that "these women are not required to stay at the house where they are hired & it is no uncommon thing on Sundays to see them dressed up in their finest clothes & walking about the village."[96] His rant continued, "Those who do not sleep in the prison are allowed to roam at large at night and can be seen almost every night in the company store and about Coalburg where ever they choose to go . . . The female convicts at this prison are a very unruly set and give a good deal of trouble. We have had them put in uniform, and try to keep them under control but it is a hard matter."[97]

In both Georgia and Alabama, imprisoned women's bodies served as critical "sites of resistance." Yet, in Alabama, the incarcerated black female body was also a site of pleasure. The practice of hiring out women prisoners, many of whom previously served as domestic workers in the free world, helped rekindle their working-class consciousness. Through dress, these women created what historian Tera Hunter refers to as an "alternative ethos." Bond servants wore prison uniforms to work that signaled poverty, lawlessness, immorality, and a sunken social status. Conforming to the habits of free domestics, when it came time to stash away the washtubs and switch off the kitchen stoves and sinks, these women removed the "sartorial symbols of servility" and criminality for clothing that reflected personal style and self-worth.[98] The next step in the process of reclaiming their bodily sovereignty involved deserting their employers' homes after dark and using their spare time to cut loose at the "company store," which doubled as a "dive."

At nightfall, storefront basements in Coalburg and throughout Jefferson County and Birmingham, the county seat, were transformed into makeshift dance halls and gathering places for the working poor.[99] Engulfed in a miasma of cigarette smoke, stale sweat, and boozy breath, black patrons released their workday tensions by dancing sensually and provocatively to the blues. In Hunter's masterful description of blues dancing, she relays the following:

> The sultry settings, dimmed lights, and prolonged musical renditions invited intimacy as couples swayed together. The "slow drag," one of the most popular dances in the 1910s, was described by one

observer this way: "couples would hang onto each other and just grind back and forth in one spot all night." The Itch was described as "a spasmodic placing of the hands all over the body in an agony of perfect rhythm." The Fish Tail put emphasis on the rear end, as the name suggested: the "buttocks weave out, back, and up in a variety of figure eights" . . . The facial gestures, clapping, shouting, and yelling of provocative phrases reinforced the sense of the dancer's glee. A woman might shout, for example, "C'mon Papa grab me!" as she danced.[100]

Even though true freedom was out of reach for black women prisoners, the "dive" acted as a liberating space where bond servants could masquerade as civilians and take fleeting pleasure in their bodies. Not unlike enslaved and working-class African American women, female convicts rejected all notions that their being had only a "fiduciary value," to be used exclusively for laboring purposes. By secretly engaging in illicit amusements, and forsaking sleep for enjoyment, "unruly" workers frustrated prison administrators' attempts to control and regulate the uses to which they put their bodies.[101]

It is evident that in Alabama and Georgia, convict women resisted the negative social effects prison clothing had in externalizing their inferior status and second-rate womanhood. Although the social ordering of black women's gender positions differed in each state, prompting dissimilar acts of resistance among female captives, the underlying purpose for opposing the commodification of their bodies and the devaluation of their womanhood is the same. Black female convicts wore their pride on their sleeves, recognizing themselves as people, not as possessions, and as citizens, not chattel.

Clothing arson and the illicit appropriation of pleasure represents two distinct ways in which women prisoners reclaimed control over their bodies. Intertwined with these acts of defiance was the custom of verbal dissent. Because Georgia's tight carceral infrastructure narrowed the route of bondwomen's resistance, female convicts were forced to use alternative strategies of defense. Within the closely guarded quarters of the Chattahoochee brickyard, where escape was virtually impossible, verbal assault was implored as an alternative to running away, and women prisoners frequently engaged in oral confrontations with the whipping boss. In one such instance, Emma Clark and Ella Gamble were flogged by "Captain" Casey for, in his words, "threatening my life." Apprised of the repercussions at hand, these women braved the whip rather than endure another moment of unmitigated terror and abuse. Other bondwomen followed suit, undermining Casey's authority by "disobeying orders."

At the Chattahoochee brickyard, "disobeying orders" was a steadily documented offense for which female prisoners were brutally chastised. Recalcitrant behaviors such as "talking back," breaking rules, ignoring commands, and refusing to work were pared down to one egregious wrongdoing—"disobedience." Fifteen-year-old "murderess" Leila Burgess was among those punished for "idleness," "failure to work," and rebuffing camp officials' attempts to commodify her body. Though a freeborn novice to captivity, she understood that lackluster laboring was a potent weapon; the more she malingered and pilfered her own bodily energy, the better chances she stood of thinning the lessee's pockets and weakening the productivity of the carceral estate. Barely one month into her life sentence, the adolescent was tanned "13 licks" for refusing to labor, initiating a long sequence of punishments. For Burgess, as well as other female convicts entrapped in Casey's lair, physical violence became a fixed way of life and an intrinsic outcome of captivity.

Sex, Sickness, and Captivity

The Chattahoochee brick plant was not only a bastion for physical and sexual cruelty but a breeding ground for sickness. At the prison camp, African American women and men were imperiled by infectious diseases brought on by gross neglect. Camp administrators were inattentive to the physical well-being of convict workers, leaving them exposed to a wide range of afflictions that caused them much grief and suffering. Between 1884 and 1886, a "scourge of unhealthfulness" swept through the brickyard. Multiple convicts died of "consumption" (tuberculosis) and pneumonia, while 149 others were afflicted with a "low form of pneumonia"—influenza. The blight of pulmonary infections that erupted in the camp started in the contaminated prison barracks, which, according to the principal physician, "leaked, wetting the bedding to a greater or less extent of a number of the convicts." Others struggled with malarial fever, "portal congestion," "dropsy" (edema), neuralgia (nerve pain), constipation, and "eye diseases."[102]

Dozens of female and male convicts at the Chattahoochee camp were exposed to occupational hazards and physical violence that left them permanently maimed, scarred, or severely wounded. Some were impaired by sunstroke, "gunshot wounds," bone fractures, sprained joints, burns, and paralysis. Skin conditions like carbuncle—a form of staphylococcal skin infection characterized by pus-filled masses—also distressed its victims. The bacteria-laden dwellings of the convict camp heightened the infectivity of prison workers and made existing physical injuries worse, sometimes leading to death.

Sickness was, by and large, an immutable consequence of prison life. But for female convicts, certain gynecological problems further complicated their ability to subsist under the harsh terms of their confinement. At the Chattahoochee camp, a duo of female convicts was badly encumbered by dysmenorrhea (painful menstruation). Month after month, these women confronted severe and debilitating uterine spasms. Other conditions like amenorrhea (suppressed menstruation), leukorrhea (vaginal discharge mingled with pus), menorrhagia (excessive menstrual bleeding), "womb disease," "inflammation of ovaries," and "prolapsus uteri" (falling of the womb) resulted in gross discomfort for more than one dozen female sufferers.[103]

During the mid-nineteenth century, scientific theories emerged that linked the quality of a bondwoman's gynecological health with her ability (or inability) to accomplish (re)productive labor. Regularity in menstrual cycles was deemed necessary not only for childbearing purposes but also for performing one's work-related duties. Missed work and barrenness were "twin problems" that required focused attention from physicians.[104] Doctors experimented with therapies for regulating abnormal menstruation and other disorders to improve an enslaved woman's ability to perform productively and reproductively.

Like their slaveholding forbears, lessees were largely influenced by antebellum notions of bondwomen's health and its implications for labor efficiency. To enhance the productivity of their workers, they recruited the services of local doctors—who were then approved by the state—to occupy prison camps and offer care to those prisoners in need of medical or surgical treatment. General practitioners with minimal expertise in treating reproductive and vaginal disorders were entrusted with the management of convict women's bodies. To reconcile their limited proficiency in curing gynecological ailments, camp physicians deferred to their peers, medical journals, or the recommendation of the principal physician in resolving women's health matters.

After the Civil War, the study of gynecology and obstetrics was still in a premature state. Clinicians were clumsy in their treatment of female patients, and they often relied on crude methodologies and antidotes to treat reproductive problems. Dysmenorrhea, the most baleful of menstrual disorders, required creative ingenuity on the part of physicians, whose suggested cures included dilating blood passages through the use of a bougie or leeches, painkillers, laxatives, and hot applications. Others prescribed cotton root, opium, chloroform, and iron.[105]

Menorrhagia, a less obtrusive yet equally undesirable condition, prompted an even more innovative response among physicians, who prescribed silver oxide, cinchona bark, carbolic acid, and quinine.[106] Although quinine's dangerous effects were well known in the medical community, doctors commonly recommended it—but "with great caution." The chemical was "dissolved in water and a little sulphuric [sic] acid," then inserted into the patient's body with a hypodermic needle. Dr. W. Greene found that, in some cases, "violent ulceration" resulted, "destroying the tissue beneath the skin, and presenting to view the uncovered muscles."[107]

Recognizing the caustic effects of quinine, some doctors opted for the use of ergotine—a substance drawn from ergot fungus found in diseased rye and cereal plants—to control excessive menorrhagia. The fluid was dissolved in "equal parts of water and glycerin" before being "injected under the skin of the thigh and abdomen."[108] Treatment was rumored to produce a spontaneous effect and was declared an infallible agent in managing excessive menstrual bleeding. It was equally "remarkable" in expediting childbirth and reducing postnatal hemorrhage.

In the treatment of amenorrhea (suppressed menstruation), Dr. Willis F. Westmoreland, a celebrated surgeon, editor of the *Atlanta Medical and Surgical Journal*, former vice president of the Southern Surgical and Gynecological Association, Atlanta Medical College professor, and principal physician of the Georgia state penitentiary (1884–90), encouraged the use of electric pessaries—devices worn inside the vagina to support or "arouse the organ"—and cheaper, more accessible, uterine cloth tents.[109] By the 1870s, tents were a particularly popular means of administering intrauterine medication, dilating cervical strictures, and priming the uterus for intrauterine injections. Strips of cloth, from one-half to one inch in width, were rolled tightly between the forefinger and thumb. The fibrous instrument was then dipped in any of the following agents: "tincture of iodine . . . carbolic acid, carbolic acid and iodine in combination, nitrate of silver solution, chromic acid solution, glycerin . . . and oil turpentine," and inserted through the cervix into the uterine canal.[110] The results of the tent treatment were mixed, as were others. Yet prison camp doctors moved ahead with recommended therapies and sometimes improvised their own curatives designed to mend women's reproductive functions so as to motivate productive labor.

Menacing Reproduction

While scores of female convicts contended with the unpleasant condition of their gynecological health, others were afflicted with a more deeply demoralizing infirmity—pregnancy and childbirth. At the time of her incarceration in 1884, twenty-two-year-old newlywed and mother Ella Gamble had been married scarcely five years and had given birth to two children, one of which was delivered at the B. G. Lockett brickyard. By the time she arrived at the Georgia state prison farm in 1899, after passing through the Chattahoochee brick plant, Bolton broom-making factory, and Camp Heardmont prison farm, Gamble had birthed a total of six infants—four living and two deceased.[111] Dr. Westmoreland confirmed that the bondwoman's circumstances were not novel. In accordance with his calculation, "dozens of bastard children had been born in the [state's] camps . . . one woman had borne seven during the fourteen years of her confinement."[112] Between October 20, 1884, and October 1, 1890, fifteen cases of childbirth and one "threatened miscarriage" was recorded at the Chattahoochee brickyard alone.

In the absence of "doctoresses" or midwives to usher expectant mothers through the painful travail of childbirth, female prisoners relied on white physicians to assist in labor and deliveries. Because the prison was an institution of power that tightly regulated black women's bodies, female inmates had no autonomy or power over the maintenance of their health—physical or reproductive. They were not allowed to utilize their own practitioners and therapies like the enslaved but, instead, had to concede to the directives of lessee's and their medical handlers.[113] As a result, slapdash obstetric techniques that threatened infertility in female patients were carelessly implemented by prison camp doctors, who were grossly inexperienced in obstetric care. Foolhardy practitioners clumsily manipulated dirty forceps, fingers, or other contaminated items inside the wombs of female subjects, causing infections and uterine collapse. In keeping with the principal physician's reports, five of the six women who gave birth at the Chattahoochee brickyard, between 1886 and 1888, were afflicted with "prolapsus uteri" (fallen uteruses), likely caused by injuries sustained during childbirth and further exacerbated by heavy labor.

Unlike slaveholders, who had an economic investment in the future re-productivity of bondwomen, lessees had no material motivation to grow their labor forces through natural reproduction. Convict workers were re-plenished by a steady stream of felons flowing in from the state peniten-tiary, not through imprisoned women's birth canals. Thus, female prison-ers were economically valued only for their ability to produce labor, not laborers. Conversely, in the antebellum South, where enslaved women were expected to labor productively and reproductively, motherhood had a com-mercial value and purpose: to literally and figuratively nourish the growth of the plantation economy.

Slave owners valued slave infants and, therefore, adjusted work routines to allow mothers to breast-feed their young and put rules in place to gov-ern the nursing and weaning of slave babies.[114] As outlined in the Georgia Slave Narratives, in a section entitled "Rules of the Plantation," "sucklers" were kept working near their infants and allowed time to "visit their chil-dren until they are eight months old, and twice a day from thence until they are twelve months old."[115] But, in the production-driven economy of the New South penal franchise, there was no designated space for mater-nity. What's more, industrially minded lessees usually didn't view them-selves as "humane and enlightened managers" or as paternal guardians in the way slaveholders did, nor did they draw a psychological benefit from being able to think of themselves in such terms.[116]

In Georgia, the hypervaluation of imprisoned black women's produc-tive labor forcefully undermined their role as mothers. Female prisoners were not given the license to nurture their children, who held no social, relational, or monetary worth to leasing agents. Children born into cap-tivity did not belong to the state, the lessee, or the rapist for which there were no legal consequences for deflowering and impregnating a black woman. These "bastard children" were, then, rendered the dispensable pos-sessions of their mothers.[117]

Twelve to fourteen hours per day, female convicts were forced to aban-don their children in dusky, dirt-laden barracks, and to ignore their baby's desperate cries for milk. With little time allowed for nursing, hungry in-fants writhed in starvation while helpless mothers stewed in their guilt. When a bondgirl or bondwoman dared to position her maternity above her role as a laborer, violent repercussions followed. In one such instance, "a mother with her two-day's-old babe sat on the ground leaning against a building in one of the camps—the birth took place there too. A guard saw her and ordered her to go to work." When the prisoner refused, she was "shot with the little one in her arms."[118] Taking into account the calculated devaluation of black motherhood, what then was to become of expendable offspring born in private lease camps?

The process of attempting to understand a youngling's place within Georgia's convict lease system has raised many more questions than answers. Did these children face a lifetime of de facto enslavement, shuffled back and forth between the carceral communities to which their mothers were bound? Or did penal authorities make provisions for disposable infants to be collected from the state's camps? According to one newspaper source, "a number of these bastard children are given away."[119] If so, who were these children bequeathed to? Kin? Childless strangers? Beyond the mere mention of their existence in the state's camps, the fate of these children remains shrouded in mystery. Yet faint traces of death perfume the historical record.

Census data, newspaper articles, exposés, and progressive orations all gesture toward the issue of infant mortality within Georgia's convict camps. For example, in her personal defense of black prisoners in the South, Mary Church Terrell spoke candidly about the predicament facing mother and child: "Women have often been placed in dark, damp, disease-breeding cells, whose cubic contents are less than those of a good-size grave, and they had given birth to children who had breathed the polluted atmosphere of those dens of vice and woe from the moment they had uttered their first cry into the world until they had been relieved from their suffering by death."[120] The informal record is flecked with similar evidences of infant death by starvation, prenatal complications, and other unnamed causes (excluding infanticide, for which there is no proof), while the official penal record remains an empty graveyard.

The physical and mortal condition of imprisoned women was meticulously registered by camp doctors, but the status of their offspring (beyond birth) was omitted from these otherwise copious transcripts. Published annual and biennial principal physician's reports, which were fashioned out of secondhand data supplied by medical personnel, exclude any mention of infant mortality within Georgia's prison camps. Questions loom over why deceased children were expunged from the official record. A deeper interrogation of the facts may provide some sensible explanation.

A series of answers can be offered to explain why babies' footprints left no impression in the annals of Georgia's penitentiary system. It is safe to assume that camp officials, including physicians, skewed certain truths to preserve their individual reputations, negate public reproach, and ensure future employment within the penal regime. Evidence of dead babies would have produced outrage among the press and opponents of leasing, who were growing increasingly critical of the system as its atrocities became more apparent. Therefore, withholding the mortal condition of infants born into the state's camps would have been firmly encouraged.

Another rationale suggests that pregnancy and childbirth were chiefly recognized as ailments sapping profitability. Illegitimate children born to incarcerated women were considered an unprofitable, unproductive, and unofficial part of the convict workforce. Infant invisibility is, therefore, as much a statement about children's perceived unworth to the convict leasing enterprise as it is an example of the way in which leasing officials (including doctors) collectively discredited the mortal condition of nonlaboring bodies. It appears that formal reports only existed to manage and document the livelihood of operable, injured, and traceable laborers, not their unworkable and untraceable progeny.

It is worth noting that the aforementioned assault on black motherhood was not universally implemented throughout the South. In Alabama's prison camps, where many of the sociocultural elements of slavery were preserved, female felons were sustained by the presence of their little ones, often imprisoned with them. They also drew an emotional benefit from consensual sexual relationships with male prisoners, many of whom were the fathers of their children.[121] In Georgia, however, no tangible evidence exists to suggest that incarcerated men and women engaged in intimate relationships, produced children, or assembled quasifamilial structures. Yet there is a glut of evidence that confirms rape as the source of impregnation among bondwomen in the state's private lease camps. This is not to suggest that male and female felons never forged bonds of intimacy or engaged in consensual sexual relations that resulted in conception. It just happens that the historical record does not support this contention. Nonetheless, it is important to look beyond the archive for meaning here, and to speculate on the scenarios that might have arisen in which bonds of affection *could* have been forged between male and female prisoners.

To be clear, the male–female convict relationship in Georgia was a forbidden one. Different from slaveholders, who had an economic basis for allowing and encouraging female–male intimacy and interaction to take place, lessees saw intercourse between the sexes as socially and economically dangerous. Deepening bonds of affection between male and female inmates increased the possibility of collective resistance transpiring across gender lines. Likewise, the risk of reproduction and the economic issues it engendered, by turning productive women into less profitable commodities, fueled lessees' desire to enforce a strict social separation between the sexes. In short, intimacies between women and men were nearly impossible to develop. Even so, one is left to wonder if, out of their natural desire for love and affection, men and women sometimes made their way out of the bolted stockades under the cover of night, or slipped beyond the view of the whipping boss to share an embrace. The answers to these questions remain unknown. But these are the types of queries historians must make in their attempts to understand the intimate lives of incarcerated men and women.

Given that the plight of incarcerated mothers, fathers, and their offspring in the postbellum South has garnered little to no attention from scholars, one can only look to historian Mary Ellen Curtin's work on African American women prisoners in Alabama to gain a clearer outlook on this subject. Her evidentiary discoveries paint a compelling portrait of inmates such as Annie Tucker, a cook and washerwoman at the Pratt mines, who raised two children while maintaining a relationship with their father, a black convict.[122] Remarkably, even after she was relocated to a different prison camp, Tucker somehow managed to cultivate a new relationship with Jack Bozeman, a "freeman," and conceived a third child. As per Curtin's findings, Tucker and Bozeman "got together night and day time," in between the woman's trips from the house to the stockade. Patterning after Tucker, several other women prisoners also "got together" with male paramours, and brought to the Walls with them nearly two dozen children.[123]

The facts suggest that, in Alabama, gender conventions were upheld in the areas of both labor *and* maternity. Even though imprisoned women found it difficult to raise their children in captivity, penal authorities did not seek to obliterate the bonds between mother and child. While the primary stimulus for relocating female felons to a centralized space derived from the "lapses in discipline" caused by integrating the sexes, there was a secondary goal to, in some way, attend to the welfare of women prisoners and their young. This was not the case in Georgia. Lessees and their hirelings not only degraded black motherhood; they disembodied it altogether for the sake of fulfilling the New South promise.

While the commercial reward of convict leasing paled in comparison to the cost of human life and dignity, southern industrialists made impressive financial gains through the exploitation of women prisoners. By un-

Female prisoners standing outside the women's building at the "Walls" at the Wetumpka prison, Elmore County, Alabama, circa 1890–99. Notice the woman on the right holding a baby on her hip. Courtesy of the Alabama Department of Archives and History, Montgomery, Alabama.

making gender positions and denying black motherhood and womanhood (except for purposes of sexual abuse), lessees were able to profit from the labors of female felons who helped fortify new industries while, simultaneously, fulfilling ancillary labor roles (cooking, cleaning, and laundering). Nevertheless, African American women consciously rejected their role as tools of profit.

In the face of horrible squalor, work-related oppression, sexualized violence, and an unquantifiable degree of physical and emotional suffering, black women prisoners waged private and collective struggles to maintain their human dignity and self-respect. These struggles transcended beyond the masculine milieu of convict leasing in the "Empire State" into the newly forged feminine terrains where women's roles were revised to meet a new set of commercial demands and to abate public dissent. Existing and future modernizing changes made to Georgia's penal infrastructure were, thereafter, predicated on black women's presence in the carceral estate.

CHAPTER THREE

The Hand That Rocks the Cradle Cuts Cordwood

Prison Camps for Women

By the time Carrie Massie arrived at the Camp Heardmont prison farm in 1892, she was no longer a young "Negro girl," but a full-grown woman who had given birth to "four children and, in each instance, the child bore unmistakable signs that the father was white."[1] After ten years confinement in Georgia's private lease camps, Massie was reduced to a "plaything of beastly passion." Even while floating in a sea of handsome women at Camp Heardmont, she still stood out as a preferred target. As reported by reformer Selena Sloan Butler, the bondwoman's captors "became so infatuated with her, that peace did not always reign within the camp among the guards."[2]

Like so many female captives, Massie's path from adolescence to womanhood was paved in pain. Everywhere her feet touched, between the quarry and the field, the washhouse and the stockade, the whipping post and the rapists' clutch, her deathbed and the dissection table, she suffered unceasing insults to her humanity. In February 1895, just one month after giving birth to her last child, twenty-six-year-old Carrie Massie and her newborn both died at Camp Heardmont. An inquest was ordered, and the two corpses were sent in for autopsy to determine their causes of death. It was concluded that the mother died of puerperal sepsis, also known as "childbed fever," a bacterial infection of the female reproductive organs caused by the introduction of contaminated forceps or other unhygienic medical implements into the bondwoman's genital tract during delivery. The infant reportedly died of starvation in the course of its mother's illness.[3]

For more than two decades, lessees capitalized on black women's presence within the industrially driven convict lease system of Georgia. In the "Empire State," where gender symmetry, occupational invariability, and physical and sexual violence were the status quo, female convicts were frequently forced to simulate black masculinity and to conform to male-centric modes of labor and dress, while still being viewed by their custodians as sexually available. But by the mid-1880s and early 1890s, reformers were beginning to take heed of what was happening in Georgia. Social reformer and criminologist Frances Kellor observed that, during this period, "more remarks were made upon Georgia's barbarous system than upon that of any other southern state, and from its history this would seem justified. In no states are there evidences of such brutality to women, for women were leased out in the same way as the men and at the same occupations."[4]

In the 1880s, white Louisiana novelist George Washington Cable was among the first to openly acknowledge the abuse of female prisoners in the South's convict camps and to publicly condemn Georgia's practice of convict leasing, using the system as the corrupt yardstick by which every other state should be measured. Before the prison congress of Kentucky, he avowed that "what is true of Georgia is true of the convict lease system everywhere. The details of vice, cruelty and death thus fostered by the states whose treasuries are enriched thereby, equals anything from Siberia. Men, women, and children are herded together like cattle in the filthiest quarters and chained together while at work."[5] Although in his writings he precluded any in-depth discussion of the impact of physical and sexual violence on female subjects, finding the details "too revolting for popular reading,"[6] what Cable penned was significant enough to help catalyze a movement to reform Georgia's penal system.

During the early 1890s, as the penal reform movement in Georgia began to catch fire, African American women activists such as Selena Sloan Butler and Ida Bell Wells-Barnett stoked the first flames of racial and gendered protest against convict leasing in the southern states. Albeit best known for her role in piloting the anti-lynching crusade of the late nineteenth and early twentieth centuries, Ida. B. Wells's social reformist agenda went beyond rescuing black men and women from the noose to casting a light on the essential legal lynching of African Americans by the criminal justice systems of the post–Civil War South.[7] In 1893, she published "The Convict Lease System," as part of a coauthored book of essays entitled *The Reason Why the Colored American Is Not in the World's Columbian Exposition*. On its pages, she branded the southern convict lease system and the "Lynch Law" as "twin infamies which flourish hand in hand in many of the United States."[8]

Though less popular than Wells, Georgia-born African American woman reformer and educator Selena Sloan Butler was one of the most outspoken opponents of convict labor in her home state, and a tutor to her fellow club women on matters related to the exploitation of black female misdemeanants and felons confined in Georgia's convict lease and chain gang camps. In *The Chain Gang System* (1897), a paper originally delivered before a group of club women in Nashville, Tennessee, Butler offered a gut-wrenching treatise on the plight of the black female offender, highlighting the ways in which physical violence, rape, disease, and masculine labor operated in the lives of Georgia's female prisoners.[9] In the years that followed, more soul-stirring exposés like Butler's were produced.

Amid growing criticism over the social intermixing of female and male captives within the state's prison camps, the braiding of men's and women's working roles, the bending of racialized gender norms, and an increasing public recognition of the system's horrors, lessees and penal authorities were strained to amend existing leasing practices while, at the same time, effectively conserving and exploiting the state's valuable supply of female workers. As a result, dozens of women prisoners were uprooted from the state's brickyards, mines, and railroad camps, and replanted into gender-exclusive and agricultural settlements. Some were distributed to a broom-making factory in Fulton County. Others were parceled out to farmsteads stretching from the east bank of the Ogeechee River to northeast Georgia. Within these colonies of female convicts, women's roles were reconstituted— but only to an extent. Female felons delivered "men's work" while robed in striped dresses, bonnets, soft felt hats, or towels "tied around the skull after the Egyptian mode."[10] But the contours of physical and sexual violence remained unaltered.

Bolton Broom Factory

In the spring of 1890, the CBC sent its thirty-person female work crew to a newly constructed broom-making plant in northwest Atlanta. The Bolton broom factory was a newfangled enterprise that promised to make Chattahoochee's chief executive, James English, even richer. The successful entrepreneur envisioned using his petite throng of women workers to "make enough brooms to sweep the state of Georgia."[11] Camp Bolton was legitimated based on its potential to secure "the most favorable conditions for morality" and, as stated by one news writer, to teach female prisoners "a valuable trade by which to earn a comfortable living ... whether they are subsequently employed in factories or not, for there are blind men in Georgia making brooms for a living in their own homes."[12] Yet, for the few African American women who outlived the terms of their sentences, their inability to traverse the occupational boundaries in their path would limit their capacity to use their newly acquired skills in the free labor market.

During the late nineteenth century, penitentiary-based broom manufactories swept across the United States. The crackle of broomcorn echoed from the halls of state penitentiaries extending from the western territories of Wyoming and Oklahoma to the northeastern states of New York and Massachusetts. By 1900, convicts at the Wyoming state prison in Laramie were churning out 720 brooms per day. At camp Bolton, one of the earliest constituents in the prison-based broom-making industry, female convicts were also primed to "produce brooms on a large scale."[13] As early as 1888, when the CBC first broke ground for the construction of its new manufactory, company executive James English began purchasing new machinery, including a trio of mechanized "winders," to be used toward tidying up the state of Georgia.

The advent of the mechanical "winder," in the nineteenth century, gradually supplanted the homespun method of broom-making. As production techniques improved toward the latter half of the era, the artisan based trade was transformed into a fruitful commercial enterprise. By investing in modern technology, James English, a sentient observer of the New South's blossoming economy, poised the Bolton broom factory to compete in the region's industrial marketplace. When added to the numbers reflected in the 1890 United States census, black women prisoners at camp Bolton comprised 3.25 percent of all (reported) female broom makers in the United States.[14]

It was in the remote settlement of the Bolton broom yard that second-generation bondwomen advanced the art of broom making—a skill first honed among their enslaved foremothers. In slavery, brooms were built to serve both a utilitarian and cultural purpose. As a cleaning implement, simple straw brooms, consisting of a handful of dried sorghum plants, were used to sweep the earthen floors of slave cabins, while sturdier brush brooms, composed of tree branches held together by cotton cloth strips, were reserved for scouring the yard. As a cultural edifice, brooms played an all-important role in authenticating slave marriages. On the word of Paul Smith, a former slave, "When a slave man wanted to git married up wid a gal he axed his marster, and if it was all right wid de marster den him and de gal come up to de big house to jump de broomstick fore deir white folkses. De gal jumped one way and de man de other. Most times dere was a big dance de night dey got married."[15]

In the New South, brooms possessed no cultural significance among bondwomen, but the industrialized production of sorghum sweepers enlisted a new socioeconomic relevance for black female convicts. Women prisoners' forcible engagement in the broom-making industry enlarged the spectrum of African American women's labor force participation in the "Gate City" of Atlanta.[16] Furthermore, like their male counterparts, female captives helped power the Chattahoochee Brick Company's economic engine while simultaneously enhancing its image as a leading light of industry in the New South.

It was springtime, 1890, when the small fleet of women landed on the sticky clay grounds of the newly constructed Bolton broom factory. Ella Gamble, Leila Burgess, and Nora Daniel formed part of the procession leading from the Chattahoochee brickyard into the secluded precinct. When the women arrived at the camp, they took in the quiet of their new surroundings. The stillness of the vacant outpost offered a sharp contrast to the brick plant. There were no work gangs scurrying under Casey's whip, ovens roaring, or moans of dying convicts reverberating from the camp infirmary—only the occasional whistle of "Boss" Cowan's whip cutting the air and the earsplitting cry of a female captive.[17]

Inside the broom factory, women prisoners were prescribed new duties. They were not to dig clay, process bricks, clean camp kitchens, or cater meals for more than two hundred famished convicts any longer. Instead, their physical fortitude, technical, and creative muscle would be reserved for industrialized broom production. Within the plant, bondwomen were delegated to perform specific functions that included hauling and sorting bundles of broomcorn, soaking the brush, anchoring the tuft to a cylindrical wooden pole, stitching the bristles with the support of a winding machine, and trimming protruding quills from freshly sutured broom bases. Albeit inexperienced with mechanized broom-making techniques, women prisoners improvised at the trade and in time became proficient workers.

The daily grind at camp Bolton mimicked the arduous labor routines of male convicts confined within the state's prison mines, brickyards, and railroad camps. Day by day, women prisoners were marshaled into multiple work squads, then collectively dispersed onto the factory grounds. From sunup to sundown, female captives hauled, stitched, cut, and processed broomcorn. In the meantime, "Boss" Cowan skulked about the prison workshop like a predacious feline.

Although classified by penal officials as "light duty," industrial broom production proved to be onerous and physically taxing. The most stalwart members of the workforce at camp Bolton were required to fulfill the herculean mission of transporting colossal bales of broomcorn, weighing anywhere from 120 to 200 pounds, each, to the main factory grounds. Once the freight was unloaded, the brush was broken apart and moistened until wringing wet, making the broomcorn pliable and ready to be sorted. Then the straw was separated by length and grade—fifteen, seventeen, and nineteen inches long, respectively. Rough, short, or crooked pieces were temporarily stored in a scrap pile, while longer tresses of broomcorn were meticulously arranged in midsize bouquets. After the brush was divided, it was then passed off to one of several machinists to be processed.

As the damp grass crawled its way toward the "wrapping station," nimble-fingered machine operators primed stacks of wooden broom handles, puncturing small holes into their bases. Once the stilts were perforated, the process of fastening the broomcorn to the shaft commenced. First, the lowest-grade grass was tightly wrapped around a timber post, forming the belly of the broom. More side corn was placed along the perimeter of the center bundle, creating a set of shoulders for the implement. To secure the wilted brush, a metal wire was implanted into an opening situated at the bottom of each broomstick. After the foundation was stabilized, the most optimum strands of broomcorn ("hurl") was used to swaddle the naked filament. Using a "kicker-winder," the graded grasses were passed through a foot-powered treadle that cinched the broomcorn firmly to its base. In a final step, the brush was "seeded," trimmed, dried, and primped for sale.[18]

While the profitability of camp Bolton is difficult to calculate, the benefits of this arrangement are clear, if unintended. For the first time, women prisoners were permitted to live and labor within an exclusively female-centered carceral space, and they were able to recoup a modicum of their much coveted femininity. In the process, black women workers gained expertise in the broom-making trade—a line of industry untapped by freedwomen in the postemancipation South.

Although ineffectual in producing long-term employment options, female convicts' engagement in the broom-manufacturing industry allowed black women to deviate from the traditional courses of labor that circumscribed their occupational identity in the New South. In negotiating black women's place (or absence) in the free labor market, it is imperative that scholars take into account the incidental ways in which African American women contributed to the industrial sector. Prison, after all, was an important conduit by which manufactured goods produced by African American women made it to the open market.

Old Town Plantation

By 1891, the industrial operation at camp Bolton was prematurely discontinued. To mollify increasing public disapproval of convict leasing, penal authorities motioned to steer black female convicts into the fields. Over and above the superficial concerns about securing black female morality, the deployment of women prisoners into agricultural work was based on a desire to exploit African American women's rich knowledge of crop cultivation. The enduring connection between black women and fieldwork, rooted in slavery, made farming a sensible and profitable way to deploy black women convicts. Rather than squander bondwomen's energies on "light duty," or part with this valuable labor supply altogether, officials adjusted leasing practices to meet commercial demands.

Before the 1890s, when agriculture became the predominant basis of female felons' work, women prisoners were scarcely utilized in the fields. Although the convict lease system of Georgia was composed of mixed economic interests that were both industrial and agricultural in nature, the dominant class of industrially minded lessees elected to use female prison labor toward executing the vision of New South prosperity. As these barons of industry set their sights on modernizing the "Empire State," a smaller yet no less important population of planters directed their focus toward recasting the Old South agrarian model of affluence. Simultaneously, James English painted the "Gate City" of Atlanta in reddish-brown loaves of toasted clay while lessee T. J. James carpeted the grounds of Jefferson County in cushiony white cotton bolls.

In Jefferson County, before and after the Civil War, cotton was king. On the eve of the war, approximately 6,000 slaves, 4,000 whites, and 431 slaveholders peopled the rural hamlet.[19] Susan Matthews was "jes a chile when de white folks had slaves . . . My ma, she done the cooking and the washing fer the family and she could work in the fields jes lak a man. She could pick her three hundred pounds of cotton or pull as much fodder as any man."[20] After the war's end, Susan, her mother, and scores of other ex-bondwomen continued to labor in the fields.

Within days of Robert E. Lee's surrender at the Appomattox Court House, Jefferson County was spilling over with freedpeople, many of whom found it unfeasible or detrimental to leave. Ergo, white planters seeking a tenable source of cheap labor plunged into the county's ceaseless pool of prospective tenant farmers and sharecroppers. Other bold entrepreneurs, such as "Captain" T. J. James, capitalized on the county's emergent market in convicts. He purchased his stock from the Old Slave Market in Louisville, where, as Z. V. Thomas recalls, "it was customary for officers of the court to conduct legal sales." As in antebellum days, "slave" property was "here put upon the block and sold under the hammer."[21]

The Old Town settlement, the future site of Thomas Jefferson James's prison plantation, had a long and seedy background. The farmstead was initially founded in the 1760s when George Galphin, an Irish immigrant, acquired the then fourteen-hundred-acre land tract. Over the course of ten years, the planter/rancher enlarged his holdings by purchasing adjoining parcels of farmland, eventually accumulating a healthy 1,850 acres. To sustain his enterprise, Galphin made generous use of slave labor to shepherd thick herds of black cattle and to satiate the greedy corncribs and cotton sacks feasting on the farm.

When George Galphin died in 1780, all except twenty-nine slaves and most of his cattle and horses were carried off by raiding parties.[22] The remainder of his assets was divided among his five offspring. John Galphin, a son, inherited the largest share of the Old Town estate. But within a few years time, he was forced to sell his fourteen-hundred-acre cut to satisfy outstanding debts. He ceded his share of the property to Robert Forsyth, who, upon his death in 1794, willed the plantation to his two sons—Robert Jr. and John.[23]

John Forsyth claimed the greatest interest in perpetuating his father's resources. He lavished the homestead with extravagant gifts, including a "one framed house twenty-eight feet long and eighteen broad, with covered piazzas on each side," a new stable, carriage house, barn, smokehouse, dairy, and kitchen that stretched "twenty-four feet long and fourteen wide."[24]

In the fall of 1801, he became entangled in a prolonged legal scrimmage with Thomas Galphin, a competing claimant of the Old Town estate. At the heart of the contested court struggle between John Forsyth and Thomas Galphin was the latter's claim that, following his brother John Galphin's death, the legal right of ownership shifted to him. In 1807, a federal court ordered in his favor. However, within two years, the insolvent rebel was forced to surrender the property in a public auction.

After the hammer landed and the auction subsided, Christopher Fitzsimmons walked away with the deed to the Old Town estate. Fitzsimmons and his heirs made copious use of the land, converting the settlement into one of the largest short-staple cotton plantations in Georgia. The estate included a state-of-the art sawmill, gristmill, one hundred slaves, an eight-room "big house," an overseer's cottage, "sixteen double framed Negro houses with brick chimneys, commodious stables and barns" and a gin house.[25] But when the Civil War struck, the property was looted and its buildings torched. Even so, the plantation managed to rise again—this time on the backs of convict workers.

Female farmworkers posing in a cotton field, Ben Hill County, Georgia, circa 1896–98. Courtesy, Georgia Archives, Vanishing Georgia Collection, ben139.

In 1878, Old Town adopted the southern convict lease system. The plantation's new emissary, Thomas Jefferson James, made it his personal ambition to restore the estate to its early prominence. In doing so, he erected stockades, a new "big house," several outbuildings, an overseer's cabin, corncribs, stables, grain bins, and a gin house. His most essential investment included the lease of sixty-five prisoners.

T. J. James adopted a hybrid approach to convict leasing, segmenting his labor force into two spheres: one part agricultural, the other industrial. "Stout and healthy" male workers were used to assist in grading the Georgia Midland Railroad, while "fifteen or twenty women" steered the fields and governed the plow, aided by a few "feeble male convicts."[26] African American women's sovereign position in the fields of Old Town was anchored in the prevailing notion that slavery's mothers and freedom's daughters were "built" for farm labor.

Agents of the New South agricultural empire, such as T. J. James, enlisted black female convicts on the basis of their physical power and gender. Some white planters summoned Old South images of enslaved women like Patsey, who, in Solomon Northrup's words, could turn "as true a furrow as the best, and at splitting rails there were none that could excel her . . . Such lightning-like motion was in her fingers . . . that in cotton picking time, Patsey was queen of the field."[27] Others mused over the way female slaves prevailed in cotton-picking contests. As described by historian Jacqueline Jones, "Picking cotton required endurance and agility as much as physical strength, and women frequently won regional and interfarm competitions conducted during the year."[28] Black women's inordinate level of agricultural experience was reified through slavery's portrayal of bondwomen as "human hoeing machines" who could "work hard, plow and go and split wood jus' like a man."[29] Attuned to the preconceptions regarding black women's muscularity in the fields, and confident in their ability to "outplow a man," James set about building his cotton-based agrarian enterprise on the spines of female felons. Trained during slavery, more than one-half of these women were accustomed to furrowing enormous landscapes where cotton-capped waves stretched to the horizon.

Planting time at the prison farm possessed an uncanny likeness to the scenes played out on slave plantations stretching across the Cotton South. Bondwomen like Amanda Hill, Caroline Crittenden, Sylvia Washington, and Mary Puckett guided listless plows through springtime soil while being forced along by anxious mules. When the incisions were made and the ground sufficiently pleated, seeds were laid into earthen creases; then the dirt was folded back into place. Once the impregnated earth gave birth to its first seedling, the scraping procedure began.

Female farmers drove their hoes like sledgehammers, slicing up the grass and unripe cotton, then crafting miniature mounds where the stalks could gestate until they reached full bloom. To protect the growing plants from being strangled by weeds and grasses, the land was periodically spaded. By late summer, when the cotton flowers outgrew their prickly sacks, harvesttime commenced.[30]

Mary Puckett, Amanda Hill, Caroline Crittenden, Laura Johnson, Rose Jackson, Nancy Morris, Lucinda Evans, Ida Harris, Sylvia Washington, Laura Mitchell, Matt Vincent, Adeline Henderson, and multiple others soldiered through the harvest season at Old Town. Though already adept at picking cotton, they dreaded the routine all the same. Watching the moon retreat to its resting place and daylight's shift begin, these women braced themselves, each morning, to face off against a new day's weariness.

At the crack of dawn, farmhands marched into the fields with their cotton-picking sacks and baskets in tow. Large canvas bags were hitched to their torsos by a two-foot shoulder strap intended to support the pending load. When the day's work was set to begin, the gang moved into a half-bowed stance and began mowing the fields. With the indignant burs gnawing at their fingertips, harvesters peeled cotton bolls, one by one, stuffing the silken plunder into their coarse satchels. Twelve to fourteen hours later, the spoils were inspected and weighed. The next stop was the gin house.

Despite the fact that, by the late nineteenth century, the cotton gin (short for engine) had undergone substantial technological improvements, ginning short-staple cotton was no simple task. During harvest season, thousands of pounds of cotton were manually fed into the machine, whose circular saws separated the viscous green seeds from the fiber. Once processed, the seedless cotton was packed and baled for sale. In 1880, alone, eight hundred bales (four hundred thousand pounds) of cotton were harvested at Old Town, valuing more than $45,857.[31]

Mimicking the sights in Bayou Bouef, Louisiana, where "Queen" Patsey wore the crown, female felons took part in every stage of agricultural production. In addition to raising cotton, imprisoned women grew other consumption-based agricultural commodities, such as corn, potatoes, peas, and turnips; managed the farm's livestock; and attended to domestic duties (cooking food, cleaning camp buildings, and laundering soiled garments). A couple of women were promoted to trusty status, and they were "allowed to go to Mr. James' house half a mile away and cook and wash and do other work."[32]

When one house servant, Laura Heard, became pregnant after several years detention in the James residence, she was hurriedly extradited to the fields. The camp physician was certain that paternity belonged to the lessee but had no grounds to confront him. He, too, played a part in undermining the sexual integrity of black women prisoners. While it was customary for whipping bosses and guards to molest bondwomen, it was less common for a lessee or camp physician to engage in intimate improprieties with female captives. But, at Old Town, each member of the triangular alliance formed between T. J. James, Dr. David M. Houk, and William E. Smith (the whipping boss) took turns violating, corporally and sometimes sexually, female convicts.

In 1885, Dr. Houk was hired to serve as the camp physician at the Old Town plantation. A graduate of the Atlanta Medical College (1882), and a protégé of Principal Physician W. F. Westmoreland, the newly minted surgeon was publicly graded as a respectable and qualified candidate to oversee the medical condition of the state's prisoners. Within the private enclosure of the prison farm, Houk sustained a more sinister reputation; female felons knew him as a sexual marauder.

During an 1887 penitentiary investigation committee hearing, Houk's character was placed on trial. G. H. Williams, a former superintendent of the Old Town camp and "next in authority to the lessee," testified that the doctor had a "falling out" with the whipping boss, William E. Smith, because he "locked him out of the door of the woman's department, and issued orders that he was not to go in there without witness or Mr. Smith with him. This order was issued because two of the women had given birth to children which they swore were Dr. Houk's."[33] Williams went on to explain that the lessee, T. J. James, "knew as much about it as I did . . . I didn't tell the Principal Keeper or the Principal Physician any better, because I didn't think it was any of my business, and because of my friendliness for Dr. Houk. I was willing to help him cover it up."[34]

To the doctor's relief, one of the children he fathered was "born dead." He attributed the child's death to its mother's alleged illness during pregnancy. But immediately following the stillbirth, the woman "got well of the dropsy," and Houk resigned from his post as camp physician, citing his inability to work with the whipping boss and a refusal to "remain longer without change in the management of the convicts."[35]

On the surface, William Smith's willingness to take partial responsibility for the intimate safety of female convicts makes him a heroic figure. But the whipping boss's uncontrollable temper and fetish for cruelty compromised his apparent nobility. At the Old Town prison farm, enfeebled male and able-bodied female felons lived in terror of the lash. Physical violence was generously tendered by "Boss" Smith, "an old slave driver in antebellum days, who imbibed a strong prejudice against the Negro race and improved every opportunity to abuse them to the utmost."[36]

In 1887, per Dr. Houk's witness, Smith was brought before the penitentiary investigation committee for his involvement in the whipping deaths of two ailing convicts. Peter Jackson was "in a very bad condition, a mere skeleton," when Smith thrashed him with the hide. He "died within a few days." Ben Mix was also "in a bad way" when the "boss" assailed him for not working. He perished in less than a week.[37] Smith also took out his aggressions on "idle" women workers.

At Old Town, female prisoners were customarily flogged for "failure to work." Rose Jackson, a thirty-year-old Muscogee County sharecropper, was convicted of "larceny from the house" in 1881 and issued a six-year sentence at the prison farm. She was described as a five-foot-two, 150-pound woman with "good health" and no identifiable scars on her person. When she was released in 1887, Jackson had a chokecherry tree of twenty branches permanently engraved on her back. Smith lashed the bondwoman ten "strokes" for "bad work," five "strokes" for "neglect of work," and five "strokes" for "failure to work."[38]

Twenty-two-year-old Laura Johnson, a Sumter County "burglaress," and thirty-eight-year-old Mary Puckett, a convicted arsonist and life-term felon, were also repeatedly whipped for their careless work habits. Johnson was flogged three times in less than one month for "failure to work." Puckett was beset with the same level of brutality for "bad plowing" and "neglect of work."[39] Multiple others were also reprimanded for slacking in their labor assignments.

The patterns of violence stitched onto the backcloth of camp Old Town were identical to those quilted into the fabric of Georgia's industrial prison camps. Nonetheless, the standing infraction for which these women were punished provides a key to understanding the art of resistance. The practice of malingering was the most common means of opposition, and it was broadly adopted by female captives at the Old Town prison farm. By working slowly, clumsily, or avoiding labor altogether, bondwomen attempted to undermine the viability of the prison farm and to impair its profitability. While unable to change their condition as involuntary laborers, and ultimately forced to acquiesce to the labor demands imposed by the lessee, imprisoned women nonetheless internally rejoiced at a momentary victory by asserting themselves and rejecting being transformed into human commodities.

Raucous Infectivity

The inexorable specter of violence, coupled with the breakneck pace of labor and unfavorable environmental conditions, produced adverse physical consequences for imprisoned women. Blights of infection and injury razed through the prison farm like a tornado, wounding female captives trapped in its path. As stated by Dr. Westmoreland, Old Town plantation was "regarded as all other places on this [Ogeechee] river, as unhealthy, as malarial fever prevails from four to six months in the year."[40] During the warmer months, fieldworkers were blitzed by infected mosquitoes that bred along the stagnant waterway. Wasted by the effects of their onslaught, female patients hobbled back and forth between the fields and the camp infirmary to be treated for a myriad of agonizing symptoms: fever, chills, vomiting, diarrhea, joint pain, headache, and breathing difficulties. The camp physician successfully treated sufferers with an injection of quinine and, within a few day's time, sent them back to work.

Malarial fever terrorized its victims, and other ailments, such as "rheumatism," dogged the older workers. Caroline Crittenden (fifty-five) and Sylvia Washington (fifty) were saddled by the long-term complications of the arthritic disorder. The chronic slog of plantation slavery brought about years of wear and tear on their bodies. Once taken in by the South's system of penal vassalage, these women were already aged and struggling with physical debilities related to "rheumatism": inflamed muscles and joints, stiffness, soreness, swelling, difficulty bending, and chronic pain. Dr. J. M. Johnson, Houk's replacement, bewailed his inability to exact a permanent cure for Sylvia Washington. "This woman is a great sufferer & I have only been able to palliate her condition."[41]

As was the case at the Chattahoochee brickyard and other private lease camps stationed throughout the state of Georgia, gynecological problems abounded among female captives at Old Town. Between 1884 and 1891, five cases of "womb disease," two cases of "prolapsus uteri," six cases of dysmenorrhea, one case of menorrhagia, one case of leukorrhea, and two cases of amenorrhea (one fatal) were reported.[42] While suppressed menses alone did not result in death for female patients, untreated "womb disease," which frequently caused menstruation to cease, did result in death. If a foul vaginal odor or abdominal pain were absent during an examination, a uterine infection could be carelessly mislabeled according to its symptoms (e.g., obstructed menstrual flow), as opposed to the true origin of those symptoms—an infected womb.

Based on medical proof, the influx of uterine infections (also referred to as "womb disease") stemmed from hygienic negligence during labor and delivery as well as from physicians' incompetent indifference toward rendering obstetric care to imprisoned patients. Other causes may have included multiple miscarriages, traumatic vaginal intercourse, or complications arising from an untreated sexually transmitted disease, such as gonorrhea. But, even with their health imperiled and their humanity under siege, female prisoners fought desperately to survive the Old Town horror. And they were not alone.

Smithsonia

In Oglethorpe County, James Monroe Smith, Georgia's captain of agriculture, managed an estate stretching thirty square miles.[43] His empire covered twelve counties, but his Smithsonia plantation in northeast Georgia was the nerve center of his farming operation. Until 1879, he relied exclusively on his "Negro workmen," tenant farmers, "white foremen," and three hundred "fine mules" to cultivate the grounds of his massive plantation. An established planter, former Georgia governor, U.S. senator, and railroad developer, Smith was already a rich man when convict leasing became an option. As a baron of agriculture in the "Empire State," he felt compelled to join in the business of renting prisoners.

By 1880, Smith purchased a healthy 125 share interest in Penitentiary Company No. 3, which tilted the balance of his ownership to 25 percent. One quarter of all prisoners apportioned to the prison company were funneled directly into the lessee's hands to be used in any way he deemed fit. With his holdings, he built a multimillion-dollar agrarian enterprise, intensely predicated on the exertions of black convicts.

At Smithsonia, approximately one hundred prisoners occupied the fields, plowing, sowing, hoeing, and reaping corn, cotton, small grain, potatoes, peas, and cane. Four members of Smiths' labor force were "Negro women . . . all convicted of arson or murder. One with a six-weeks-old baby had killed her husband."[44] Two others were serving life sentences, one for poisoning and one for murdering a white woman "for a few dollars." The fourth woman was condemned for "ordinary burglary."[45] As per historian Ellis Merton Coulter's findings, there was also "a white girl of eighteen, convicted of murder. Her work was light 'but her degrading situation preyed on her mind, and finally led her to suicide,' by drowning herself in the Beaverdam Creek."[46]

Like "Captain" T. J. James, Smith lived in close proximity to his labor force, and he relied on a network of whipping bosses and guards to levy order in the camp. To dissuade escape among female convicts, who were "the worst class to deal with," or to recover male runaways, "Colonel Jim kept bloodhounds, and his principal guard [Bud Asbury] saw to it that they were well trained."[47] Smith insisted that his hounds "could follow a trail twenty-four hours old and that no convict was clever enough by the application of herbs to his feet or by wading in creeks, to throw the dogs off the trail."[48]

Smith was commended for his managerial proficiency at Smithsonia. The grand jury of Oglethorpe County, an assembly of white men put in charge of visiting the county's prison camps twice annually and reporting on the conditions found therein, permanently upheld the lessee's utopian facade. In scripted fashion, the jurists made the same assessment during each visit: the convicts are "well fed," "treated humanely," have "good water," have "decent bedding," are allowed to bathe and change clothes weekly, are not overworked, and "look cheerful."[49] Swollen from the battery of compliments, and well informed about the sexual indecencies prevalent in other penal colonies, "Colonel" Smith boasted, "No bastard children were ever born in his camp." This proved not to be the case at his Oglethorpe plantation. Sometime between 1888 and 1890, an unnamed female convict gave birth to a child at the prison farm and perished shortly thereafter. The cause of death was maladroitly labeled "amenorrhea."[50] It is almost certain, however, that her death was triggered by a fatal case of puerperal sepsis ("childbed fever") which invariably derived from an untreated uterine infection.

In the beginning, camp Oglethorpe was regarded by Principal Physician W. F. Westmoreland as "one among the best camps [in Georgia], with the convicts generally in a healthy condition and presenting a good and healthy appearance . . . The prison building is a roomy one for the number of convicts . . . The hospital is sufficiently large for the number of convicts, well lighted and comfortably furnished."[51] Although there were, in fact, two deaths at the camp during its first two years (1882–84), "one from a gun-shot wound that produced death in a few hours, the other from an ovarian tumor of malignant character," Westmoreland proudly denoted that "not one death had occurred from ordinary or acute diseases."[52] Evidently, his goal to remake the prisoners of the Georgia state penitentiary into the "healthiest class of people in the state" was paying off at the plantation. But by May 1885, the camp suddenly became "very unhealthy."

The insalubrious condition of the camp's prisoners resulted from a multiplicity of factors: administrative failure on the part of the lessee and his entourage, poor diet, and famine. According to Dr. Westmoreland, "Almost every convict I talked with said they did not get enough to eat . . . The convicts have had no fresh or any other kind of beef since the latter part of last fall . . . The only fresh meat that has been served to them, as I learn, was a few messes of the fifth quarter of the hog"—intestines, ears, trotters (feet), and stomach. He added, "Vegetables have not been as plentiful as heretofore, and have not been served to the convicts in quantities sufficient during the winter, and for the past five or six weeks, as I have been informed, no vegetables have been issued to the prisoners."[53]

Oglethorpe's malaise was rarely attended by "Colonel" Smith, who made infrequent visits to the camp. In his absence, he accorded guards and whipping bosses full reign over the abandoned province and its eighty incarcerated subjects, most of whom were men. A small handful of women lived and labored on the plantation, and they were given work assignments "adapted to their health and strength." Mary Battle, a forty-four-year-old "murderess" and life-term prisoner, was enlisted as a cook, while Mary Martin, a nineteen-year-old 130-pound "burglaress," spent her five-year sentence tilling the grounds of the Oglethorpe plantation.[54]

In general, age was not a relevant factor in determining a bondwoman's labor assignments in Georgia's private lease camps. Yet, at the Oglethorpe prison farm, it appears that maturity, in addition to fitness and perceived strength, factored into the delegation of female work roles. As in the case of Mary Battle, age was sometimes intertwined with one's health status and cast as a form of debility. Past her prime, camp officials rendered the bondwoman useless in fieldwork.[55] Gender, on the other hand, formed no basis in this decision-making process; sex was rarely ever esteemed as a disability for black women prisoners.[56] Moreover, neither gender *nor* age had any influence on the extent of violence meted out against female convicts.

Older women such as Mary Battle were met with the same level of physical hostility as young women such as Mary Martin. In August of 1885, Battle was mauled by the whipping boss for being "filthy about cooking."[57] Prison camp kitchens were, as a rule, mired in filth. But poor housekeeping was a fault that was seldom, if ever, punished. Even so, Battle's case may be an exception, demonstrating the subjectivity used by camp overseers in effecting punishment. An alternate and more plausible scenario, however, involves abuse as a consequence for defiance.

It was not unfeasible for a disgruntled cook, bound or free, to add toxic and nontoxic agents into an oppressor's meal. Spit, urine, feces, and poison were sometimes used by black women in slavery and freedom to enact revenge, physically injure, or kill their white employers. Thus, Battle may have "seasoned" the boss's personal food with excrement or some other "filthy" spice certain to excite his taste buds and stir up his anger. But the whipping boss' displeasure with nasty kitchens or polluted food was not the only source of his fury. The use of profane language, especially when directed toward him, was equally upsetting. In one instance, young Mary Martin drew "8 licks" from the strap for "cursing."[58] Although born one generation apart, and separated by distinct spheres of labor, Mary Battle and Mary Martin had much in common; they shared the same first name, belonged to one lessee, incurred similar abuse, labored strenuously, and were knitted together by the same spirit of animosity.

De Meanest Man Dey Is

As early as 1874, propositions were made to Principal Keeper John T. Brown to have Georgia's women prisoners "gathered up from all the present lessees and sent to some farmer in a healthy location, who may be qualified and is willing to give bond to take as special care of their morals as of their persons."[59] Having witnessed firsthand the gendered cruelties evinced by convict leasing, several other principal keepers of the Georgia state penitentiary also whispered their desires to see a rational and moral gesture made by the state government toward applying female convict labor in an economically productive and socially satisfactory way. Nearly twenty years after the first suggestion was made, to round up all Georgia's female felons and disburse them to a centralized women's prison camp, the proposed scheme was finally put into practice. In 1892, Governor W. J. Northen mandated sex segregation within Georgia's private lease camps, and he ordered female prisoners to be delivered into the hands of William H. Mattox, "the meanest man in Georgia."[60]

In Elberton's Elmhurst Cemetery, William Henry Mattox's remains rest, calmly, in an isolated grave marked by a weatherworn white headstone. Its inscription reads, "William H. Mattox, Co. 1, 15 GA. INF., CSA [Confederate States of America]." Gone but never forgotten, Bill's memory lives well in the minds of the descendants of persons who knew him and in the script of a local folksong that commemorates his barbarity: "Bill Mattox is yo' marster / Bill Mattox is yo' frin / Bill Mattox totes de long cowhide / An' nebber fail to len."[61]

Steeped in folklore, the "Bill Mattox" song had been sung by slaves and local planters. According to John McIntosh, one day, while in Augusta, Mattox "chanced to be walking down Broad Street when to his surprise he heard Negro workmen singing, 'Bill Mattox is yo' marster.' He stopped and listened for a moment. Then walking over to the Negroes he inquired where they learned that song. 'Marster,' one of them replied, 'ain't you nebber heard of ole Bill Mattox? 'Dats 'de meanest man dey is!'"[62]

On January 5, 1836, William H. Mattox was born in the "big house" of the Mattox family plantation in Elbert County. Crowned a son of privilege, baby William's adoring father, Henry Page Mattox, a prosperous planter and former state legislator, took great care to formally educate his son and to also school him in the fine art of slaveholding. After graduating from Franklin College (now University of Georgia) in Athens, young William began laying the groundwork for his entrée in to the family business.

By the time he reached his twenty-third birthday, he owned more than one thousand acres of land and seventy-eight slaves: forty-two women and girls, and thirty-six men and boys, all ranging from ages six to sixty-eight.[63]

During the antebellum period, Elbert County was a "slave society" where black bondpeople made up the majority of the population. By the dawn of the Civil War, 5,711 slaves, 25 "free colored," and 4,697 whites inhabited the area.[64] Mattox thrived in his small corner of the cotton kingdom. Through the use of enslaved labor, most of which was female, he established himself as one of the most successful cotton planters in Elbert County.

At the close of the Civil War, Elberton's ex-planters tiptoed their way back to economic safety. But Mattox was an exception. The economic calamity wrought by the war allowed the entrepreneur to grow in a season of poverty. While the battles were still raging, he borrowed $10,000 specie (Confederate currency) from Mildred "Miss Millie" Gray, a well-to-do relative and fellow Elbertonian.[65] No longer interested in wearing the outdated brand of Old South prosperity, Mattox used the money to invest in the New South vision.

A short time after the war subsided, Mattox embarked on his first economic venture. He assembled a gristmill on his land near the Savannah River. It was a lucrative undertaking for the businessman. The one-hundred-horsepower turbines at Mattox Mill could grind up to two hundred bushels of grain a day.[66] From his earnings, Mattox purchased more than two thousand additional acres of land and secured personal assets in excess of $22,000. But a chance encounter with Henry Woodfin Grady on July 23, 1889, changed the course of his destiny.

Grady's visit to Elberton inspired a "carnival-like atmosphere." Hordes of people congregated in the streets to hear from the famed speaker. His electrifying message kindled a fire of optimism in the hearts of ambitious entrepreneurs like William Mattox, who rated Grady's speech "the best and most forward thinking I've ever heard."[67] That same day, the *Elberton Star* announced that Mattox and a group of investors planned to deliver more of the New South to Elbert County.[68] Soon afterward, the venture capitalist mortgaged his gristmill and used the funds to invest in a more enterprising project: Heardmont Cotton Mill.

By the late nineteenth century, the textile industry in Georgia was evolving at a rapid pace. The expansion of the railroad fueled the growth of cotton mills in the state. With a more efficient system of transportation in place, industrialists could transport their goods to distant markets. Anticipating an economic windfall from his new investment, Mattox began purchasing machinery in the Northeast. He bought eight carding machines and spinning frames for one thousand spindles. The venture was an experimental one. But, if successful, his mill would become one of the largest in the South.[69] However, three short months after the mill opened its doors it was struck by a bolt of lightning and burned to the ground. With no fire insurance, Mattox experienced a devastating financial loss. Two years later, he concocted a new—and extreme—business scheme in hopes of reestablishing himself as a front-runner in the New South.

Camp Heardmont

To outside observers, Camp Heardmont prison plantation appeared to be yet another chancy endeavor undertaken by W. H. Mattox. Cynics were doubtful of his ability to advance Henry Grady's New South mission with his peculiar labor force. But the slaveholder turned lessee was immoderately adept at managing "Negro women," and secure in their ability to give him "more than value received for their hire."[70] After spending $12.50, per head, to rent Georgia's female felons, Mattox was reassured by Principal Keeper George Jones that women prisoners "as a rule, make good farm hands, and adapt themselves to the work to the perfect satisfaction of the officials."[71] In a short period of time, the lessee began reaping the benefits of Jones's prediction. He found that leasing women prisoners was "entirely satisfactory as a financial venture . . . They are workers that would put strong men to shame."[72]

In the winter of 1892, Mattox, hired sixty-four "colored females" and two "white females" from the state penitentiary to labor on his sprawling six-thousand-acre plantation in the northeast Georgia piedmont, in Elberton, 118 miles east of Atlanta. Camp Heardmont, Mattox's newest commercial exploit, spanned the distance of eight square miles, with the Savannah River forming the eastern boundary. In the center of the farmstead, several prison camp buildings were staggered on "the crest of a hill" on "a piece of ground about the size of a large city lot enclosed with a ten foot fence."[73] The outer edges of the estate were littered with scores of wooden shacks, where one hundred sharecroppers and tenant farmers retreated when they weren't slogging in the fields.

On the inside of the main enclosure, hidden behind a large gate, was a bulky whitewashed wooden stockade, which acted as the women's sleeping quarters. The windows were covered with iron bars, and the beds made of "straw and excelsior," blanketed by a pair of white sheets and two thin spreads. In this inhospitable space, female captives were slept like cattle with "nothing in the room but beds and the coverings." Mattox alleged that, for a time, he allowed "chairs in this room, but took them out so that in case of a fight between the women the chairs could not be used as weapons."[74]

To mitigate conflicts and to prevent escapes, a night guard slept in the vestibule of the building "on a cot" that was placed "across the barred door" leading to the women's sleeping quarters.[75] Mattox slept in the "big house," in earshot of the quarters. Adjacent to the main garrison were several ten-by-twelve-foot shacks that doubled as bathhouses and dressing rooms. Every Sunday morning the women were expected to wash. But, according to Mattox, "there are many who take a bath twice each day."[76] The lessee's conceited implication is that his influence on the women led to a turnaround in their hygiene. Women prisoners took personal pride in their appearances, anyway, and simply capitalized on the resources provided for them (assuming that Mattox's statement is true).

Camp Heardmont carries significant weight in the history of Georgia's penal system. It was the first centralized women's prison camp in the state and the first in a complex sequence of reform initiatives introduced during the late nineteenth century and early twentieth century. The plantation served as a proxy for Georgia's missing women's reformatory and blended slavery's leftovers with the New South convict lease system. The farmstead was, indeed, a "queer colony of female convicts." It was a place where, in Mattox's words, "the hand that rocks the cradle cuts cordwood," but the woman who "spits [snuff] upon the scoured floor must suffer the penalty of carrying water on the Saturday half holidays."[77] The lessee's innovation marked the final stages of convict leasing for black women. It also signaled the genesis of a new trend toward penal restructuring.

Beyond its capacity as an instigator of New South modernism and an accessory to the penal reform movement, Camp Heardmont was a sociological innovation. When female felons were exported from various lease camps, across county lines and city borders, into this incarcerative setting, they brought along with them their traumas, resentments, frustrations, impatience, resistance politics, and skills. Camp Heardmont joined together strangers, friends, foes, and past acquaintances. The old cohabited with the young, the married with the unmarried, the ex-slave with the second-generation captive, the illiterate with the semiliterate, the dying with the living, the brick mason with the farmer, and the cook with the mechanic.

Sketch of women prisoners at Camp Heardmont prison plantation. From the *Weekly News and Courier* (South Carolina), 1897.

While the full extent of community formation among the prisoners of Camp Heardmont is uneasily accounted for in the historical record, it is apparent that bonding did play a vital role in these women's lives. The best way to understand how female convicts may have used their network as a site of protection is to look at the ways in which space, environment, and labor shaped the social context of their lived experiences. In railroad camps, brickyards, and prison mines, where women were grossly outnumbered by men, incarcerees' work lives rarely followed a traditional pattern of sex segregation. Yet their social world only involved other female prisoners. Women ate together, slept in the same barracks, traded jokes, gossiped, cried, conspired, laughed, prayed, sang, and fought. In the absence of male friendship and protection, these women also looked to one another for emotional support.

In gender-exclusive spaces, like the Bolton broom factory, Old Town prison farm, and Camp Heardmont, long-term female felons almost certainly built on the relationships forged in male-dominated lease camps while, at the same time, establishing new connections. The group identity they created would have combined two sets of consciousness; one framed around the slave community experience and the other derived from the working-class background. With this fact in mind, the tensions that sometimes arose between imprisoned women, who were exposed to varying degrees of freedom and unfreedom and possessed different thresholds for disrespect or betrayal, were to be expected.

Unable to fully defend themselves against their oppressors, inmates sometimes channeled their rage toward one another. Beyond personal antipathies, women prisoners fought over stolen goods and for other unintelligible causes. Although the historical record does not allow for a deep interrogation of the sources of internal strife among black female convicts, there are a series of conceivable explanations that can be made to account for violent behavior among detainees. Emotional duress caused by confinement and physical and sexual violence may have elicited hostile behavior among female inmates. The compounding of psychological stress, exhaustion, and unrelenting work routines also made for a combustible outcome.

In the absence of legislative restrictions intended to limit or decisively characterize the nature of convict women's work in the state's camps, W. H. Mattox cleverly restored indiscriminate occupational demands on Georgia's black female felons while, simultaneously, invoking the paternalist ethos of the Old South plantation regime. He dressed his laborers in loosely fitted striped gowns, cotton in the summer and wool in the winter, and whipped them in all seasons if they disobeyed. The lessee opined that it was his interest to incorporate into his camp "every idea of reformation . . . They [female prisoners] are sober because there is no drink to be had; they are industrious because they have every incentive to work; they sing gladsome songs in the field because they are happy and satisfied . . . The convicts appreciate what I am doing for them, and they work with a will at a word now."[78] But, in reality, black female felons were disenchanted, restless, and rebellious, and they reserved no feelings of loyalty or "gratitude" for their new "marster." What's more, the "gladsome songs" they allegedly sang were spirituals and work songs. These uplifting tunes were designed to alleviate the difficulty of their circumstances, not to express complacency for the given situation.

Mattox's embellished testimony is just as contradictory as his perspective on the laboring identity of African American women prisoners. On one hand, the lessee acknowledged the feminine potential black female convicts possessed and sought to exteriorize their womanhood through dress and the presentation of "good manners." On the contrary, he assented to the status quo and reinstated masculine work habits for female felons. Once more, African American women prisoners were forced to navigate between "men's" and "women's" labor duties: cooking, farming, cutting and hauling cordwood, blacksmithing, operating gristmill machinery, and aiding in the overall composition of New South modernity.

"Colonel" Mattox's workforce entered Camp Heardmont already equipped with a wealth of industrial, agricultural, and domestic skills. For the most part, their duties were deputized by the lessee according to the previous order of their labor. But differences in the labor economy of the plantation caused their titles to become slightly altered. Some former cooks became field hands, former broom makers became log drivers, and railroad builders became lumberjacks. Mattox implemented subjective choice in the delegation of work assignments, and he ignored the keeper's orders that each convict "be assigned such duty only as he or she may be able to perform without injury."[79] In his estimation, there was no task that a black woman could not physically perform; her strength had already been proven in the state's brickyards, railroad camps, mines, and plantations. White women, however, were granted amnesty from "Negro" women's work and afforded limited authority over their racial subordinates.

In the summer of 1892, Pearl Pendergast (forty-three) and Alice White (seventeen)—both white women—were arrested in Savannah for kidnapping Ella Holmes, a "little 14-year-old country girl," and "sending her to a disreputable house for immoral purposes."[80] White was given a five-year prison term, while Pendergast, the accused ringleader in the crime, was dealt a seven-year sentence. On account of their arrival, a scheme of segregation was promptly implemented at Camp Heardmont. Both White and Pendergast were separated from "Negro women" at work and rest; they slept in an isolated wing of the stockade, used different bathhouses, and worked in vocations atypical of their "second-class" peers. In essence, the racial division of labor and leisure that was applied among the two classes of female felons at the prison farm was drawn from the same system of racial caste that was being legally cemented beyond the invisible walls of the penitentiary.

Pearl Pendergast is the most revealing example of how a structure of racial hierarchy was imposed at Camp Heardmont. Thinly insulated by the cult of "True [white] Womanhood," which remained intact as long as she subsisted alongside "scandalous" Negro women and gave the lessee no trouble, Pendergast was spared the exertions of fieldwork, lumberjacking, blacksmithing, and so on, jobs exclusively reserved for black women prisoners. Instead, Mattox made her the seamstress and "matron" of the camp, claiming she was "too feeble to work in the field."[81] As a low-level supervisor, Pendergast was expected to "look out after the dormitory . . . She is separated from the Negro women and is their superior, as she has the counting of the convicts morning and evening intrusted [*sic*] to her care and is given minor authority in the camp."[82]

Alice White entered Camp Heardmont with a similar level of racial favor. Like Pendergast, she was employed as a seamstress but, according to Mattox, "could not learn to do even the simplest thing well."[83] Even so, the lessee kept her in a privileged category until, one day, she became "unruly" and attempted to escape. After she was captured, White was demoted—occupationally and socially—to "measuring wheat at the threshing machine" in the company of black women prisoners. Several months later, she was pardoned by Governor W. J. Northen after she protested that she had been "outraged [raped]" by the officers of the camp.[84]

She Wields an Axe with Great Proficiency

In the spring of 1892, Ella Gamble, Mary Battle, Leila Burgess, Caroline Crittenden, Martha Williams, Lummy Long, and nearly two dozen others were put to work in the fields of Camp Heardmont, clearing new ground, pulling fodder, running plows, milking cows, grooming mules, and so on. A handful of additional women were left to govern the kitchen and washhouse. The remaining members of the camp were preserved for a more ambitious project, to assemble a small-scale lumber mill for commercial and domestic purposes.

Between 1870 and 1910, lumber grew faster than any other industry in the American South, and employed more laborers than any other enterprise in the region.[85] African American men—convict and free—comprised the majority of the southern lumber workforce and played a key role in the industrial transformation of the southern states. Although completely excluded from historical discourse on the subject, owing to a shortage of available evidence, this chapter section puts forth an initial attempt to understand black women's contribution to the thriving timber industry of the New South.

At 3:30 each morning, when the "big bell" rang, the women of Camp Heardmont hurriedly put on their zebra-striped uniforms and scuttled out the door to the "messroom" for a quick breakfast of fried meat, biscuits, and syrup. After they guzzled down their rations, the workers were lined up in pairs and led to their posts. The plowgang stepped at a "brisk gait" to the stable, about a half a mile away, to gather their mules.[86] Next, they trooped into the fields with one guard in front and the other at the rear, while a group of sowers and hoers moved in the opposite direction "followed by a guard carrying a pistol in his hip pocket."[87] In the distance, a team of loggers trailed a camp guard into the dense pine forest.

Working in small clusters, female lumberjacks felled heavy trees, shaved their limbs, and "bucked" the collapsed wood by cutting it into logs of a desired length, usually four feet. In order to sever the trees from their bases, two women had to hack away at the trunks repeatedly with razor-sharp felling axes. As each severed torso made its descent to the ground, the woodcutters scrambled for cover, then returned to the scene to inspect the carnage. Next they hacked off the branches of the down logs, then loaded the cut trunk pieces into several mule-powered wagons. When the carriage beds were full, the timber was transported to the camp sawmill for processing.

Lumberjacking was an extremely dangerous and unsparing occupation, ordinarily restricted to strong, practiced men. Inexpert at the trade, and, in many instances lacking the physical power to fell the trees or maneuver their limp corpses, female convicts were often severely wounded. Some were crushed by falling logs, while others were dismembered by misdirected axe blades or aggrieved by the pain of dislocated bones and muscle tears.

Rose Henderson was nineteen years old when she acquired her freedom and thirty-four when she lost it. In 1877, she was convicted of murder by a Lumpkin County judge and outsourced to the Grant and Alexander firm. The first part of her life sentence was spent laboring on the Air-Line Railroad.[88] By the time she reached William Mattox's snare in 1892, Henderson was forty-seven years old and, ostensibly, in decent health. On March 19, 1896, the lumberwoman was "hurt by a falling tree" and laid up in the camp hospital for six days before being driven back into the forest. In a similar instance, forty-four-year-old Sarah Johnson, convicted of attempted murder in 1893 and condemned to five years' detention at Camp Heardmont, was nearly crushed to death by a falling tree. Standing at five feet and two inches tall, weighing 165 pounds, the short, stocky axe handler was no match for the wooden giant. After the accident, she spent close to one month convalescing in the infirmary.[89] As shown in Table 2, an average of twenty-one injured and sick female inmates cycled in and out of the camp infirmary on a yearly basis. Nearly 5 percent of these patients died from their ailments.[90]

The pine forest was a harrowing space for female lumberjacks. Sometimes in their haste to dodge collapsing bodies of timber, they made costly

TABLE 2 Showing Rate of Injury, Sickness, and Death at Camp Heardmont by Number of Reported Cases, 1892–1897

Illness	1892	1893	1894	1895	1896	1897	Deaths
Abscess	1	—	1	—	—	—	—
Amputation	—	—	—	1	1	—	—
Boil on Head	1	—	—	—	—	—	—
Broken Hand	1	—	—	—	—	—	—
Bronchitis	—	—	—	—	1	—	—
Catarrh	7	—	—	—	—	—	—
Catarrhal Fever	1	—	—	—	—	—	—
Childbirth	2	—	—	1	—	—	—
Cold	4	—	—	—	1	—	—
Confinement	1	3	2	2	—	—	—
Congestion of Lung	—	—	—	1	—	—	1
Cut Foot	—	—	—	—	—	1	—
Cut Hand	—	—	1	—	—	—	—
Cut Thumb	—	1	—	—	—	—	—
Debility	1	—	—	—	—	—	—
Deranged Menstruation	1	—	—	—	—	—	—
Dysentery	1	1	4	—	—	—	—
Dysmenorrhea	1	—	—	—	—	—	—
Dyspepsia	—	—	—	—	—	1	—
Facial Neuralgia	1	—	—	—	—	—	—
Fecal Impaction	—	—	—	—	—	1	1
Gastritis	1	1	—	—	—	—	—
General Debility	1	—	—	—	—	—	—
Gun-Shot Wound	—	1	1	—	—	—	—
Hepatitis	—	—	—	1	—	—	—
Hysterical Neuralgia	—	—	—	—	—	—	—
Indigestion	3	—	—	—	—	—	—
Influenza	1	—	—	—	—	—	—
Injured by Falling Tree	2	—	1	—	1	—	—
Intercostal Neuralgia	—	—	—	—	—	1	—
Kicked by Mule	1	—	—	—	—	—	—
La Grippe	2	—	10	—	1	—	—
Leukorrhea	1	1	—	—	—	—	—
Lumbago	1	—	—	—	—	—	—
Malarial Fever	3	1	—	—	—	1	—
Mammary Abscess	—	1	—	—	—	—	—
Measles	—	—	—	1	4	—	—

(*continued*)

TABLE 2 (*continued*)

Illness	1892	1893	1894	1895	1896	1897	Deaths
Menstrual Period	1	—	—	—	—	—	—
Miscarriage	1	—	—	—	—	—	—
Neuralgia	1	—	—	—	—	—	—
Overheated	1	—	—	—	—	—	—
Pneumonia	—	—	1	—	—	1	1
Prolapsus Uteri	—	—	—	—	1	—	—
Puerperal Sepsis	—	—	—	1	—	—	1
Remittent Fever	2	2	—	—	2	—	—
Rest	4	—	—	—	—	—	—
Rheumatism	2	—	—	—	1	—	—
Sore Leg	—	—	—	1	1	—	—
Sporadic Cholera	—	—	—	—	1	—	1
Sunstroke	—	—	—	—	—	1	1
Tuberculosis	—	—	1	—	—	1	1
Typhoid Fever	1	—	1	—	—	—	—
Urethritis	1	1	—	—	—	—	—
Uterine Fibroid	—	—	1	—	—	—	—
Uterine Trouble	1	—	—	—	—	—	—
Total	54	13	24	9	15	8	7

mistakes. Fannie Drinks, a thirty-six-year-old "yellow" murderess and for-mer sharecropper from Lowndes County, was so terrified of being crushed by a falling log that she miscalculated the swipe of her chopping partner's axe. When the blade fell, Drinks's arm was nearly sliced off. With her limb barely attached, the bleeding bondwoman was rushed to the camp hospital, where a surgical "amputation of the arm" was performed.[91]

Other less evasive injuries also proliferated among female lumber workers. Emily Brown, a teenager, was sent to the sick bay for a sprained knee after an accidental fall. Dilly Echols, sentenced to life for infanticide in 1889, developed an acute case of "lumbago" from lifting heavy tree trunks and hauling them to the wagon bed. The pains in her middle and lower back, likely emanating from a muscle strain, were so bad she had to be checked into the camp hospital for four days and placed on bed rest. After the infirmary, the next step for Brown, Echols, and numerous others was the sawmill. There the "mulatto murderess" of Quitman County, Eliza Randall, was chief engineer.

Eliza Randall, the Other Only Woman Blacksmith

Late one October evening, Joe Randall was sitting on his front porch chatting with his nephew Ben Randall. As he was "bending over making out by way of explanation, a plan for building a gin dam," his daughter, Eliza Randall, allegedly "crept up behind them."[92] In a flash, the teenage girl swiped her father across the top of his head with a "club axe," knocking him to the floor. With the "aged man" dying at her feet, Eliza turned to her cousin Ben and saluted his astonishment with these words: "I hit him and I intended to kill him, and before I will have my skin cut I will die and go to hell."[93]

Joe Randall had promised his teenage daughter that he was "going to whip her for having disobeyed him." According to Eliza, her father was physically abusive toward her and forced her into "improper relations" with him. The nighttime ambush that she staged was, therefore, a lethal act of self-preservation. "If she didn't kill him he would kill her."[94] In December of 1887, Randall was tried in the Superior Court of Quitman County. A journalist, who was on-site at the time of the ruling, said, "The jury was out but a short while before it returned a verdict of murder, without recommendation to mercy."[95] On the eve of her scheduled hanging, Governor John Brown Gordon decided to commute the seventeen-year-old's sentence to life imprisonment.

Eliza's crime caused quite a media stir. In conservative newspapers, such as the *Macon Telegraph*, writers vilified the young woman and attacked Gordon's decision to, in their words, "shield this female demon under the state's name of woman" and to "insult the noble women of our country upon whom she [Eliza Randall] has forfeited every claim of woman by the atrocity of her most unnatural crime."[96] Others sided with Gordon, proclaiming that "hanging was too good for her. She is now condemned to the Georgia chain gang [convict lease system] for life. Under these circumstances even Eliza Randall commands our sympathies."[97] Free from the noose yet still wound up in the media, Randall made her move to the Chattahoochee brickyard, where she was leased as a cook. Not long after her confinement, she was accosted by E. B. Stanley, "Boss" Casey's replacement, for "cursing and fighting."[98] Faithful to her declaration to never have her skin cut again, the feisty teenager devised a terrific plan of escape. Two years into captivity, she seized her chance to be free.

In 1890, when the Bolton broom factory was completed, Eliza Randall and her peer inmates were relocated to the camp, along with one overseer and one guard, Miles M. Bollen. Moderately fortified and lightly armed, camp Bolton was a reasonably escapable site. But reduced munitions and modest surveillance did not improve Eliza Randall's confidence that liberty could be achieved through ordinary means. Unconvinced that a solo prison break could deliver long-standing victory, the young woman chose a more promising, albeit unfamiliar, gateway to freedom; she absconded with a prison guard.

Miles Bollen and Eliza Randall's tryst began shortly after their arrival at the broom yard. Evidence of how the relationship began or evolved exists far beyond the reach of historical text. But subtleties arise in the printed record that suggest an amicable and intimate relationship did mature between the two. Even so, the extent of Randall's passion for her hired captor is questionable. Had she bartered her sexuality for freedom and maneuvered the guard's infatuation until his zeal carried her beyond the stockade into a sovereign life? Had she rendered herself "unrapeable" and, as stated by historian Kali Gross, "embraced the illicit in an attempt to dismantle sex as a potential instrument of violation?"[99] Or had her unintended pregnancy with Bollen's baby prompted her to seek liberation for herself and security for her unborn child? While it is arguable whether or not amorous feelings influenced Randall's decision to engage in a consensual sexual relationship with her appointed subjugator, it is a patent fact her beau "played the fool and erred exceedingly" when he broke the covenant of white racial hegemony.[100]

When the summer night sky descended on the broom yard, the couple jetted northward. The next day, James English assembled a search party, offering a two-hundred-dollar reward—the required sum for all escapes in the state's camps—for the outlaws' return. The pair made it seventy miles northwest of Atlanta before they were apprehended near Rome, Georgia, on a boat rowing down the Oostanaula River. Eliza Randall, alias "Evergreen Smith," was found "dressed in boy's clothes to escape detection." She had been passing as a man.[101] Once Bollen "saw that the jig was up," he pled guilty to the crime of "assisting a convict to escape." He was sentenced to four years in the penitentiary and sent to the Dade coal mines, while Randall was carried back to the Bolton broom yard. Less than six months after her return, camp Bolton was eliminated and Randall was sent on to Camp Heardmont.

William Mattox was unhappy about inheriting Eliza Randall. Aside from her "infernal" blackness and history of violent crime, two critical factors helped shape the lessee's particular disdain for the bondwoman: she blatantly defied the code of white supremacy by voluntarily perpetuating a forbidden interracial affair and was carrying a child bred of miscegenation. In addition, the scandal connected with Randall's disappearance became fodder for Georgia's conservative newspapers, causing much embarrassment to statewide defenders of the carceral estate. Offended by her audacious actions, Mattox took bonus measures to entice the bondwoman's fear and to censor her cheeky manners.

On January 5, 1892, approximately one month after arriving at Camp Heardmont, Eliza Randall gave birth in the prison camp hospital. Her nameless nursling was the first of three children born at the prison farm, and the first to die.[102] Bud Hilley, a former guard at Mattox's camp, recollected that "on more than one occasion . . . a convict would give birth. No time could be spared for a nursing mother, so on Mattox's standing order the newborn was simply taken to the river and thrown in."[103]

Once Randall's baby was disposed of, and her body, time, and energy unclogged, Mattox made full use of the bondwoman's energies in the lumber mill. The "engineeress" and her handful of assistants waded through piles of "bucked" lumber. Some were set to manually chopping and bundling wood, an abundance of which was sold by the cord. Others helped Randall navigate smooth logs through hydropowered blades to make planks. Both processes were daring and perilous. Mary Washington's "amputated finger" was proof of this fact.

In addition to governing the sawmill and cotton gin, Eliza Randall was made the machinist for the camp and required to operate a fifty-horsepower engine. "She runs the big gristmill . . . and does about half of the blacksmithing for the farm," noted one journalist.[104] As part of the vindictive ordering of her work and gender representation, the lessee outfitted Randall in a suit of male stripes. According to one reporter, "Captain Mattox thought that if the woman was dressed in the apparel of a man there would be less chance in her clothing becoming mixed up in the machinery of his cotton gin and grist mill . . . he concluded that Eliza Randall, the life-time convict, was too valuable a hand to have killed by the machinery or even hurt in any way."[105]

Although this was not the first time Randall "shoved her lower limbs into a pair of pants" and "in the matter of appearance completely changed her sex,"[106] it was the preliminary moment in which she was masculinized against her will and socially raped. If given the choice, it is highly probable that Randall may have elected to wear men's garb and, quite possibly, garnered esteem from doing so. But in this situation, as in the case of

Mattie Crawford, compulsory defeminization served a pragmatic and punitive purpose. It was a way to amplify the bondwoman's labor productivity while, at the same time, debasing her femininity. Furthermore, by dressing Randall in men's clothes, officials could easily identify the disaffected convict if she took flight. Coincidentally, when the time did arrive for her to run away (as was predicted), she was hastily pursued by a pack of light-footed bloodhounds and a trigger-happy guard who shot her on the spot. Clinging to life, Randall was seized and confined to the camp hospital for three weeks while she recovered from the "accidental" gunshot wound.[107]

A Troublesome Property

Escapes were prevalent at Camp Heardmont. According to Mattox, the prisoners were "always watching for a chance to get away" and many succeeded. In 1893 alone, six women slipped from the lessee's grasp. Some critics blamed the escapes on his amateur approach to managing female convicts, whom he purposely chose because they were, presumably, less likely to flee than males were. Mattox failed to realize that the majority of his labor force was birthed on the bed of freedom and exceedingly desperate to mature outside the bounds of captivity. In the same way, formerly enslaved women were inordinately antsy to be recradled in liberty's bosom. No longer constrained by the rigid borderlines of the state's industrial camps, female dissidents profited from the farm's unusual insecurity and Mattox's naïveté.

Nora Lay, a "handsome mulatto girl," was one of the first to quit Camp Heardmont. Convicted of arson in April 1891, and interned at the Bolton broom factory for an anticipated lifetime, the seventeen-year-old quickly harvested a reputation for walking off. A few weeks detention at the broom yard was enough to "dull her appetite for penitentiary life." As relayed by a reporter for the *Macon Telegraph*, "In broad daylight in the merriest fashion she climbed the high fence and deliberately walked away . . . The woman is reported to have been seen on the Western and Atlantic train since her escape."[108] Within a week's time, Lay was recovered and returned to the prison camp. Less than one month later, she "took her departure a second time" and had to be recaptured. The rebel's flight from Camp Heardmont marked the third episode in a trilogy of spontaneous jailbreaks.

Lay was the "pet" and informant of Camp Heardmont, and, according to *Atlanta Constitution* journalist Frank Weldon, "strongly disliked by the other convicts. They thought that she gave them away, so they held a meeting on a Sunday and resolved that she must run off."[109] Facing pressure by her icy colleagues, she evidently "slipped out of the lines as the women were marching into the gate and off she ran. It was dark and somehow her absence was not noted. She went to the [Seaboard] railroad and followed it a few miles until she came to the second station . . . She hid under the platform until the train came along."[110] Next the fugitive slipped an "old wrapper over her convict garb" and boarded the first train headed to Atlanta.

In the "Gate City," Nora Lay found herself penniless and stranded. A native of Rome, Georgia, the bondwoman had no family or friends nearby and suddenly found herself in a tight spot. Her dream of being free instantly turned into a nightmare. In a panic, Nora made an unprecedented decision that she almost certainly regretted later on. "She went to the statehouse and hunted up Colonel Jones [the principal keeper] and told him that she had run away, but that she had been compelled to do it by the other prisoners."[111] She was sent back to the camp, whipped, and downgraded from the plow team to the hoeing gang, where she could be more closely watched.

Alice White, the ham-handed seamstress turned wheat measurer, was among the last of the six who escaped Mattox's camp. The details of her risky getaway read like this:

Alice's room overlooked the yard in which the hounds are kept. Every day she would carry something to her room and call the hounds to her window and divide with them. She made a special pet of Reed, the best hound in the pack . . . The day Alice slipped away the dogs were not in the field. They were brought hurriedly and soon on the trail . . . For a mile the trail was followed. It led deep into a tract of woods along the river. Great was the surprise of the guards when Reed suddenly appeared from the bushes wagging his tail. He went off and laid down in the water. Nothing could induce him to resume the search. He was through . . . When Alice was captured fifty miles distant and brought back she said that when Reed came up on her in the bushes she just patted him on the head and he thought that he belonged to her . . . so he wagged his tail and walked off. Alice does not feed the dogs now.[112]

Alice was apparently joined by two other deserters who were discovered trying to cross the Savannah River on a flatboat. As escapes abounded at Camp Heardmont, it became more evident that, as Weldon declares, "It is riskier to trust a woman than it is to trust a man. Few women can resist the temptation to run away if they got a fair chance."[113] Harried by the shrinkage of his workforce and the mounting fines accruing from the state, Mattox upped the ante by purchasing more hounds that could "tear a man or woman to pieces," hiring more guards, and arming them with Winchester rifles instead of revolvers to overawe their opponents. Several of the women were also shackled at the ankles. According to one eyewitness, "On Sundays they rest and are allowed to go out into a lot, carefully enclosed by a barbed-wire fence, and watched over by guards."[114]

Along with escape, sexualized resistance may have also had its place among female captives. When Dilly Echols arrived at Camp Heardmont in 1892, she was completing her third year of a life sentence for the crime of infanticide. No sooner had her feet touched the ground than she was raped and impregnated by a guard. It is unclear how long her pregnancy endured. On November 24, 1892, Echols was admitted to the camp infirmary for a "miscarriage."

While the heavy fieldwork she was forced to perform may have contributed to her failed pregnancy, it is not inconceivable that Echols could have had a hand in uprooting her unborn seed by chewing on cotton root, ingesting turpentine, or resorting to the use of some other natural abortifacient found on the plantation.[115] It is a well-known fact that, in slavery, bondwomen utilized herbs and other natural elements to prevent conception, induce abortions, and to remedy a wide range of illnesses. Less apparent, however, is how the use of subversive medical tactics factored into the lives of imprisoned women after the Civil War. Hence, one is left to ponder how, why, and with what level of frequency female convicts resorted to abortion.

In view of the fact that ex-slaves and freeborn women coexisted within Georgia's private lease camps and prison farms, herbal wisdom could have been easily conferred by the mature to the young on how to expunge an unwanted pregnancy. Yet it is not beyond reason to believe that some youthful women, like Echols, may have arrived in the state's camps with a previously acquired level of homeopathic knowledge. It is a well-known fact that freedwomen and their daughters relied on home remedies passed down from older generations to treat health problems. This practice inspired a sense of autonomy among ex-bondwomen, in particular, but was also a necessity for a group of people too poor to afford medical treatment anyhow.[116] Since the scholarly record is quite thin as it pertains to African American women's use of folk medicine during the postemancipation period, one is left to rely on ex-slave narratives to validate the use of slavery-based healing rituals among freedwomen and their offspring.

In the 1930s, Works Progress Administration interviewer Louise Oliphant made a record of the surviving "folk remedies and superstition" among black Georgians. Her collected testimonies reveal how ex-slaves and their progeny continued to make liberal use of natural cures to treat a host of infirmities, including measles, hiccups, "bad blood," stomach worms, nosebleeds, toe corns, fevers, colds, constipation, hives, and asthma. While most suggested therapies were non-gender-specific, a handful of gynecological solutions were disseminated by female interviewees. One woman advised Oliphant to wear a "raw cotton string tied in nine knots around your waist" to alleviate menstrual cramps. Another woman extended advice on how to eliminate leukorrhea by drinking "tea made from parched egg shells or green coffee."[117] As one might expect, female interviewees carefully avoided any mention of natural contraceptives or abortifacients. Even so, their testimonies provide persuasive evidence that ex-bondwomen arose out of slavery with a concentrated level of homeopathic intelligence and transferred this knowledge to their female descendants.

While it is difficult to pinpoint exactly how and to what degree imprisoned women aborted their offspring, it is much easier to explain why an individual would have pursued such drastic measures. Taking into consideration the precarious nature of bondwomen's maternal condition in Georgia's prison camps, it is quite plausible that female convicts induced abortions to expel their rapists' spawn, to prevent their children from being killed or disappearing, or to avoid watching their infants waste away from malnourishment while they labored from the crack of dawn till eventide. Abortion may have also served as a way to reclaim power over one's sexuality and reproductive autonomy. Given that sex was not a "work role," and there was no economic motive on the part of the state or lessees to advance the penal system through reproduction, sexualized resistance in particular had more to do with African American women's desire to defend their bodily autonomy than it did a yearning to impair the political economy of convict leasing.

In excess of abortion, feigning illness was another, more popular, method of "everyday resistance" utilized by female captives at Camp Heardmont. From the point of their arrival at the plantation, work hands plotted ways to sidestep their duties. In this regard, some bondwomen elected to "play off sick." By pretending to be in poor health, overtaxed laborers hoped to gain temporary relief from backbreaking work routines, and to rest their tired limbs in the sick bay. Faking illness also served as a way to undermine the lessee's ability to profit off the use of their bodies.

During the first four months of Camp Heardmont's existence, it appears that the camp physician, A. E. Hunter, gave women prisoners a modest degree of latitude when they complained of being sick. On the whole, doctors found it impossible to determine if bondwomen were actually ill or faking, especially when no visible symptoms were present. But even in instances where a clear diagnosis could not be made, Dr. Hunter took his patients' word for it. Case in point, Nancy Morris was granted a four-day stay in the infirmary when she claimed to be stricken with the "all-overs."[118] Numerous others were admitted overnight for "general debility" and "rest"—generic terms used by the physician to describe undiagnosable ailments.

Five months into his employment, Hunter either resigned or was released from his duties, and he was replaced by Dr. John S. Christian. It seems as though Christian brought to Camp Heardmont a stricter level of intolerance for female convicts' tendency to "play possum," and, like Colonel Mattox, grew immune to their claims of illness—legitimate and false. Based on the uptick in hospitalizations for serious medical conditions and the complete halt on admissions for ambiguous or unverifiable illnesses, one might reasonably conclude that Christian's indifference, coupled with escalating work demands imposed by the lessee, is what altered hospitalization patterns and frequencies. It is also important to mention that, because Mattox underwent an entrepreneurial conversion after his slaveholding days and was no longer economically invested in bondwomen's reproductive abilities, there was no added leverage to female prisoners' claims of pain or disability.[119] Still and all, the camp physician's dismissal of seemingly benign medical conditions and Mattox's deepening exploitation of bondwomen's working bodies had a detrimental, and sometimes fatal, impact on their health. One is left to wonder if Lummy Long or Martha Williams would have "died in the field" had their complaints of fatigue and faintness been taken seriously. Or maybe Mary Battle would have survived her bout with "sporadic cholera," instead of dropping dead at the doctor's feet on the same day she was finally admitted to the camp clinic.[120]

Sadly, Mattox's and his practitioners' anxieties about being hoodwinked cost several female felons their lives. Reflecting on his managerial successes, the lessee claimed to have ultimately mastered the art of handling women prisoners—even if he lost several in the process.

While few claims made by leasing officials can be trusted, Mattox resolutely maintained that, by ruling with respect, he succeeded in taming otherwise ungovernable female convicts. In his words, "Escapes are unknown since I have ruled with kindness and consideration" and "the women no longer play off sick . . . I know nothing about the management of male convicts, but I do know that it is the nature of a woman to rebel if she is treated cruelly. Take a woman and beat her with the lash and she becomes stubborn, hysterical, cowed and browbeaten."[121] The lessee confessed that he made many mistakes in the beginning: "I tried driving at first. The convicts gave me trouble. They rebelled and mutinied under the sting of the lash" and "would shirk every task possible." But once the "meanest man in Georgia" relaxed his whip and, instead, placated the women with civil manners, a positive change allegedly occurred. The rate of escapes fell, and Mattox learned a valuable lesson: female convicts "must be treated humanely."[122]

The experiment forged at Camp Heardmont came to a close in 1899, with the founding of the Georgia state prison farm. Additional factors also played a role in the state's decision to liquidate Mattox's bound labor force. After years of fiscal mismanagement, combined with an inability to fully recover from the depression of 1893, which sent cotton prices crashing, the lessee was eventually forced to declare bankruptcy. In 1898, one year before the state's female felons were removed from his grab, the Equitable Insurance Company, a New York–based investment bank, sued him for his debts, and the majority of his foreclosed property was sold at a public auction in Elberton for $16,000.[123] Overdrawn, and unable to afford to renew his lease, Mattox amicably surrendered his rented chattels to the state. Two years later, the entrepreneur's cheerless soul was put to rest when he was shot to death by his son-in-law in a duel over a stolen horse.[124] Although Mattox ultimately failed in his final venture, Camp Heardmont set an important precedent that helped shape the future of penal reform in the "Empire State." The slow movement of female felons from the private lease camps to the public agricultural realm, culminating with the inception of the state prison farm in 1899, marked the closing of one modernizing experiment and the opening of another.

CHAPTER FOUR

Sustaining the "Weak and Feeble"
Women Workers and the Georgia State Prison Farm

In the summer of 1911, A. H. Ulm boarded a Friday morning train out of Atlanta, bound for the Georgia state prison farm. A contributing author for the *Atlanta Constitution* newspaper and a noble son of the South, the essayist traveled to the farmstead seeking fodder for a news story that would combine the literary fluency of folklorist Joel Chandler Harris and the paternalistic temper of Georgia-born historian Ulrich Bonnell Phillips. In Ulm's words, it was time to "convey a few impressions gained upon a visit to those penal-philanthropic institutions located on state-owned land in Baldwin County" that "are not as well-known as they should be."[1]

Ulm's ninety-eight-mile day trip through the woodlands of central Georgia ended at a bustling depot in the heart of Milledgeville, two short miles from the state farm. After "Captain" Joseph Williams, then warden of the penal complex, received his visitor on the platform, the two men sailed down the dusty red clay roadway. As the pair coasted through the main gate of the four-thousand-acre settlement, they were welcomed by undulating rows of immature cotton buds, shiny ears of ripened corn, and the sight of several domestic workers promenading around the front porch of the warden's family residence; it was their assigned duty to make a decent showing for the "Captain's" special guest. In the yard, a coterie of reformatory inmates was lined up to be photographed. "Boys, all of you who intend to grow up and be good men, hold up your hands," they were asked. "Every palm was raised in an instant."[2]

"Bring out the music," Chairman Davison requested as Ulm and the warden settled onto a wooden bench in the men's quarters, where "convicts old and worn in the service and no longer fit for roadwork" were detained, and where the "afflicted and dying" were cared for.[3] On cue, "a semi-blind white boy came out with his mandolin, and to the accompaniment of a guitar picked by a [so-called] Negro murderer, began to make the quiet evening air resound with the doleful strains of prison music."[4] Guards and trusties were invited into the makeshift amphitheater to hear the two-man band. The next morning, the amusements continued. The chairman rallied up a small choir, "all in stripes," and "asked if they wouldn't sing for a bit." Led by an ex-preacher who was serving a life sentence for wife murder, they raised their voices and "shook the rafters of the old cow barn."[5] As the byre trembled at the sound of baritone vocals smacking against its timber frame, female prisoners, working on the opposite end of the farm, were stirred by the internal sound of sorrow.

Ulm's voyage to the women's quarters of the state prison farm was unlike any of his previous excursions. There was no jesting, music making, mock civilities, or simulated "paternal care" exchanged between Mr. Maxwell, keeper of the women's department, and his female staff. Instead, "while visiting there on Sunday morning, when the sun was pouring down rays of heat that sent the mercury in search of 100," Ulm found, in his words, a "big black giantess," curled up and "sleeping soundly" in a wooden cage, which doubled as a makeshift solitary confinement chamber. Based on this sinister scene, the reporter must not have been surprised when "a group of women hovered around the visiting party, begging for help to get out."[6] He impassively ignored their pleas for assistance. Contrariwise, he pitied and praised Mr. Maxwell for handling the "class of female prisoners with whom he has to deal . . . noting the semi-savagery predominant in the aspects of most of them, I would say that occasional use of the lash is not only necessary, but entirely humane," stated Ulm.[7]

A. H. Ulm's narrative is significant for what it reveals as well as what it conceals. On one hand, it shows that black female prisoners had few allies in the form of southern white men, who dismissed them as unruly and dangerous "representatives of the lower strain of their race,"[8] and abused them according to these fixed racialized assumptions. The report also gestures toward the essential role African American women workers played in the cultivation and expansion of the state prison farm, but, all at once, it ignores the impact their incarceration posed on the state's penal reform movement. As it happens, the modernization of Georgia's prison system during the first decade of the twentieth century was, to some degree, framed around the laboring bodies of black women prisoners.

Under the cover of humanitarianism, the state farm—Georgia's first active residential public incarcerative facility to be established after the Civil War—was, like the private lease camps, structured as a for-profit carceral entity. African American women were the "mules of men" at the industrial plantation, where they toiled from morning to night in the fields and supported the young, handicapped, and unhealthy male prisoners—the majority of whom were untrained or incapable of hard farm labor. Black female convicts also served as labor substitutes for a handful of white women who were "weakened by their race" and thus exempted from heavy fieldwork.

The twentieth century ushered in a new wave of farming technologies and a fresh set of occupational demands for Georgia's incarcerated workforce. Black women prisoners, to the greatest extent, were forced to apply their agronomic expertise and technical proficiency in old and new ways, while also coping with work-related abuses, bodily exploitation, and violence. This chapter foregrounds the lived and laboring experiences of black female inmates detained at the Georgia state prison farm, and it explores how African American women's labor supported the formation of New South modernity in a chiefly agrarian context. Although this chapter places female convicts and their burdens at the fore, it also considers, for the first time, the plight of "weak and feeble" men, and it lays emphasis on the difficulties faced by juvenile offenders swaddled in the state's care.

A New Era of Reform

By the close of the nineteenth century, the southern convict lease system was a popular subject of discourse among progressive reformers, newspaper reporters, and advocates of free labor.[9] Horrifying details of prison camp life saturated the pages of local and national newspapers, pamphlets, and essays that slandered the system and its perpetrators. These expositions provided chilling details of the gratuitous violence and deplorable living and laboring conditions convicts faced, and they also underscored the malevolent actions of leasing officials who habitually subjected women and girls "to the grossest indecencies and exposures."[10]

On Sunday, January 26, 1902, Helen Pitts Douglass, widow of prominent abolitionist, writer, orator, and champion of civil equality Frederick Douglass, graced the pulpit of the Second Baptist Church in northwest Washington, D.C. For more than an hour, she held her listeners in "rapt attention" while she recited the horrors of convict leasing in Georgia and Alabama and described scenes that, according to one spectator, "have not been exceeded in pathos by George Keenan on 'Siberia' or by the tales of weylerism in Cuba."[11] Echoing passages from her unpublished essay on the southern convict lease system, Pitts Douglass publicly denounced the "especial atrocity" committed at the hand of Georgia's lessees. "With tragic intensity," she exhorted her audience to acknowledge how "cruelly and how brutally ignorant we have remained of the terrible condition of things in our Southern states . . . Could there have been since 1870, an invisible marching through Georgia, what horrors would have been witnessed, of things testified to in court; cruelty and vice and filthiness unutterable; insufficient and filthy food; beds and people alive with vermin; inhuman punishments . . . Bastard children—25 in one camp. One convict for 14 years said that she had had 7 children. One lessee testified that 'such irregularities as bastard children would occasionally occur as long as women were guarded by men.' "[12]

The woes of incarcerated women served as an essential catalyst in Georgia's early penal reform movement. Reformers and journalists (local and national) used the exploitation of female convicts as a focal point in their appeals and editorials. Semiconservative white newsprints invoked the plight of women prisoners in dramatic exposés, while black newspapers, such as the *Cleveland Gazette*, candidly (and paternalistically) defended black womanhood, reproving Georgia's leasing officials and the state for underwriting the exploitation of female inmates. "Ought Georgia be permitted to so debase womanhood even if an ignorant Afro-American is the victim?" asked one reporter. "Would any northern state permit either black or white woman, intelligent or ignorant, to be so maltreated?"[13] From women reformers, especially, the rejoinder to this question was a resounding no.

Georgia's unusually hostile system of convict leasing engendered a high level of female social activism. During the progressive era, as women's roles began to change, white women who were once hindered by the cult of domesticity began to engage in social affairs and were granted a sturdy platform whereby to express their political views on women's suffrage, prohibition, and other social issues of the day. The National American Woman Suffrage Association, General Federation of Women's Clubs, and Woman's Christian Temperance Union (WCTU) greatly enriched the lives of white women seeking an outlet to advocate for the female sex. Nevertheless, with the exception of the WCTU, these organizations were not biracially composed or hospitable to black female reformers. Thus, middle-class African American women forged a separate crusade for social justice. Unable to detach race from their "analyses of power," black female reformers integrated the struggle to achieve gender parity with a more prominent mission to secure racial equality.[14]

Mary Church Terrell was one of the first female activists to vocally challenge the mistreatment of black women prisoners in the southern states, particularly in Georgia, where she found "the convict lease camps of no state in the South have presented conditions more shocking and cruel."[15]

She bewailed that fact that many citizens in the North, West, and East remained unaware of the atrocities associated with convict leasing. "A striking illustration of this fact occurred while I was addressing the Baptist Women's Missionary Society in Beverly Massachusetts," asserted Terrell. "I had been invited to speak on the Progress and Problems of Colored Women. During this talk I referred to the Convict Lease System . . . Mrs. George W. Coleman, the president of the Association, interrupted me to explain what I meant by the Convict Lease System . . . 'How many in this audience,' she asked, 'know anything about the Convict Lease System to which the speaker has just referred?' . . . Not a hand was raised."[16]

To combat ignorance and indifference toward Georgia's convict labor problem, Terrell did much to inspire and mobilize African American club women against the maltreatment of women and youth ensnared in the South's prison camps. As reflected in the minutes from the 1895 and 1896 meetings of the NACW, members were encouraged to take account of affairs in the state of Georgia and to follow the lead of Selena Sloan Butler, who, according to Terrell, "does not turn aside from her work exclaiming: O, I cannot touch such a subject. It makes me shudder!," and to, instead, bring their "mighty influence to bear for the abolition of the convict lease system."[17]

One by one, female critics—black and white—hurled stones at the system's already broken frame. The "Empire State" hung its head in shame as local reformer Rebecca Latimer Felton unleashed an arsenal of criticism against the system and its supporters. Born on June 10, 1835, in DeKalb County, Georgia, to a family of slaveholders, Felton was a daughter of privilege. She attended and graduated from Madison Female College in Madison, Georgia, in 1852 and, afterward, married William Harrell Felton, a U.S. congressman and member of the Georgia state legislature. In 1886, Felton began to take a leading role in local and national reform movements. She became active in the national women's suffrage campaign and in the prohibition movement of Georgia. She was also a blunt critic of the state's convict lease system.

From the apathetic citizens of Georgia, Felton demanded, "How are you conserving—preserving if you please the honor and good name of the state of Georgia—in thus allowing a woman—be she white or colored—thus beaten by a creature appointed by our prison commission—and continued in brutal authority—by the very same do-nothing commissioners. Why do you sluf over your rights and privileges and to give such a woman the treatment of a dog—in the prison camps of your state? Are you citizens—

voters—or are you numbsculls?"[18] Revolted by the presence of "bastard children" and women "in their advanced stages of pregnancy" roaming the camps, Felton rounded off her tirade by asking, "Where is the possibility of reformation in a system—where men and women are chained together and we are annually raising a number of children from mothers who are on the chain?"[19]

While publicly calling for the expulsion of the convict lease system and the reformation of its female victims, Felton also advanced her personal campaign to eliminate race mixing. She is a clear example of how some southern white progressives used the penal reform movement to promote their own social and political agendas, which were often steeped in racist logic. In Felton's opinion, convict leasing exemplified the "basic wrong of miscegenation" and accentuated the worst features of the Old South slavery system, where "mulattos were as common as blackberries."[20] Furthermore, sexual intercourse between white men and black women threatened to undermine the white woman's position as a mother and wife. Hence, at the core of Rebecca Latimer Felton's crusade to abolish convict leasing in Georgia was a more deep-seated motivation; she hoped to stop the spread of miscegenation and the negative social effects it levied on the white race—particularly women—by separating black women prisoners from the control of "unprincipled" white men in the state's camps.

While Felton attacked Georgia's convict lease system from within the state, some of the most bellicose demonstrations against the system were waged by northern "interlopers." In her pamphlet *The Crime of Crimes* (1907), Clarissa Olds Keeler, a liberal white social reformer, culled together information collected from various newspapers and official reports and assembled a scathing state-by-state denunciation of America's justice system. She laid bare the atrocities inherent within the South's convict labor regimes and highlighted the deplorable working, living, and health conditions found therein. What's more, she spoke candidly about the impact of violence on the region's felony and misdemeanor convicts. Of Georgia's penal system, Keeler had the following to say: "The convict lease system in Georgia has been fraught with evils, in some respects, unparalleled in American prisons . . . Female convicts have been the greatest sufferers" and have "helped pay the price with their virtue and their blood."[21]

Whereas the majority of Keeler's writings were publicized through secular mediums, she periodically articulated her feelings to religious audiences. In her essay "Let the Singing of the Prisoner Come before Thee," read before a meeting of the National Convocation for Prayer in Saint Louis,

Missouri, in 1903, she critiqued the level of Christian indifference to the condition of the South's prisoners, boldly declaring that "while the good people are praying for the outpouring of the Holy Spirit on other lands may they not forget that we need a baptism of fire right here in our own land. Our Saviour's last act of mercy and forgiving love was shown toward a Prisoner and shall we imitate His example, or shall we not?"[22]

Although evangelical participation in the struggle to abolish convict leasing is understated in the historical literature, prison evangelist (and affiliate of Clarissa Olds Keeler) Elizabeth Ryder Wheaton's example of righteous discontent, in particular, offers some insight into the ways in which religion influenced the penal reform movement. During the 1880s and 1890s, Wheaton journeyed throughout the South, proselytizing and surveying the condition of the region's convict camps and its prisoners. In her memoir, *Prisons and Prayer, or a Labor of Love* (1906), she documented her observations, placing special emphasis on the predicament of female captives. Throughout her travels, Wheaton met with women who had been physically and sexually exploited and forced to engage in heavy work unsuitable for any woman to perform. As per her recollection, "In some instances, women are made to do the farm work, work in brick yards, and do other kinds of hard work. At one place in the South, the women cultivated a thousand acres of cotton, doing other farming and caring for the stockade, horses, mules, cows, and hogs and having only men to guard them. They were not allowed a woman matron to care for them when they were sick or dying. I found them in rags and tatters and looking almost like wild beasts."[23]

One of Wheaton's worst memories involved the day she stumbled across an "old colored woman" who had been "tied to a log and severely whipped on the bare flesh" for either defying orders or failing to execute her labor duties in an efficient manner.[24] In response, "I went to the governor of that state and pleaded with him for my own sex," says Wheaton. "I begged him to protect the poor women from such cruel treatment and brutal punishment. I asked him to have them taken in from the farm where they were clearing up the land and compelled to carry logs, to the state prison at the Capitol, and given proper work and humane treatment."[25] But what Wheaton failed to realize is that, in the southern states, agricultural labor on state-run prison farms *was* considered "humane treatment."

By the 1900s, public prison farms cropped up in all the southern states. This new model of incarceration emerged from and represented a unique trend in penal experimentation and reform advanced by southern prison officials, governors, and penologists at the turn of twentieth century.[26] For

the most part, state-run custodial institutions were spaces where (theo-
retically) "dead hands," female, youthful, old, and sick prisoners could be
cared for and supervised in one centralized location and worked in a healthy
and humane way.[27] In principle, by reinstating state control over state prisoners a more efficient regulation and inspection of prison facilities would
follow, thereby enhancing the physical, medical, and material welfare of
felony inmates.

In Florida and Georgia, state-run penal farms were primarily instituted
on humanitarian and reform-centered grounds. However, in Texas, Louisiana, and Mississippi, prison plantations were the states' final answer to
the convict lease question. To allay the dissenting voices of free labor pro-
ponents, state politicians resolved to consolidate entire prison populations
on state-owned lands rather than to allow lessees to continue to flood the
free labor marketplace with cheap prison labor.[28] Yet this modernizing aim
toward penal restructuring did not eradicate the states' fiscal interest in
convict labor. Southern officials still saw convicts as capital-bearing commodities. Furthermore, despite the South's claim to "progressive penology," plantations, chain gangs, and prison industries prolonged rather than
diminished race, labor, and gender exploitation.[29]

Baptized by Fire

On December 21, 1897, the Georgia General Assembly introduced a new
act that limited the lease of able-bodied felons to a period of five years,
substituting the state's newly expired twenty year lease. The abolition of
the principal keeper's position and the creation of a governor-appointed
three-man prison commission also factored into the assembly's reorganization scheme. One of the first orders the newly elected commissioners' received was to allocate $50,000 toward the purchase of four thousand acres of
land in Milledgeville, a "ginnery, a mill for grinding corn, a depot, warehouse," plows, mules, wagons, harrows and other farming essentials, along
with materials to build several stockades to house the state's female convicts,
juvenile boys, and "old and infirm men, who were not able to be hired out."[30]

Sixteen months after the state signed the deed on its new prison plantation, seventy-one female felons—sixty-eight black and three white—set
out on one last forced migration across the Georgia countryside. This
time, the women were shipped, in groups, ninety-six miles south from
Elbert to Baldwin County. For Leila Burgess, Nora Lay, Ella Gamble,
Rose Henderson, Amanda Hill, Nancy Morris, and more than one dozen

others, the trek from Elberton to Milledgeville—Georgia's fourth capital and the seat of the state government during the Civil War—was the last leg of a quadrangular passage from one of the state's male-occupied private lease camps, to the Bolton broom factory, to Camp Heardmont, and finally to the state prison farm. But for most of the others, the plantation was their first or second voyage through unfreedom's wilderness.

To persons familiar with its pre–Civil War topography, Milledgeville at the turn of the century appeared much different than it did during the war. The old penitentiary square was now home to the Georgia Normal and Industrial College for women (present-day Georgia College & State University), the old capitol building was the new site of Middle Georgia Military and Agricultural College (renamed Georgia Military College), and the once-destroyed depot building and Oconee Bridge were rebuilt and in pristine condition. But with all its improvements, the former capital city still did not measure up to the industrial prosperousness of its successor, Atlanta. Nevertheless, its large tracts of arable land made it a promising space for the state's newest modernizing venture: to create a "self-sustaining colony of convicts."[31]

From January to April of 1899, superintendent of the Georgia state prison farm, "Captain" K. C. Foster, acted on the state's orders to get the farmland in working order. He hired a team of approximately one hundred men to prep the fallow grounds for future cultivation. As described by a correspondent for the *Atlanta Constitution*, workers "dug and delved and whacked bushes and burned bramble and filled ditches and gullies until they had rendered arable more than a thousand acres reclaiming as good farming land tracts that had remained barren for more than ten years."[32] When the land was sufficiently primed and the buildings nearly complete, all Georgia's sick, disabled, and female prisoners, and a fraction of the state's underage convicts, were settled into their respective quarters of the farm. One hundred and fifty-seven "aged, infirm, and diseased" men were moved into a building on a secluded hillside. Nineteen juvenile boys "of fifteen years of age and under" were lodged on a different part of the plantation, separate from the men. Across the way, "about a half mile from the railroad . . . across Fishing Creek,"[33] the state's sixty-seven able-bodied female inmates were stashed in a "very large" one-room dormitory-style wooden stockade—but not for long. On the seventh day of December, the women's quarters were baptized in a pool of fire and reduced to a pile of ashes.

In the fourth annual report of the Prison Commission, submitted to Governor Allen D. Candler, Commissioners Joseph S. Turner, Tom Eason, and Clement A. Evans detailed the incident as follows:

> The women who were engaged in the burning, were short term women, one white, serving a term of eight months for larceny from the house, and two colored, with terms of two years each, for similar offences. The white woman concocted the plot, and stood watch, while the two colored women applied the fire underneath the building, between the weather-boarding and the ceiling. Within a few days after the fire, sufficient evidence had been secured to convict them, and the two colored women confessed the crime. At the January term of the Superior Court, of Baldwin County, they were indicted and placed upon trial for arson, and although there was no doubt whatever of their guilt, the evidence outside of the confessions, being sufficient to establish the same beyond all reasonable doubt, the jury trying them, acquitted all of them, in total disregard of the evidence, and apparently without reason, unless it was thought that convicts had the right to burn the prison in which they were confined, and were amenable to no law therefore.[34]

The scorching of the women's stockade with no legal consequences to follow was a rare and welcomed (yet short-lived) victory for the arsonists and their disgruntled associates. With no fire insurance or system of waterworks in place, the state was forced to pay $4,875.49 to install a water main and $2,500 for cement, lumber, and hardware to build a fireproof stone prison dormitory for the farm's female incendiaries.[35]

Reflecting the symbiotic relationship between the state's private and public laboring regimes, more than one dozen leased felons were rented to quarry stone on the farm, set up a water supply at the women's prison, build a "large store smoke-house, two two-room frame guards' cottages, and several larger barns and shelters for storing farm products," while a number of stonecutters and masons were extracted from the lease camps for the purpose of rebuilding the stockade at no cost to the state beyond the maintenance of the workforce.[36] In the meantime, the women were housed in a separate wing of the men's building until the "weather became sufficiently warm." Afterward, they were transferred to their designated area of the farm and put to work.[37]

In my attempt to decipher the lived and laboring experiences of female inmates at the Georgia state prison farm, I find it important to, first, acknowledge *who* these women were prior to their confinement. Through the use of rare census data, which, until now, have remained unutilized by scholars, it is possible to account for the date of birth, marital status, motherhood status, literacy rate, and nativity of each prisoner. It is also possible to track key changes that took place during the term of one's incarceration. Out of these census data, fluctuations in the maternal condition of female convicts are most revealing. Women who entered prison with no children were later reported as having had multiple births and several deceased offspring. This type of demographic information is crucial to our ability to carve out an identity for these women, within and beyond captivity.

As specified in the twelfth census of the United States, on or after June 13, 1900, a total of seventy-seven women occupied the women's quarters of the state farm—seventy-three black and four white. Of the seventy-three African American women detained at the plantation, eighteen were born before 1865 and fifty-five were born after emancipation. In addition, forty-one were classified as married, thirty-one as single, and one widowed. Concerning their parental status, thirty-seven (or 50 percent) of all black female felons were mothers. Fifty-four-year-old Mary David, born in Virginia in 1846, was recorded as having the highest number of children in the bunch; fourteen total births, eleven living offspring. Seven women had five or more children, and the remaining thirty mothers had borne between one and five children. Of the four white women prisoners confined at the Georgia state prison farm in 1900, all were born before 1865, three were classified as married, one widowed, and all but one were mothers of at least one child.[38]

As it pertains to labor, the previous occupations of female felons held at the state farm between 1899 and 1910 were analogous to the former work roles performed by first-generation captives imprisoned in Georgia's private lease camps. Although official penitentiary records do not allow for a specific racial or gendered itemization of the laboring duties once held by incarcerated women, it is still possible to surmise which categories of labor female felons previously engaged in. This can be done by bearing in mind the occupational trends of the era, and by homing in on certain categories of labor that were customarily reserved for black women—cooking, housekeeping, laundressing, and fieldwork. Table 3 shows the previous occupations of both male and female felony inmates in Georgia's prison system.[39]

TABLE 3 Showing Previous Occupations of Felony Convicts and Number Employed

Occupation	1899–1900	1900–1901	1901–1902	1903–1904	1904–1905	1905–1906	1906–1907	1907–1908	1908–1909	1909–1910
Accountant	7	11	6	8	4	4	5	4	2	6
Baker	1	3	4	8	9	10	11	9	8	10
Barber	16	13	16	16	17	17	22	21	21	17
Barkeeper	4	7	7	7	3	5	11	13	11	4
Bellboy	—	—	—	—	—	—	1	5	3	9
Bill Poster	—	—	—	1	1	1	—	—	—	3
Blacksmith	19	22	19	13	14	12	16	17	16	9
Boat Hand	—	—	—	—	5	6	4	3	3	5
Boilermaker	1	2	4	5	1	—	—	1	—	—
Bookbinder	1	1	—	—	—	—	—	—	—	—
Bootblack	13	14	19	8	13	15	19	19	20	9
Brick Mason	17	13	16	17	21	22	21	—	4	11
Broom Maker	1	2	6	3	2	5	6	3	2	—
Butcher	17	18	11	15	17	14	21	23	19	17
Butler	22	33	26	6	36	32	32	37	27	15
Candy Maker	7	9	8	7	6	10	8	5	1	7
Carpenter	27	26	25	26	19	13	23	23	21	16
Chambermaid	—	—	—	—	—	—	—	—	—	4
Cigar Maker	2	—	—	1	2	1	2	1	2	2
City Marshal	—	—	—	1	—	—	—	—	—	—

(continued)

TABLE 3 (continued)

Occupation	1899–1900	1900–1901	1901–1902	1903–1904	1904–1905	1905–1906	1906–1907	1907–1908	1908–1909	1909–1910
Clerk	11	14	13	14	11	7	7	2	—	7
Coachman	10	16	17	23	17	18	20	22	1	7
Cook	56	58	44	46	28	48	46	42	33	24
Cooper	7	7	9	10	9	9	6	10	3	4
Dairyman	—	—	—	—	1	8	6	—	—	—
Detective	—	—	—	1	—	—	—	1	—	—
Distiller	2	4	4	1	3	3	2	4	4	3
Drayman	12	22	20	—	1	12	15	16	17	22
Dyer	—	1	1	1	4	1	2	3	1	1
Engineer	—	4	7	6	10	3	5	4	3	8
Factory Girl	—	—	—	—	2	1	—	—	—	—
Factory Hand	—	—	—	4	—	—	2	8	5	—
Farmer	776	681	699	603	600	571	644	650	261	377
Fisherman	—	—	—	1	2	3	3	1	—	2
Glass Blower	—	—	—	1	1	1	1	1	—	—
Harness Maker	4	4	3	1	1	2	2	1	—	—
Hostler	—	—	8	8	4	4	15	7	8	5
Hotelkeeper	—	—	1	1	1	—	1	—	—	—
Hotel Waiter	—	—	—	—	12	14	17	8	—	—
Housemaid	—	—	—	18	12	16	33	20	25	22
Janitor	—	—	—	—	—	3	4	2	—	—

Occupation										
Jockey	5	13	10	—	—	—	—	—	—	1
Laborer	981	955	1,028	1,052	1,048	1,029	989	1,054	1,418	1,319
Laundryman	—	—	—	1	4	1	1	2	—	1
Lawyer	—	—	—	—	—	—	—	—	—	—
Machinist	10	5	5	—	6	12	12	10	8	9
Mail Carrier	—	—	—	—	1	—	1	1	1	—
Marble Worker	—	1	1	4	—	—	—	—	—	—
Mechanic	8	—	4	12	8	8	5	4	3	3
Merchant	—	6	6	5	7	7	9	9	7	5
Mill Operative	—	4	—	—	—	—	—	—	—	6
Miner	—	3	3	8	5	2	4	5	4	7
Molder	3	3	3	1	2	1	3	6	4	5
Nurse	—	—	3	15	9	11	10	6	6	5
Painter	22	19	15	7	10	11	17	13	16	21
Peddler	—	—	1	4	—	—	—	1	—	—
Physician	1	2	2	2	4	2	2	2	—	—
Pilot	1	1	1	2	2	1	1	2	2	—
Plasterer	6	4	6	5	4	4	3	4	4	2
Plumber	6	3	3	5	6	10	10	3	7	3
Policeman	—	—	1	—	1	2	2	—	—	1
Porter	33	28	24	25	25	13	17	15	16	41
Preacher	8	9	16	7	7	10	7	6	3	6
Printer	1	5	3	6	4	2	3	3	2	5

(continued)

TABLE 3 (*continued*)

Occupation	1899–1900	1900–1901	1901–1902	1903–1904	1904–1905	1905–1906	1906–1907	1907–1908	1908–1909	1909–1910
Public Works	—	—	—	—	—	115	109	211	389	307
RR Brakeman	—	—	1	5	10	17	17	16	13	7
RR Conductor	—	—	—	—	—	—	1	2	20	—
RR Fireman	29	21	35	35	35	37	37	36	38	47
RR Hand	61	128	83	125	83	83	82	43	38	51
Sailor	8	6	2	8	8	6	10	12	10	4
Seamstress	—	—	—	3	3	1	1	5	5	—
Shoemaker	12	6	6	4	2	1	3	5	4	4
Showman	—	—	—	1	1	—	—	—	—	—
Silversmith	2	1	1	2	1	2	1	1	—	1
Stevedore	5	7	5	9	4	1	3	6	—	1
Stonemason	5	6	5	6	2	3	—	2	2	2
Tailor	4	6	6	9	20	11	14	15	13	7
Tanner	—	—	—	1	1	—	—	—	—	—
Teacher	7	7	4	2	3	4	3	3	1	1
Teamster	—	—	—	32	17	5	9	7	1	5
Telegrapher	—	1	1	1	3	1	1	1	2	1
Tinner	1	2	7	2	—	—	—	—	—	—
Undertaker	—	—	—	—	—	1	—	—	—	—
Vagrant	—	—	6	3	12	12	12	5	—	5
Waiter	—	4	13	10	—	—	—	—	—	—
Washerwoman	—	—	—	—	22	16	18	21	15	13
Weaver	—	—	—	1	1	—	—	—	—	—

Like their occupational, marital, and motherhood statuses, the educational levels of African American women prisoners were wide-ranging. In 1900, fifteen women had completed between forty and ninety-six months of education, seven had completed thirty-one to forty, seven completed between twenty and thirty, nine completed eleven to nineteen, fourteen completed two to ten, and twenty-one had zero months of education. With regard to the literacy rates of black female inmates, 58 percent were capable of reading on a basic level, while 42 percent were wholly illiterate. To boot, 54 percent of African American women prisoners were able to write, while 46 percent were incapable. White female convicts fared nearly the same; three out of four were able to read and write and all had less than seventy-four months of education.[40]

In reference to the "nativity" and labor practices of all female felons, black and white, 86 percent of incarcerees were born in Georgia and 14 percent outside Georgia. Of the 14 percent, six women emigrated from Alabama, two from South Carolina, one from North Carolina, and two from Virginia. Concerning the women's occupational status at the plantation, five inmates were classified as servants (three of whom were white), one as a cook, two as seamstresses, and sixty-nine as farm laborers.[41]

Between 1900 and 1910, an average of seventy-five black female felons and five white women prisoners—including misdemeanor convicts—worked the state farm.[42] The labor of these women was divided along lines of race, skill, gender, and stereotype. As a rule, white female convicts were racially "debilitated" and exempted from heavy fieldwork, which was earmarked for "Negro women." By the same token, black male prisoners were judged incompetent in the fields on account of their physical disabilities and limited agricultural skills. For these reasons, which were in many ways reinforced by the long-standing racialized and gendered presuppositions about black women's hyperproductivity in field labor, African American women were branded as "the best farmers" on the plantation. As one observer put it, "The women have always been doing farm work, while the men, except in a few cases, have been employed in mills and such like places [during the term of their imprisonment]. This is given as the reason for the difference of work between them. The authorities say that most of the men, when they were started to work, had not only to be learned to put the gear on the mules but had to be started at the very alphabet of farming, the 'gee and haw.'"[43] Commissioners Turner, Eason, and Evans corroborated this assertion, expressly stating that "the burden of farm work falls upon the women and boys who are, as a rule, strong and healthy, and who, not only make their own support, but assist to a large extent in making a support for the men, the most of whom are, by reason of age, infirmity, or disease, unable to be self-sustaining, and a very large percent of whom are unable to perform any labor whatever."[44]

Comparatively speaking, in other southern locales such as Texas, Louisiana, and Mississippi, where the prison plantation was the standard method of incarceration, agricultural work was typically prescribed for male inmates. Notwithstanding, African American women prisoners were routinely exploited in modes of agricultural labor that were gendered male and in categories of work exclusively reserved for women. At the Goree plantation in Texas, officials made it the duty of the "Negro women" to "take care of the cotton and corn crop; the white women do sewing, garden work, care for chickens and work around the place in general."[45] On the Parchman prison farm in Mississippi, black female convicts labored in the fields throughout cotton picking time in the fall and canned vegetables. But their principal duty was to make striped uniforms, linens, and mattresses in a sweat-soaked sewing room.[46] Occupationally, Parchman formed the deepest contrast to the Georgia state prison farm, where incarcerated women were almost exclusively exploited for agricultural purposes. Nonetheless, the range of agronomic labor they did perform was broad and industrialized in nature. Female felons improvised with modern technologies and, despite its modest size, helped convert the state farm into an industrial prison plantation.

Breaking the Land

The "farm factory" concept that took root in the South after World War I was not sown by the carceral state. Yet prison plantations, which also operated as farm factories, were somewhat of a test performance for the grand agricultural production of the 1920s. In keeping with historian Deborah Fitzgerald's findings, the "industrial logic" was a fundamental aspect of twentieth-century agriculture.[47] Thus, it can be argued that, within the southern penal system, the purchase of large tracts of land, the modernized farming implements, the mass production of staple crops and cotton, and the large-scale rearing of livestock were practices that merely presaged the industrial and technological transformations to come.

When compared with its southern neighbors, the Georgia state prison farm lacked in size. Even so, the farmstead upheld the "industrial logic" of the twentieth-century agricultural marketplace. From the outset, it was hoped that the "experiment" would be a lucrative one. If by the end of the new five-year lease the farm turned a sizable enough profit, it was projected that "all the convicts will be employed in the various manufacturing industries that will be established to give them work."[48] As reported by an unnamed journalist for the *Atlanta Constitution*, commissioners considered "getting figures on a broom factory, a fertilizer factory, a ginnery outfit, a cotton mill and some other industries that they think might be successfully carried on with convict labor."[49] Although, over the first ten years of its existence, multiple attempts were made to strengthen the plantation's financial yield and its industrializing potential, the farm never excelled beyond a self-sustaining state. Proceeds from the sale of cotton and excess staple crops were deposited into the state treasury to support the penal complex, its workers, and its patients; in essence, convicts managed to "earn their keep" at the farm. Nonetheless, it can be argued that agricultural practices at the state farm added to Georgia's repertoire as a modernizing force in the region.

As the twentieth century dawned in Georgia, New South boosters and progressives in the "Empire State" appealed to the state's farmers to diversify their crops and to surrender their dependency on king cotton. On the eve of World War I, before the boll weevil infestation devoured the crop, prompting the mass migration of hundreds of thousands of black and white tenant farmers out of the state's rural townships into urban and northern spaces, Georgia farmers produced an unprecedented 2.8 million bales of cotton.[50] But even with its cotton economy at a high point, industrialists still feared that the overproduction of the crop would collapse the state's agricultural economy. Consequently, these anxieties impacted the economic ambitions of the carceral state in unexpected ways.

During its first three years of operation, the Georgia state prison farm produced approximately 909 bales (454,500 pounds) of cotton, earning more than $30,000 in profit. By 1905, the farm had to curtail its cotton growth to placate local and regional competitors, who complained that the farm was undercutting the price of cotton and, at the same time, competing with free labor. Ginners lamented to *Atlanta Constitution* reporters that "it is ruinous to their business to be forced to compete with the state in the ginning of cotton. Their plants, they say, are not, in the very nature of the case, equal to the state's in equipment . . . they declare that if the state continues to engage in the business they will be forced to shut down their plants."[51] Acknowledging public discontent, and honoring the call for a modern, diversified agricultural economy, penal officials adjusted the work

Women prisoners setting out to plow a field at the Georgia state prison farm in Milledgeville, circa 1895–1920. Courtesy of the Georgia Historical Society, MS 1764.

demands of the state's convicts to reflect the mixed economic interests of the state. Instead of flooding public lands with cotton, prisoners were made to shower the earth with designated amounts of various crops. At the women's farm, in particular, the initial quantity was five hundred acres of corn and cotton, one hundred acres of peas, fifty acres of goobers (peanuts), twenty-five acres of sweet potatoes, twenty-five acres of wheat, and two hundred acres of garden products.[52]

In order to tend to the diversity of crops they were forced to cultivate, women prisoners were furnished with an assortment of old and modern farming implements: hoes, axes, long- and short-handle shovels, pitchforks, harrows, plow stocks, horse-drawn Chattanooga plows, large heel scrapes, mowers, turners, reapers, threshers, scooters, hatchets, binders, cross cut saws, and so on. Newfangled machineries such as guano distributors, two-horse middle buster plows, and cotton planters were also put into action on the farm.[53] To warehouse the harvest, feed, livestock, and equipment, a twenty-by-sixty-foot three-story granary was built to store and cure roughly three thousand to four thousand bushels of wheat at a time. Multiple stables, one of which was one-hundred-by-fifty-four feet, was designed to hold up to four thousand bushels of corn for feeding purposes, and thirty-six stalls for livestock.[54] Without a doubt, the plantation profited immensely from "strong and healthy" women who were backbone of settlement. They grew the food that the other prisoners consumed, and were a much needed help to the indigent and unskilled. White female seamstresses—albeit extremely few in number—and skilled workers, such as Mattie Crawford, also contributed to the advancement of the penal estate.

Operating in a world far different from that of her underprivileged, overburdened counterparts, Mattie Crawford's experience at the state prison farm was a welcome reprieve. Away from the Chattahoochee brickyard, she was allowed to use her blacksmithing skills as a pathway to trusty status. Gradually, Crawford shifted from welding while wearing pants to welding herself to male clothing as a potential site of protection and elevation. On the word of one penal custodian, "after she had them [the pants] on awhile she became attached to them as to refuse absolutely to take them off."[55] Masculine garb and "professional" competency were key ingredients to her survival. Perhaps, in her mind's eye, Crawford secretly hoped that if she was ever liberated from the clutches of captivity, she may be able to bypass the rigid social boundaries circumscribing black women's labor and apply those skills in the free labor market.

As was the case in penitentiary systems throughout the South, an incentive program existed at the Georgia state prison farm. Certain convicts that exemplified "good manners" and a superior work ethic were elevated to "trusty" status and afforded privileged positions within the penal colony. These choice inmates were granted greater mobility, more manageable workloads, preferential treatment by penal authorities, and an improved livelihood when compared with their angst-ridden peers.

The labor hierarchy instituted at the farm was divided into three tiers: domestic service, skilled labor, and agricultural work. Trusty-servants acted as aides in the household of the farm superintendent, where they cooked, cleaned, washed, and so on. In 1919, Pink "Pinkie" Gardner was forced to work as the private servant of the warden after she killed Emma Bovine for "trying to wreck her home." The woman claimed that Bovine "had made her brags that she had her husband and was going to keep him."[56] Fortunately, seven years into her prison term, Gardner was approved for parole and restored to her "two little children." Officials seemingly honored the fact that she "had born a good reputation [with the warden]; that she was an industrious hardworking woman."[57]

Further down on the servant ladder were the dog handlers, whose principal role was to feed the bloodhounds and manage the kennel. "Half guards," who were also grouped into the servant class, functioned as the eyes and ears of the camp. "Without the help of the prisoners, we couldn't employ guards enough to hold them here," declared "Captain" Burke, general superintendent of the farm.[58] In this position, which was as much predicated on race and gender as it was the level of one's obedience and submission to authority, white male prisoners were armed with revolvers and granted permission to pursue would-be deserters.

In a class of her own, Mattie Crawford was situated at the top of the occupational pyramid at the state farm. As the settlement's sole ironsmith, she was the most highly esteemed trusty-artisan in the lot. But her remarkable ascent to the top was not a haphazard occurrence; it was hewn out of several years of oppression, opposition, and hard labor at the Chattahoochee brickyard. By excelling as a blacksmith, she tilted the scales of southern injustice in her favor and transformed her persecution into social promotion.

Artisans possessed great social and economic value to the carceral estate. In Crawford's case, mastering a masculine skilled trade allowed her to accrue a certain level of acclaim for her work. The camp warden praised her as "one of the best blacksmiths for miles around. She can hit the iron while it's hot and bend it into any shape she desires . . . She does all of the blacksmith work on the farm and much for the people all around."[59] By feigning deference, and shielding the truth of her inner self from her subjugators, Crawford also secured a greater level of mobility. Imprisoned for life, she utilized her skill to intermittently free herself from the physical and representational limitations of prison life. Just the same, by embracing masculine garb and performing male-oriented labor, Crawford contested the imposed heterosexual violence wielded against the black female body. It is quite possible that she used her dress and vocation as a blacksmith to redirect the glare of her captors and to refashion the way in which her body was regarded by her keepers and the system at large.

At the state farm, Mattie Crawford was successful in her attempts to escape punishment. But such was not the case for a number of her workmates—male and female. Unfortunately, everywhere convicts traveled, violence, neglect, and work-related abuses followed. In the summer of 1908, an investigation of the prison department revealed that convicts at the state farm were severely flogged, fed rotten food, maggot-filled meat, and wormy meal. One white male prisoner testified that, on top of being fed spoiled food, he was "maimed in one of the delicate organs of his body [presumably his penis]" after receiving a whipping.[60] The investigation also showed that a disabled "Negro convict" died after being "forced to the field to work, over his protest . . . When he arrived at the place to work, he was in no condition to work." The man laid down "in the shade, and in a few hours was a corpse."[61]

A cursory reference to the plight of women prisoners was made in the 1908 investigative report, which revealed that female convicts were cursed and flogged. A 1922 probe at the state farm uncovered an even deeper level of neglect and maltreatment. Investigators claimed that the bunks in the "colored female ward were deplorably infested with chinches [bedbugs]. We also found in the female colored ward sweat boxes just large enough for a person of normal size to be confined for punishment; said sweat boxes containing chains for the purpose of preventing the prisoners incarcerated therein from assuming a squatting position."[62]

Perhaps the most damning evidence of the abuse of women prisoners at the state farm is tucked inside the personal papers of investigative journalist, communist, and author of the famous exposé *Georgia Nigger* (1932), John L. Spivak.[63] So far untapped by scholars, the September 1931 "Georgia Penitentiary Report of Convicts Employed at the State Prison Farm Female Camp, Punishment Report"—which was excluded from Spivak's widely referenced appendix of illustrations—is the most crucial and sole piece of official documentation available in the historical record that catalogs, in detail, the nature of gendered violence (and resistance) at the Georgia state prison farm. Table 4, drawn from the report, chronicles the methods of discipline utilized against female convicts, and shows how modes of punishment became more elaborate over time.[64] Why Spivak omitted these data from his publication, therefore rendering women prisoners invisible in his critique of Georgia's carceral regimes, is unknown. Nevertheless, this report proves that, inasmuch as the state farm was branded as a progressive, humanitarian innovation, the institution was slow to fully discard the abuses and immoralities that necessitated its establishment in the first place.

Example of the type of solitary confinement chamber ("sweat box") that would have been used at the women's quarters of the Georgia state prison farm. Photograph by Duane Perkins, courtesy of the State Archives of Florida.

Wayward Boys and Hardened Men

In 1897, essayist Sarge Plunkett posed a critical question to the nation's reformers. He asked, "Are we all hypocrites?" The inquiry was made in response to the unsettling issue of "wayward boys" being intermingled with "hardened men" in Georgia's convict lease and chain gang camps, and the indifference shown on the part of reformists to this matter. To prick the conscience of the state's activists, Plunkett used his personal observation of a mother mourning the loss of her son to a county chain gang. In his words,

> A deep impression was made upon my mind by watching a poor
> old mother that passed every day for weeks to spend her time in the
> neighborhood of where the county chaingang was at work. A very
> feeble little son of this old mother had been convicted of some
> petty theft and was serving a term on the chaingang . . . The boy
> was not strong enough to do more than carry water for the rest of
> the criminals, and to this work they had put him. The old mother
> would repair there every day and take her seat at the root of a tree

TABLE 4 Showing Punishment of Female Convicts at Georgia State Prison Farm, September 1931

Date	Name	Punishment	Duration	Offense
Sept. 1	Lara Sims	Dungeon	5 Days	Disobedience
Sept. 2	Ada Robertson	Punishment Stool	1 Hour	Fighting
Sept. 5	Ethel Perry	Dungeon	24 Hours	Feigning Illness
Sept. 5	Sara Thomas	Dungeon	24 Hours	Feigning Illness
Sept. 5	Rose Roberts	Dungeon	24 Hours	Feigning Illness
Sept. 5	Ella Mae Flemming	Dungeon	24 Hours	Feigning Illness
Sept. 7	Minnie Prator	Dungeon	24 Hours	Feigning Illness
Sept. 11	Mary Hart	Stocks and Dungeon	15 Hours in Stocks, 10 Days in Dungeon	Feigning Illness and Impudence to Guard
Sept. 11	Hattie Mae McKinley	Box	24 Hours	Feigning Illness
Sept. 14	Mattie Lou Williams	Punishment Stool	1 Hour	Talking in Dining Room
Sept. 14	Rosa Small	Punishment Stool	1 Hour	Talking in Dining Room
Sept. 15	Louise Riley	Punishment Stool	1 Hour	Talking in Dining Room
Sept. 15	Jessie Mae Christian	Punishment Stool	1 Hour	Talking in Dining Room
Sept. 16	Bessie Russell	Box	24 Hours	Feigning Illness
Sept. 16	Carrie Roberson	Box	24 Hours	Feigning Illness
Sept. 16	Johnnie Mae Burley	Box	24 Hours	Feigning Illness
Sept. 16	Ruby Clarke	Box	24 Hours	Feigning Illness

(continued)

TABLE 4 (continued)

Date	Name	Punishment	Duration	Offense
Sept. 17	Ruby Ray	Punishment Stool	3 Hours	Disobedience
Sept. 18	Mattie Parker	Box	24 Hours	Feigning Illness
Sept. 18	Catherine Parker	Box	24 Hours	Feigning Illness
Sept. 18	Bertha Thomas	Box	24 Hours	Feigning Illness
Sept. 18	Annie Singleton	Box	24 Hours	Feigning Illness
Sept. 22	Ruby Mitchell	Box	4 Days	Fighting
Sept. 23	Rosa Small	Box	24 Hours	Feigning Illness
Sept. 23	Florine Stanberry	Box	24 Hours	Feigning Illness
Sept. 23	Hozie Walker	Box	24 Hours	Feigning Illness
Sept. 24	Mary Hart	Box	24 Hours	Feigning Illness
Sept. 24	Annie Singleton	Box	24 Hours	Feigning Illness
Sept. 25	Rosa Small	Stocks	15 Minutes	Fighting
Sept. 25	Hozie Walker	Stocks	15 Minutes	Fighting
Sept. 25	Bertha Roberson	Box	24 Hours	Feigning Illness
Sept. 25	Hattie Hightower	Box	24 Hours	Feigning Illness
Sept. 25	Ella Harden	Box	24 Hours	Taking Food from Table
Sept. 28	Thelma Thomas	Stocks	15 Minutes	Fighting
Sept. 28	Mattie Lou Williams	Stocks	15 Minutes	Fighting

near the spring. Here the little son would come with his bucket, a heavy chain rattling upon one of his legs . . . the old mother would drop her knitting, bid the boy sit down, and she would dip the water. When the bucket was full she carried it away up the hill and to nearly in sight of the "bosses." Day after day while this boy served his term, this old woman performed this labor of love, and in all that time the only consolation that she received was that her boy should not have been a thief.[65]

Plunkett's narrative offers a rare glimpse into the interior world of a woman who was victimized by the state, not as a prisoner but as a disconsolate parent. Often left unrecognized in the historical narrative, mothers of incarcerated daughters and sons, as well as the wives and children of imprisoned men, were left to shoulder intense emotional and economic burdens in the absence of their loved ones. In one Georgia county, a wife grieved the loss of her husband to the state after he was blamed for stealing a bale of cotton. Once her spouse was taken from the jail to a coal mine to serve out his sentence, the "illiterate and poor" woman returned home to her father, "broken down in health, branded in character, and with a three-months-old baby to raise and care for."[66] Still, looking beyond the plight of forlorn mothers and wives, Plunkett's essay is most essential for the way in which it exposes the dilemma faced by juvenile offenders ensnared in Georgia's penitentiary system. Child prisoners, albeit marginalized in the historical discourse, were preyed on by the southern criminal justice system. The state of Georgia was just one of many spaces where boys and girls were punished like men and women.

In her 1898 essay *The Progress of Colored Women*, Mary Church Terrell wrote, "The colored youth is vicious we are told, and statistics showing the multitudes of our boys and girls who crowd the penitentiaries and fill the jails appall and dishearten us."[67] Terrell's sentiment was shared by numerous champions of the "black child-savers" movement, a campaign instigated by black social reformers, namely, club women, to enforce a more humane and less exploitative treatment of African American youth in the South's penal systems. Unquestionably, Jim Crow (in)justice afflicted every strata of black society. But poor, (potentially) parentless, uneducated, unskilled African American adolescents were, arguably, the most vulnerable targets of the carceral state.[68]

As early as 1894, a bill to establish a state reformatory for juvenile offenders was introduced in the Georgia legislature. Responding to reformers and prison commissioners' petitions to have boys, in particular, separated from "hardened criminals" and offered a true chance at reform, the state began to conceptualize how it would respond to this crisis without de-incarcerating its youth population entirely. In effect, the laboring bodies of teens and preteens were as much an asset to the state as those of adult men and women. Over a period several decades, hundreds of adolescents (a majority African American) were used to work on county chain gangs as punishment for vagrancy, larceny, and other minor offenses, while others were chaperoned through the state's convict lease system. In 1896 alone, 144 juveniles, sixteen years of age and under, were detained in the state penitentiary system.

Before 1907, adolescent boys confined at the state farm worked and slept in a separate zone of the plantation (girls were never separated from women), ate in the same dining room as adult male prisoners, spent their Sundays in the yard with them, and worked full days with no time spared for education and "moral instruction." In essence, a large field was the only partition used to divide the lived and laboring experiences of youth captives from those of "hardened men." Race, on the other hand, was an added delimiting factor put in place to divide black and white youth inside the bounds of their private world at the farm. Notwithstanding, all juvenile workers performed the same types of labor and the same level of inattention to their education and moral welfare was paid.

By way of an executive proclamation issued on January 1, 1907, an official reformatory for youth was instituted on the grounds of the Georgia state prison farm. With an appropriation from the state, prison commissioners secured a contract with McMillan & Son, at the price of $10,000, to furnish materials and erect a brick dormitory, with the help of healthier convicts from the farm, to accommodate 125 inmates and provide for a "complete separation of races and sexes."[69] Abiding with the law of Jim Crow, penal authorities mandated that "white and Negro" be "fully separated socially and otherwise."[70] In actuality, the reformatory ideal—to offer "industrial, mental, and moral training" to underage inmates—was initially conceived with Caucasian boys in mind.

In the facility's formative stages of development, prison commissioners preferred that white boys be exclusively housed at the reformatory, believing that "they would have afforded the best material for the experiment, with better chances for permanent success." But judges, "in exercise of their discretion under the law, saw fit to commit both white and negro boys from their courts."[71] During its first year, the state reformatory admitted sixty-three inmates; thirty-four white boys, twenty-eight black boys, and one white girl. By 1911, the numbers were reversed: sixty-five African American males, thirty-eight white males, and one white female.[72] Evidently, in the absence of a state home for "wayward girls," the state farm was seen as the only appropriate place to send the lone youngster.

Though it was labeled a reformatory, the juvenile ward of the state farm didn't have a dedicated teacher and a reduced workday at the farm until 1911, four years after it was established. Previously, child prisoners were given two months of education per year and then spent the rest of their time slogging in the fields. As itemized in the thirteenth annual report of the Prison Commission, the following crops, in the stated acreage amounts, were grown on the reformatory premises: 140 acres of corn, 65 acres of cotton, 30 acres of wheat, 60 acres of oats, 10 acres of sorghum, 12 acres of sweet potatoes, 4 acres of alfalfa, 1½ acres of rye and vetch, 6 acres of bur clover, "5 acres of truck, including cabbages, onions, collards, tomatoes, rape, Irish potatoes, okra, beans, squashes, and melons," 1½ acres of ribbon cane, ¾ acres of Japanese cane, and 4 acres of cowpeas.[73]

On the whole, able-bodied African American women and boys were the "muscle" at the Georgia state prison farm. But disabled men also contributed their share to the expansion and operation of the carceral estate. Drawing on historians Dea Boster's and Jenifer Barclay's scholarship on slavery and disability, it can be forcefully argued that disabled long-term felons were partial producers in the South's postwar penal regimes.[74] While health as a category of analysis is still inching its way into convict labor studies, state prison farms function as, perhaps, the most critical site of inquiry for understanding how wounded, blind, and physically impaired workers fit into the southern penal economy. The phrase "dead hand," widely used in the southern penal idiolect, was merely a misnomer. Disabled prisoners were not idle or "worthless"; they engaged in light farmwork and domestic duties in lieu of heavy labor. Thus, one's debility did not preclude him or her from working successfully in the state farm. Unless an individual was in a dying state, administrators tailored one's laboring roles to fit the scale of his or her disabilities.

At the Georgia state prison farm, everyone was required to work. One eyewitness described the laboring world of the plantation as one in which "a man [or woman] must be in an absolutely helpless condition to be exempt from work."[75] Unless one's debilities necessitated round-the-clock hospitalization, his or her hands were not spared from the hoe or the washtub. In the men's department a "washing crew" was assembled to launder garments for the "hospital gang," which was composed of slightly healthier male inmates who were employed in fieldwork. The crew was made up of three men, two of whom were responsible for doing the washing, and one whose duty it was to bring the water and hang the clothes to dry. In describing the men's daily routine, as well as their infirmities, a writer for the *Atlanta Constitution* indicated the following: "One of the scrubbers is absolutely blind; he does the first scrubbing, while the one that does the wrenching and gives the stripes the finishing touches is minus both legs, one being cut off at the hip and the other at the knee ... The water carrier and clothes hanger for this rather afflicted laundry crew has one useless arm."[76]

Disabled washermen clearly contributed their share to the operation of the state farm. But even those who were hospitalized were expected to work in a limited capacity. Under Dr. Dozier's watch, convalescents were taken from the hospital to work for a short period of time, then taken inside during the warmest hours of the day.[77] This was considered a therapeutic measure. Penologists and southern physicians alike believed that outdoor work was beneficial to the physical welfare of the state's ailing inmates. Yet this ideology was racialized and principally applied to African American detainees. Physically disabled white male workers were often employed in indoor skilled or professionalized vocations. In fact, the camp's bookkeeper, telegrapher, and stenographer was a white male convict. He was described by "Captain" Foster as "an indispensable article that the camp could hardly get along without. He has lost one leg."[78] By and large, tubercular and dying patients—women included—were the only persons exempted from laboring on the state farm.

Sick and Tired

The day-to-day trials of sickly and moribund women prisoners are rarely addressed in Prison Commission reports, where female felons are portrayed, nearly exclusively, as laborers and seldom as patients. Yet clemency applications offer a more complete representation of the dilemmas faced by indisposed workers. Although the state prison farm was an environmental upgrade, especially when compared with the state's private lease camps and chain gangs, it was far from infallible. It appears that wherever incarcerated women lived and labored, sickness and death were sure to follow.

Dr. Dozier's mission, and that of subsequent physicians at the farm, was to restore as many of the state's ailing prisoners to optimal health as possible, so they could labor productively. But he saw no hope for those who were completely paralyzed, bedbound, infection laden, or "in the final clutch of tuberculosis." These persons were a "human wreck" and a burden on the state. Even so, owing to the length of their sentences, the severity of their accused crimes, and the state's unflinching devotion to punishment, clemency was only offered up as an answer to one's dying request.

As she lay withering in the camp hospital, forty-four-year-old Eliza Cobb appealed to have her twenty-one years of "good and faithful service" recognized by the state of Georgia, and to be dispensed with so she could "spend the remaining few years of her life a free woman among her people."[79] Her ordeal began in January 1889 at the Upson County Superior Courthouse, where then twenty-three-year-old Cobb was indicted, tried, and convicted of infanticide and sentenced to life imprisonment in the state penitentiary system. In a petition submitted to the Prison Commission on Cobb's behalf, attorneys John T. Allen, W. Y. Allen, and James R. Davis relayed the facts in the defendant's case, citing the following:

> The evidence introduced by the state upon the trial of this case was purely circumstantial, there being no eye witnesses to the death of the child . . . About the eighth of November 1888 a dead baby was found under the privy of the defendant's parents and whose appearance indicated that it had been born alive but had been killed by someone and placed under this privy to conceal it. Petitioner contended upon the trial of the case and still contends now that the baby was born while she was at school and that it was born dead and that she did not kill it as she was charged with doing. She only concealed the death because she had been very much abused by her mother who did not want an unmarried daughter to bring disgrace upon her home by bearing a child there.[80]

Cobb's first application for clemency, submitted May 10, 1909, was rejected by the commission chairman, Joseph S. Turner, who stamped "decline to recommend" across her petition.

As the months passed, the "growth upon the back of her neck" grew "larger and larger." Petitioners argued for Cobb's release on the grounds that the cancerous tumor "will eventually cause her death unless something is done to check it and that confinement in the penitentiary is detrimental to proper treatment of this growth and if she could be released that she could get medical treatment that would remove this growth."[81] Diligent in their efforts to get the dying woman's sentence "commuted to present service," solicitors Allen, Allen, and Davis submitted another application for executive clemency to G. R. Hutchins, the new chairman of the Prison Commission. Fortunately, Hutchins consented to recommend that Cobb's sentence be commuted, agreeing that she had "atoned for what she did by long and hard suffering."[82] On September 9, 1910, Governor Joseph M. Brown approved Eliza Cobb's application. At last, the bondwoman got her wish to live out the remainder of her life as a free woman.

Disease and death were rude and unwelcome callers at the state prison farm. The pair showed up unexpectedly and often lingered at the bedside of sufferers such as Sarah Dixon for years at a time. For four years, Dixon was confined to a bed in the camp hospital while "catarrh or some other dreadful malady of the face, and head, mouth, and throat"[83] ravaged her body. She was incarcerated in April 1902, after being found guilty of murdering her husband. For a lifetime, she was expected to work hard for the state. But her "malignant disease" turned her into a "confirmed invalid." As relayed by petitioners and the camp physician, Dixon's ailment was incurable. In their words, the disease made it "impossible for her to swallow anything, her throat and mouth being in such a serious condition with two holes in the roof of her mouth, that she can neither eat or drink without great pain and suffering. Petitioner further shows that said disease has eaten out one side of her face and nose to such an extent that the side of her face and nose have fallen in, everything being eaten away except the skin and bones."[84]

Petitioners in Dixon's case begged that her pardon be "prayerfully considered . . . in order that she may spend the few remaining days in God's sunlight, and among her loved ones, especially that she may live a few more days with her three small children in order that they may at least know and feel the fond embrace of a mother."[85] Kept alive by a cocktail of "stimulants and opiates," Dixon was incapable of ever working again, let alone surviving another week. On her deathbed, her pardon was finally satisfied. What was left of her "broken, ruined, and wrecked" body was returned to her family.[86]

Dixon's case exemplifies how tightly the state clutched its long-term felons, unwilling to offer mercy until death arrived. Regrettably, for all its modernizing advancements, the Georgia state prison farm reproduced many of the ills that existed in the state's private lease camps, proving that the public and private realms of captivity may have been spatially and economically disparate, but they engendered the same detriments. Women prisoners worked long and hard, were steered by violence, and were subjected to insufficient living standards and medical care. Nonetheless, the state farm paled in cruelty when compared with Georgia's infamous chain gang system.

As the twentieth century progressed, the state did away with convict leasing and a decentralized chain gang system took its place. For thousands of short-term black female misdemeanants, being placed on the chain produced disastrous results. The perils of captivity were concentrated into a compact sentence, and it was deployed with unrestricted vengeance. Consequently, scores of female workers had their bodies and minds "broken, ruined, and wrecked." But unlike Eliza Cobb, Sarah Dixon, and multiple other female felons, short-term offenders were typically released with minimal delay. Parsimonious county officials found no benefit in maintaining unviable women workers.

CHAPTER FIVE

Broken, Ruined, and Wrecked

Women on the Chain Gang

On September 19, 1908, the General Assembly of Georgia passed a law abolishing the lease of convicts to private parties and decentralizing the state's chain gang system. The act required that "all male felony convicts, except such as are now required by law to be kept at the State Farm, may, after March 31st, 1909, be employed by the authority of the several counties and municipalities upon the public roads, bridges, or other public works."[1] Concerning female prisoners, all felons were to be forwarded to the state farm. Misdemeanant offenders, on the other hand, were held at the mercy of trial judges. As a result of the Georgia legislature's amendment of section 1039, volume 3, of the code of 1895, it was decided that "if the [misdemeanor] convict be female, the presiding judge may, in his discretion, sentence her to confinement and labor in the woman's prison on the State farm in lieu of a chaingang sentence, not to exceed twelve months; provided that the trial judge shall have the discretion also of sending any person convicted of a misdemeanor to the State Farm."[2]

On September 28, 1908, during the same month and year that the new chain gang law went into effect, Mattie Black was accused of "larceny from the house" and tried in the city court of Americus, in Sumter County, Georgia. The trial judge found her guilty of the crime and opted to sentence her to ten months hard labor on the county chain gang, as opposed to sending her to the state farm. Unable to "keep the lick" and match the labor output and velocity of her male co-laborers, Black was subjected to brutal acts of violence that left her body destroyed. Within six weeks, a clemency application was filed by Joseph S. Turner, chairman of the Prison Commission, petitioning for her release. On November 18, 1908, Black's sentence was commuted to "present service" and she was set free.[3]

During her term of service, Mattie Black was 1 of 5 African American women sentenced to labor on the Sumter County road gang, and 1 out of 105 African American women working on public roads throughout the state of Georgia.[4] As was the case in the state's convict lease camps, gender conventions were of no consequence. Chain gang women helped clear lands, built roads, harvested turpentine, grew food, cooked meals, laundered garments, and fulfilled whatever labor demands were required of them by camp authorities. When they refused, or failed to carry out their duties in a way that was right and proper in the eyes of their custodians, they were ruthlessly attacked.

During the November meeting of the Sumter County Board of Commissioners of Roads and Revenues, a resolution was passed to release Mattie Black from the county chain gang on account of her "critical condition" and "worthlessness." Board clerk W. L. Thomas transcribed the proceedings, homing in on the magnitude of the woman's infirmities: "it appears from the evidence of the County Physician, Dr. B. Mayes, that the said Mattie Black is suffering from the result of a fracture of the breast bone, and of the seventh and eighth ribs on the right side, and the results of injuries received internally when said fracture was occasioned . . . and the said Mattie Black being further afflicted with *hysterical convulsions* [seizures] that in his opinion is incurable and in her physical state she is worthless as a laborer on the Chain-gang."[5]

Black's inability to "do any work at all" and "constant and continuous" need for medical attention made her an expendable, non-profit-bearing commodity. Such was the case for dozens of incapacitated misdemeanant female offenders who were of no value to the carceral state. This chapter gives emphasis to the lived and laboring experiences of women prisoners entrapped in Georgia's chain gang system, and it highlights the ways in which excess labor, debilitating violence, and psychological terror impacted female subjects. This chapter also examines how broken black female bodies were treated by the state, and how clemency endorsements and rulings were often rendered on economic terms.

Bad Women Make Good Workers

By the 1890s, enthusiasm over convict leasing began to wane as the free labor problem took the zest out of the economic enterprise. Aggrieved citizens and reformers alike shared concerns over the competition convict labor posed with free labor. Free labor advocate W. E. B. Du Bois summarized the feelings of many when he stated, "Without doubt, work, and work worth the doing—i.e., profitable work—is best for the prisoners . . . At the same time, his work should not be allowed to come into unfair competition with that of honest laborers, and it should never be an object of traffic for pure financial gain."[6] Among farmers (who desired better transportation), advocates of organized labor, reformers, the press, progressive politicians, populists, and advocates of the Good Roads Movement, there was a consensus that it would be in the best interest of all parties if convicts were made to labor on public roads.[7]

Amid the free labor problem and mounting public criticism, southern business leaders in Georgia grew increasingly skeptical about the future perpetuation of the lease system. By the 1890s, the railroad boom, on which much of the system rested, began to decline. Railroad companies started to merge and consolidation plans were aimed toward New York, not Atlanta.[8] In 1897, given the diminishing popularity of convict leasing, the Georgia state legislature decided to carry on with the lease but to limit the term to five years. But the depression of 1907, coupled with the gradual economic decline of convict leasing, dealt a death blow to Georgia's industrialists. Brickyards, mining companies, sawmills, and turpentine stills were forced to close, leaving lessees with a pool of laborers that they were still responsible for taking care of.[9]

Along with the economic challenges posed by convict leasing, the nationwide thrust toward road improvement had a direct effect on how Georgia went about reframing its carceral structure. The Good Roads Movement, albeit birthed in the North, was adopted in all the southern states during the late nineteenth century. Private citizens, local and state politicians, engineers, college professors, and persons from nearly every strata of southern society saw bad roads as an impediment to the region's economic advancement, prompting them to support all aims to repair and modernize the region's inadequate thoroughfares. But farmers, many of whom were seeking to bypass the railroad in favor of transporting their goods to market more cheaply, along smooth, traversable roads, held a deeply vested interest in seeing improvements made to the region's physical infrastructure. As long as roads remained unpaved, growers ran the risk of getting their wagons stuck in the mud or jammed in potholes left behind by other farm carts or, worse, having their wagons, crops, and bodies capsize onto a bumpy dirt road.[10]

By the 1910s, when the automobile became a more accessible commodity in America's consumer society, the Good Roads Movement morphed into a highway movement. Farm-to-market roads threatened to narrow the route of economic progress in the New South. To highway progressives, good roads in the South spelled tourism, which in turn translated into economic growth.[11] Although farm-related issues were still invoked in the Good Roads Movement discourse, the modernization of public roadways promised to benefit a much broader cross section of the population:

drivers, auto dealers, rural farmers, merchants, bankers, northern investors, and, of course, the carceral state. In view of this fact, by 1910 every southern state legislature authorized local governments, county and municipal, to utilize convict labor in the repair and construction of public streets.[12]

Between 1904 and 1909, the state of Georgia more than doubled its improved road mileage with the use of convict labor. Pleased by this fact, the director of the Office of Public Roads, Logan Waller Page, boasted that "if all the state and county prisoners of the South were placed upon the roads . . . a wonderful reformation could be brought about with a comparatively small cash outlay."[13] So, as Georgia's industrialists backed away from the convict leasing enterprise, the state decided to gather up its foreclosed "property" and parcel it out to counties looking for cheap labor to build good roads.

In the moments leading up to the abolition of convict leasing in the "Empire State," the proposition to place convicts on public roads came to be viewed as a fair and economically sound substitute for convict leasing—but only after an alternative was reached on how to dispose of the state's engorged felony population.[14] Although state politicians remained divided on the issue, with some favoring the continuation of the lease system and others calling for its extermination altogether, the state senate reached a decision. On September 19, 1908, convict leasing was abolished in Georgia and the chain gang system decentralized. The following year, approximately five thousand misdemeanor and felony convicts were put to work on county roads.[15]

Overall, convict labor was a crucial tool used to reshape the New South landscape. Whereas the convict lease system mostly benefited private industrialists and the state, the chain gang system profited citizens who reaped the rewards of having new or improved roads fabricated in their districts. By 1915, Georgia had more surfaced rural roads than any other southern state, and it boasted the fifth highest number of miles of surfaced roads (thirteen thousand) in the nation.[16] But the pathway to modernity was not plied with male hands alone. Between 1900 and 1936, roughly 2,139 female misdemeanants helped clear, flatten, and grade "good roads." Others worked in sawmills and turpentine camps, while a smaller number aided in the construction of railroads, assisted in public works projects, engaged in fieldwork, and performed domestic duties.

Prior to 1900, Georgia prison commissioners, Clement A. Evans, Thomas Eason, and Joseph S. Turner, encountered immense difficulty in their attempts to collect data on the state's chain gang camps. The subleasing and illegal renting of misdemeanant prisoners to "wildcat camps" added more frustration to an already vexing situation. In a report issued to then Governor Allen D. Candler, commissioners complained that the inspection of county chain gang camps had not been as effective as desired. Because they lacked the power to compel authorities in charge of the camps to complete and return documentation on a regular basis, reports often went undone. Chain gang authorities also failed to notify commissioners when camps were created or suspended. Officials expressed their annoyance, citing that "it has frequently happened that a visit is made to inspect a camp previously visited, and the same is found to be discontinued. In other instances new gangs have been organized and operated for months before any knowledge is had of their existence."[17] The spontaneous relocation of chain gangs from one locality to the next, and the "onerous" and expensive nature of inspections, was an ongoing source of irritation for commissioners.

Despite these challenges, in 1900 commissioners began producing full reports that included aggregate numbers of chain gang prisoners held in each county. Table 5, which is made up of data culled from annual and biennial reports of the Prison Commission, shows the number of female convicts employed in most of Georgia's misdemeanor camps between 1900 and 1936, the counties of their employment, and the types of work they engaged in.

Based on these data, 91 percent of black female chain gang laborers engaged in the construction of public roads. Roughly 1 percent of women were employed in turpentine camps, 2 percent in sawmills, nearly 3 percent on private farms, and less than 1 percent on railroads. The remainder performed domestic work, as well as other forms of labor left unspecified in official reports.[18]

Statistics reveal that the highest number of misdemeanor arrests and convictions were made in Atlanta (Fulton County) and Savannah (Chatham County). This is due, in part, to the demographic makeup of these two cities, both of which were densely populated with black migrants from the rural enclaves of New South Georgia. More African American women, men, and children flocked to these metropolises than any other cities in the state. As reflected in the U.S. Census, in 1900, the total population of Atlanta was 89,872. Of the city's inhabitants, 54,145 (60 percent) were white and 35,727 (40 percent) were black. In Savannah, the ratio was nearly the same. Out of 54,244 total residents, 28,090 (51 percent) were African American.[19]

TABLE 5 Number of Female Misdemeanor Convicts, Location of Chain Gangs, and Work Engaged In, 1900–1936

County	Black Female	White Female	Total	Work Engaged In
Baker	5	0	5	Turpentine
Baldwin	19	0	19	Road Building
Berrien	5	0	5	Sawmilling
Bibb	91	0	91	Road Building
Burke	22	0	22	Road Building
Chatham	602	8	610	Road Building
Clarke	24	0	24	Road Building
Clinch	6	0	6	Sawmilling
Cobb	20	0	20	Railroad Grading
Coffee	12	0	12	Road Building, Turpentine
Columbia	2	0	2	Road Building
Decatur	62	2	64	Sawmilling, Road Building
Dooly	10	0	10	Sawmilling
Dougherty	57	0	57	Farming, Turpentine
Early	3	0	3	Road Building, Turpentine
Echols	3	0	3	Turpentine
Elbert	2	0	2	Farming
Floyd	31	0	31	Road Building
Fulton (Atlanta)	1,183	2	1,185	Road Building
Glynn	26	0	26	Road Building
Greene	4	0	4	Road Building
Irwin	12	0	12	Road Building
Jefferson	4	0	4	Road Building
Johnson	5	0	5	Road Building
Lowndes	15	1	16	Road Building
Miller	7	0	7	Turpentine
Muscogee	30	0	30	Road Building
Newton	3	0	3	Road Building
Oconee	3	0	3	Farming
Oglethorpe	18	1	19	Farming
Pulaski	3	0	3	Road Building
Richmond	195	0	195	Road Building
Spalding	24	0	24	Road Building
Sumter	42	0	42	Road Building
Thomas	42	0	42	Sawmilling, Road Building
Tift	5	0	5	Sawmilling

(continued)

TABLE 5 *(continued)*

County	Black Female	White Female	Total	Work Engaged In
Troup	5	0	5	Road Building
Walker	24	0	24	N/A
Walton	7	0	7	Road Building
Ware	8	0	8	Turpentine
Washington	4	0	4	Road Building
Whitfield	34	0	34	N/A
Wilcox	1	0	1	Farming
Totals	2,680	14	2,694	RB: 2,466 TP: 34 SM: 41 FM: 75 RR: 20 N/A: 58

Generally speaking, the mass arrest and incarceration of black city dwellers in Atlanta and Savannah was attributed to the same social, economic, and political issues: racism, economic competition, poverty, unemployment, occupational exclusion, political disenfranchisement, and legal injustice. In both spaces, working-class African Americans also felt the tightening effects of Jim Crow. Even before segregation became a legal system, restrictive covenants were put in place to regulate black mobility by limiting access to jobs, resources, housing, transportation, or access to public amenities such as restaurants and theaters. This was especially the case in turn-of-the century Atlanta, where race relations were exceedingly volatile and black autonomy was met with hostility. The Riot of 1906, which resulted in the death of at least thirty-two blacks and three whites, is a clear expression of how growing tensions over black independence sometimes erupted in violence.[20] Yet, more often than not, contests over black freedom were won through mass arrest and incarceration.

In Atlanta, black men, women, and youth were arrested in droves for a wide range of misdemeanor offenses: public drunkenness, petty theft, vagrancy, loitering, prostitution, quarreling, violating public ordinances, "idling," and disorderly conduct. Between 1898 and 1903, more than sixty thousand black arrests were made in the city alone.[21] Of those arrested, roughly 25 percent were female—75 percent of whom were between the ages of fifteen and thirty. Approximately 2,470 black women were taken into custody in 1898, 1,654 in 1899, 2,086 in 1900, 2,960 in 1901, 2,888 in

1902, and 2,619 in 1903.[22] Included in these totals are those whose cases were dismissed or settled by paying a fine, as well as those who were arrested on more than one occasion and/or sent to the chain gang.

In the "Gate City," black women were routinely arrested for social crimes: disorderly conduct, quarreling, public drunkenness, and prostitution. Their inability to remit fines—large and small—meant many months spent on the county chain gang. When Ida Roberts and Della Stewart were arrested for allegedly engaging in "disorderly conduct, quarreling," and "using profane and vulgar language," the women were brought before a county magistrate, who found them both guilty and fined each woman $5.75.[23] Unable to pay the penalty, the two women were put to work on a local chain gang. In a similar instance, Amanda Conley was arrested for "disorderly conduct and throwing socks."[24] She too was ordered to pay a $5.75 fine. Incapable of satisfying the debt, she joined Roberts and Stewart on the chain.

White police officers surveyed alleys, side streets, dives, saloons, and "disorderly houses," where many working-class blacks spent their free time, drinking, dancing, singing, quarreling, and purchasing and selling sex. Peters and Decatur Streets were hotspots for pleasure seekers as well as arresting officers who stalked would-be offenders.[25] The Atlanta police court docket of 1886 is filled with the names of black men and women like Violet Palmer and Georgia Wright, who were arrested, fined $3.75 apiece, and sent to the chain gang for roaming "drunk on the street" and exhibiting "disorderly conduct."[26] Others were detained for prostitution.

The sex work trade, particularly for white women who controlled many of Atlanta's brothel houses, was a blooming industry in late nineteenth-century Atlanta. As stated by historian Tera Hunter, white women gained success by tying their trade to the fortunes of "real estate companies, landlords, police officers, and politicians" who secured a cut of the profits.[27] African American women, on the other hand, engaged in the sex industry in very limited numbers and saw modest profits. Even so, they were the primary targets for arrest.

Police officers frequently raided "disorderly houses" on Decatur Street, the red-light district of Atlanta, and arrested madams, workers, and patrons. If found guilty, brothel owners were usually rendered stiffer penalties than the sex workers themselves were. This was definitely true in the case of Rosa Sims, who was arrested for allegedly "keeping a disorderly house." The judge in her case returned a hefty ruling: pay a $10.75 fine or do six months on the chain gang.[28] With no other options, Sims chose the latter. In a similar case, Sallie Soloman (a suspected prostitute) was taken into custody for merely "occupying a portion of a house used as a house of ill fame" and fined $5.75.[29] But even with a reduced fee, Soloman still could not afford to buy her way off the chain.

By comparison, the rate of arrest for white women in Atlanta was much lower than black women. Statistically, they made up only 16 percent of all female arrests. Even so, poor, working-class white women still felt the rigid effects of social control and gender regulation. Because the standards for white female morality were higher than they were for black women, some white women offenders suffered stiffer penalties than their black female counterparts did. This disparity is most visible in the case of Melvina Finley, a white woman, who was arrested and fined $10.75 for being "drunk," practicing "disorderly conduct," and "using profane and vulgar language."[30]

By comparison, working-class women's lived and laboring experiences in the city of Savannah were a little less morose—but not much. In this urban environment, black and white women were socially policed and arrested for crimes that defied the social or moral order of the city.[31] Criminal registers are filled with examples of women being arrested, fined, jailed, and/or sent to the chain gang for crimes like public "drunkenness," "fighting in the street," "disorderly conduct," "cursing in a loud and boisterous manner," "improper conduct," disturbing the peace, "walking the street for licentious purposes [prostitution]," and engaging in "disreputable" forms of leisure.[32]

Drayton and Broughton Streets, in downtown Savannah, were popular spaces for working-class women to enjoy city nightlife. Yet these streets were also high policing zones for arresting officers, who intercepted domestic disputes and fights that sometimes broke out in the streets and preyed on female city dwellers who failed to exercise "moral conduct." When Sarah Edwards and Amelia White were found "fighting in the street," they were both arrested and fined for "disturbing the neighborhood."[33] Hannah Levy met a similar fate when she was reportedly discovered "drunk lying in the street at 12:05 A.M."[34]

While a fine ranging from five dollars to fifteen dollars or a short-term jail sentence—of one to three months—was the usual disposition for female misdemeanor offenders, the chain gang was also suggested on occasion as an alternative to a fine. Although this type of ruling was rare, and sparsely reflected in official documents, some cases do exist. Clara Lawrence is one of the best-recorded examples of how Savannah officials chose to deal with "immoral" black women. On the evening of January 7, 1877, Lawrence was accused of behaving in a disorderly manner and "allowing disorder in her house thereby disturbing the neighborhood."[35] When she appeared before the judge for sentencing, she was provided two options: pay a twenty-dollar fine or do thirty days on the chain gang.

Whipped with a Rawhide

Misdemeanant women from all over the "Empire State" helped build New South Georgia. The disfiguring physical and emotional scars they received in the process dug deeper than any chisel could reach. Unfortunately, conditions for the state's prisoners were not improved under the revised system. Arguably, circumstances grew worse. By their very nature, chain gangs were volatile, noxious spaces. For female offenders, being on the chain proved to be ruinous to one's physical and psychological welfare.

On March 1, 1897, Lizzie Boatright, an eighteen-year-old "Negro girl," was convicted in the Superior Court of McDuffie County, Georgia, for the crime of burglary and sentenced to serve six months on a local chain gang. On the word of Judge E. H. Callaway, who ruled in the case, Boatright and another young woman were "found in possession of certain articles of clothing that had been stolen from a house near the Georgia Railroad which had been burglarized."[36] The teenagers swore that the four or five dollars' worth of garments "had been given to them by a boy," and that they held no involvement in the robbery whatsoever. But their pleading was in vain. Out of options, the pair agreed to "take a verdict of guilty with a recommendation that they be punished as for misdemeanors—they were each sentenced to pay a fine of fifty-dollars, to include the [court] costs or to serve six months on the chaingang."[37] The relatives of "the other girl," whose name is beyond the reach of historical inquiry, managed to pool their meager resources and remit her penalty. Sadly, however, Lizzie Boatright's relatives were not able to pay her fine and she had to serve out the sentence.[38]

Two weeks following her conviction, Boatright was transported to a convict camp operated by W. H. and J. H. Griffin. Therein, she labored in the fields and performed other arbitrary male-oriented duties as prescribed by her captors. One day, while fast at work digging a ditch, Boatright was spotted by the special inspector of the misdemeanor convict camps, Phill. G. Byrd, who found her "clad in male attire, wearing the same make of coat, pants and shoes as were worn by the male convicts. She was working as a man, the only difference being that she used a short-handled spade while the men used long-handled shovels,"[39] said Byrd. Initially mistaking her for a "half-grown boy among the men," the inspector "called her out from the gang and away from the guard and lessee and asked her how often she had been whipped, by whom and how."[40] She stated that the former guard, Bob Cannon, whipped her and another "Negro woman" twice for "trivial offenses." In one instance, the women were flogged "because our feet were sore and we stopped on the side of the road to fix the rags so as to protect them from the heavy brogan shoes we were wearing."[41] "Mr. Cannon made me take down my britches and lean over and then he whipped me," said Boatright. She continued: "The other convicts were all around us. One time when he started to whip me I was sick with my monthlies and I told him so and begged him to take me away from among the men, but he cursed me and made me drop my britches and he whipped me there close to the men convicts."[42]

After collecting Boatright's statement, Inspector Byrd inquired of Cannon when, how, and why he whipped the young woman. The guard corroborated the inmate's claims and admitted to whipping her with the same strap that he used for punishing male convicts, and making her strip her pants down like he did the men. But flogging her "while on her catamenia [menstrual cycle]," in the presence of men, Cannon vigorously denied. Even so, his actions inspired a stroke of compassion in the heart of Governor George Atkinson. Lizzie Boatright was granted executive clemency and released from bondage.

In Georgia's chain gang camps, short-term female offenders were subjected to horrific forms of physical and sexualized brutality. As was the case in the state's private lease camps and at the state prison farm, violence functioned as an essential tool of control, humiliation, and coercion, and it was used to induce embarrassment, invoke fear, and enforce labor among enervated workers. Women (as well as elderly and frail men) who were incapable of managing the titanic workloads imposed on them were assailed for being weak, their physical incompetence being construed as a sign of impudence or laziness. It was not uncommon to see a chain gang laborer "forced to work till they fell upon the ground, dead."[43]

In January 1904, a fourteen-year-old girl was "sent home to die" after being repeatedly flogged by a guard. Six months prior, the juvenile had been arrested and convicted of larceny by a Bibb County trial judge and sentenced to twelve months' labor on a road-building crew of the county chain gang. Midway into her sentence, she was granted executive clemency. In keeping with reformer Clarissa Olds Keeler's firsthand account, "The scars on the girl's body corroborated her dying testimony that she 'had been whipped to death.' The verdict of the coroner's jury was 'her death was the result of cruel treatment.'"[44] In a similar case, a young girl was sent to a chain gang camp in Wilkes County. For any trivial offense, the guard would "beat her on her bare back before the male convicts—her pleading would have no effect on the white 'boss.' The Governor pardoned this unfortunate girl that she might be relieved of her sufferings."[45]

Acts of violence against female prisoners were carried out in the open air and within the enclosed quarters of county jails. Inside the Fulton County stockade, where several dozen black female misdemeanants and more than 150 black and white male felons and misdemeanor inmates "ate their evening pittance" and slept in a filthy "atmosphere redolent of indescribable stenches,"[46] diseases spread and so did violence. In December 1909, an official investigation of Atlanta's city stockade uncovered grisly evidence of convicts, male and female, being fastened into a custom-made "whipping chair" and flogged until they were "hysterical." As conveyed by Keeler, "A witness was called by the city of Atlanta, in the investigation into the charges made by the *Georgian* in reference to cruelty and mismanagement at the city stockade . . . He told of a little thirteen-year-old Negro girl being placed in the whipping chair invented by Superintendent Vining. She was brought downstairs with only two thin undergarments on and placed in the chair. The front was fastened and it was turned over on its face . . . A white man whipped her with a strap . . . until when she was released from the chair she was hysterical. She said something in this hysterical condition, she knows not what, and the superintendent ordered her placed back in the chair and again whipped."[47]

Evidently, as Atlanta became more modernized so too did the processes by which penal officials elected to punish and torture the city's inmates. The "bucking machine," as the contrivance was also called, was a high-tech substitute for the antebellum style of "bucking" across a log. A solitary confinement chamber, another newfangled contraption, was also installed at the female stockade. Yet and still, these upgraded technologies of terror did not completely supplant classical forms of cruelty; they merely complemented them.

As it pertains to sexual violence, it is rather difficult to determine the extent to which female misdemeanants were raped. But rare examples do surface in the historical record. For instance, in 1898, an unnamed "Negro woman" was found guilty of disturbing the peace and sentenced to forty days of "hard labor" in a chain gang camp. As relayed by social reformer Clarissa Olds Keeler, one day, "the guard commanded her 'to go to the rice barn with him in private to carry out his wicked design.'" She refused, and "the next morning she was compelled to go there, and then was strung up by her wrists until her feet scarcely touched the floor and her clothes tied over her head." She was then "whipped with a rawhide until the blood ran down."[48]

Disposable Bodies

With shackles on their ankles and the millstone of terror around their necks, chain gang women's lives and laboring bodies were ravaged by violence and its long-lasting effects. Acts of cruelty, together with medical neglect and excessive work demands, weakened female prisoners' immunities and susceptibility to disease, aggravated preexisting medical conditions, and created a new set of health-related challenges. Although sickly, unproductive, and unprofitable female workers ultimately benefited from being expelled from county convict camps, prison commissioners' endorsement of medically related clemency applications and the affirmative rulings that emanated from those endorsements were not purely officiated on humanitarian terms. Goodwill was merely a drape used to cover a more pressing economic issue; ailing women workers, who were physically incapable of advancing the New South vision of modernization and prosperity, were a drain on county resources. They were "disposable" because of their costliness to treat and maintain and their inability to produce labor, not because they *deserved* to be set free "for the sake of humanity."

The most disposable class of laboring women were those whose medical conditions were incurable and fatal. Laura Blake, a "colored woman," was four months into her twelve-month sentence on the Fulton County chain gang for "running a disorderly house" when she developed a critical case of "cardiac dropsy" (congestive heart failure). According to Dr. Paul McDonald, the county physician, Blake's condition was "chronic and incurable," requiring that she be "kept in the hospital continually" and making her "physically unable to perform manual labor."[49] Incapacitated and unworkable, her sentence was "commuted to present service."

In Cobb County, Lizzie Teasley (Curry) was in the latter stages of tuberculosis when her husband, Joe Curry, succeeded in securing a pardon for his dying wife. Unable to read and write, Joe relied on Attorney H. B. Moss to prepare a petition in the interest of his wife, convicted under the name "Lizzie Teasley" at the March term of the Cobb County Superior Court for "selling liquor." Teasley was condemned on the witness of Hattie Ward, who claimed that "Lizzie sold her one ten cent drink."[50] Afterward, she was sentenced by the court to serve a six-month term on the chain gang, without an alternative fine. According to Attorney Moss, not long after her confinement, Teasley "developed tuberculosis in the Cobb County camp and is now in a very serious condition not expected to live but a short time."[51] Joe Curry promised to "take reasonably good care" of his wife "if he had her at home, and might, perhaps, prolong her life by good treatment." He begged to "be allowed to have his wife freed from the chaingang that he may try to take care of her until she dies, which, from appearances, will not be long."[52] Curry signed his petition with a capital "X." Two weeks later, he reclaimed his wife from the camp hospital and took her home to live out her "dying days" in comfort.

In the case of Lizzie Teasley, and that of other tubercular patients, it was "heartily recommended" that she be pardoned "as soon as possible." As a rule, highly infectious inmates were perceived as an environmental and economic hazard. Unwilling to sacrifice the welfare and output of its healthy profit-bearing assets, the entire Cobb County Board of Commissioners of Roads and Revenues, with support of the county physician, endorsed Teasley's request for executive clemency. The same was true in the case of Annie Cuyler, who was convicted of "simple larceny" and sentenced to twelve months' labor on the Glynn County chain gang. Within one month's time, she grew deathly ill and unable to work. On June 7, 1904, the Commissioners of Roads and Revenue of Glynn County sent an official petition to Joseph S. Turner, chair of the Georgia Prison Commission, urging a pardon for Cuyler "on the grounds that she is afflicted with an incurable disease [presumably tuberculosis] and is practically in a dying condition."[53] In both cases, these women's infectivity, dying status, inability to produce labor, costliness, and inconvenience of their prolonged care made it improvident to keep them around.

On occasion, the sheer inability and complexities involved in accommodating female prisoners (able-bodied or disabled) in a cost-effective way prompted favorable clemency decisions. In 1922, Mamie Cason, Mattie Davis, and Areta Fluker, all convicted of "having whiskey," were sentenced to twelve months of labor on the Johnson County chain gang. After a few months, the women succeeded in getting their sentences commuted to a fine of twenty-five dollars each, based on the recommendation of county authorities, who protested that "the accommodations of our chain gang were built for male prisoners only, and part of the time, at least, for the lack of accommodation these prisoners are thrown together . . . The presence of the women is more or less demoralizing to the male prisoners. The

County being unprepared for the care and use of women prisoners works a hardship on all the chain gang attendants to properly look after these three women. The expense of looking after these three prisoners, under prevailing conditions amounts to more than their services are worth."[54]

More often than not, the lack of gender-specific lodging was an unstated concern among county officials. It appears that authorities found a way to modify their chain gang camps to accommodate women workers. In the day, female convicts generally worked side by side with male prisoners. But at night they were locked away in "cages" or other makeshift stockades. As a rule, one's profitability as a laborer mattered more than her gender orientation did. Yet sources have shown that an individual's maternal condition *did*, in fact, make a difference to chain gang operators, who found it impractical and fiscally disadvantageous to retain pregnant workers.

In May 1904, Leila Blackman was convicted of "larceny from the house" and sentenced to pay a twenty-dollar fine or serve six months' hard labor on the Muscogee County chain gang. Unable to pay the penalty, the five-months-pregnant woman was sent to the chain gang. Owing to her advanced state of pregnancy, authorities found her unproductive as a chain gang laborer and opted to send her to the county jail instead. But confinement did not serve her much better than the chain had. In a letter to Joseph S. Turner, Dr. J. C. Evans—the county physician—described Blackman's condition in the following terms: "Blackman, a negro woman who has yet to serve about four months of her sentence on the county chain gang . . . is about seven or seven and a half months pregnant and is reportedly having pains in attempt to miscarry. She is in a bad physical condition . . . I suggest that you ask a pardon for her."[55] Commission Chairman Joseph Turner supported Blackman's application for clemency and recommended her pardon on the basis of her physical condition, notably because, in his words, "she has been unable to labor in a chaingang . . . and it is appearing that owing to her health she will not be able to labor on the chaingang during the term of her sentence."[56]

On the contrary, chain gang authorities sometimes opted to preserve pregnant workers for domestic duties, making as full use of their laboring bodies as they could. This can be seen in the case of Pearl Black, who was convicted of "adultery" in July 1908 and sentenced to serve twelve months on the chain gang of Sumter County. Four months pregnant at the time, but capable of working, Black was put to work in the camp kitchen. Once she reached her eighth month of pregnancy, officials began to agitate on her behalf, citing that "the party is now likely to give birth to the child at any time being on her feet cooking at the camps and of course necessarily suffered pain in her condition, having to do the work as a cook."[57] The county physician concurred that Black "is in no condition to be laboring as a cook in a chain gang camp." To the relief of chain gang officials, who probably recoiled at the thought of quartering a newborn babe and its nursing mother, Black was pardoned just weeks before giving birth.

Beyond pregnancy, other non-life-threatening medical conditions prompted the exoneration of feeble women workers. In 1904, Minnie Black's time on the chain was cut short because of her recurring "fits" (convulsions), which left her "badly afflicted, not able to do heavy work from the effect."[58] The exact origin of Black's epilepsy is left undocumented. Yet, based on medical evidence, it can be safely concluded that Black's sickness was triggered by a combination of neurological, environmental, and/or injury related factors. Understanding the violent milieu in which she lived and labored, it is not beyond the bounds of reason to believe that her recurring seizures were the consequence of a traumatic brain injury, stemming from a violent physical attack. Then again, Black may have suffered from epilepsy previous to her incarceration. The stress and strain of chain gang life may have merely aggravated her condition. This was certainly true in other cases, where women prisoners entered captivity in an unwell state and left in an even worse one. But forasmuch as life and labor on the chain worsened preexisting conditions, it also created new ones.

Although sparsely documented in the historical record, evidence of mental breakdowns among female chain gang workers does manifest in official correspondence. Case in point, in the spring of 1911, Mary Dykes was tried for vagrancy and sentenced to twelve months on the Dooly County chain gang. Months later, she was removed to the county jail and a recommendation for clemency was filed on "the ground of her mental illness." In keeping with the county physician's report, Dykes "became insane since her conviction and unable to work."[59] While the source of her insanity is not conveyed in official reports, it is safe to conclude that the hostile atmosphere in which she lived and labored nurtured mental and emotional disability.

Investigative reports are littered with incidences of convicts being gunned down by ill-tempered guards, flogged to death, and subjugated to other grotesque forms of violence—pre-mortem and postmortem. Even after death, some inmates' bodies were mauled by the dogs and left to publicly decompose. Dykes's case offers crucial insight into the ways in which incarcerated subjects—male and female—processed violence, as recipients and witnesses of it. Her example allows scholars to safely conclude that mental breakdowns were an anticipated, yet highly unfortunate, after-effect of unharnessed terror and violence.

While it is evident that many unproductive and unprofitable chain gang women were supported in their attempts to garner executive clemency, this was not the case for many able-bodied women whose applications were denied, thinly supported, or commuted for a hefty price. In 1899, Leila Everett was convicted of "forgery" and "simple larceny" and sentenced to two consecutive sentences: twelve months on the Dougherty County chain gang and four years of labor at the Georgia state prison farm. Understanding the gravity of the ruling, Everett endeavored to pacify her keepers through obedience and compliance, perhaps hoping to soften the blow of imprisonment or, better yet, merit a reduced sentence. While awaiting sentencing in the Dougherty County jail, she was praised by officials for leaking information regarding a "plot upon the part of prisoners confined therein to break jail, which was rendered futile by reason of the said Leila Everett informing the officers of said jail of the intention of the said prisoners to escape."[60] Once on the chain, she continued to prove herself through hard work and diligence. As stated by the petitioner in her case, "Since her incarceration upon the chain gang of said county she has conducted herself in such a manner as to be of invaluable assistance to the chain gang authorities."[61] Yet, in spite of her orderly conduct and superior manners, Everett was still denied clemency. Alas, her quest to prove herself obedient, industrious, and resourceful made her more riveted to the carceral state.

From the turn of the twentieth century to the downturn of the Great Depression, the chain gang system was a critical source of infrastructural and economic expansion in New South Georgia. But, like its antecedent—the convict lease—the chain gang system slowly relented to social and economic forces.[62] Foremost, the financial calamity wrought by the Depression drained county resources. With no access to federal relief funds, which were earmarked for the expanding free labor road force, cash-strapped counties were forced to return their convicts to state custody.[63] The impact of the economic breakdown was further strengthened by the 1932 publication of Robert Burns's *I Am a Fugitive from a Georgia Chain Gang*, which thrust Georgia's corrupt penal system in a national spotlight and ushered in a new wave of reform. The cruelty experienced by Burns, a white man, stirred up enough dissent to close the book on Georgia's chain gang system. *Chained in Silence*, on the other hand, opens up a new chapter in the study of coercive labor in the post–Civil War South.

Epilogue
The Sound of Broken Silence

This book has been my attempt to give voice to a group of women who had theirs taken away. But the process of creating voice was much more difficult than I expected. In order to tell these women's stories, I had to rely on other's interpretations of events, reading between illegible lines only to still be confronted with what I began to think of as a broken silence. At times I questioned whether the work was even possible. No matter how deep my research, certain aspects of these women's lives would remain forever obscured. But I had to honor the unknowable and move forward.

This study represents my endeavor to push beyond the epistemological strongholds that have kept southern African American women prisoners, literally and figuratively, chained in silence. It is a corrective to a history that has, for the most part, excluded the female perspective. Not unlike the enslaved, but to a much lesser degree, black women prisoners were "everywhere, yet nowhere" in the postemancipation South.[1] They were scattered in railroad camps, prison mines, lumber mills, brickyards, turpentine camps, plantations, kitchens, stockades, washhouses, and chain gangs. Yet their lives are nearly impossible to trace in writing from the post–Civil War era, and they still remain largely outside the historical literature's field of reference. Nowhere is this absence more deeply felt than in the masculinist realm of convict labor studies, where a woman's worth is least regarded.

It is within this historiographical space of convict labor studies that women prisoners' contribution to the forging of New South modernity has tended to be measured in terms of productivity and profit alone. While *Chained in Silence* has shown that female convicts did in fact supply a rich source of labor and profit to southern industrialists, there are other considerations to be made in our assessment of a woman's worth to the postbellum carceral state. From an institutional perspective, the black female presence helped foster significant changes to the penal system of New South Georgia and was the catalyst for early prison reform movements. Albeit by force, African American women prisoners also executed new forms of labor that remained untried in the free labor marketplace, therefore broadening the overall scope of black women's work in the postemancipation South. These facts, among others, make it difficult to deny that gender is significant to the study of convict labor in the post–Civil War South.

It has become quite clear to me that without the female perspective, it is difficult to fully grasp the complexities of this history. The reality is that incarcerated women experienced captivity in uniquely gendered ways. For them, life in a convict lease camp or on a chain gang was in many ways worse than slavery, for reasons that extended beyond their decline in material worth after the collapse of slavery or the excessive violence that followed. Unlike their male counterparts, imprisoned women were much more privy to sexual assault, pregnancy, and menacing reproduction. The decline in African American women's procreative worth also made their laboring bodies susceptible to new forms of reproductive exploitation.

All things considered, it is my firm belief that it is the inclusion of women in the historical discourse that best complicates the static notion that convict labor was nothing more than slavery by another name. Through the female lens, we are able to clearly witness the dramatic shift from conception to conviction as a means of growing bound labor forces in the New South. While I am aware that the rich gendered nuances that underlie the female experience may also be true of men, I find it difficult to ascertain what those peculiarities are when the female perspective is excluded. All the more reason to give voice where there previously was only broken silence.

Understanding that it is impossible for this one book to completely break the chains of silence that have circumscribed black women's historical and historiographical realities, I hope future discourses will grow out of this foundational work. One area of exploration I would like to see expounded on is the postcarceral experience, and the ways in which African American women's lives were shaped in the aftermath of imprisonment. It would be useful to know how people's social and economic lives were affected upon their release. The research questions I would pose are as follows: Did women return to the counties of their birth? Were they socially resurrected upon their return? How were they received by their community, family, and friends? How did ex-prisoners cope with the lingering psychological effects of captivity, terror, and sexualized violence? How did they respond to the limited job prospects waiting for them on the outside? If they became gainfully employed, were they relieved to be reintroduced to feminine modes of labor, and disinterested in applying masculine modes of skilled work in the free labor marketplace?

Forasmuch as the postcarceral experience is a crucial element to consider in future analyses, there are other ways the historical narrative can be enriched. The examination of prison culture, as well as African American women's experiences of—and contributions to—the cultural milieu of the postbellum carceral estate, is rarely emphasized in the historical literature. While studies of the Parchman prison farm in Mississippi, and the dynamic cultural tradition that evolved in that space, have led us much closer to understanding how women expressed themselves through song, there is still much work to do in this area. Although my personal study does not take up these matters, there is an opportunity to use the 1930s and 1940s Alan Lomax recordings of prison workers singing, some of whom were female, to understand women prisoners' contribution to Depression era musical traditions, such as work songs and the blues.[2] This cultural interrogation could also lead to discoveries about spirituality, religion, and spiritually centered forms of resistance.

As scholars carve out new roads of understanding, it is important to remember the implications of this history. Today, black women are still afflicted by the social, political, and economic vices that predisposed them to arrest, conviction, and incarceration in the past. The post–Civil War South—where the majority of the nation's black female incarcerees were once imprisoned—is an essential historical reference point. In order to better understand the modern carceral state and the complex relationship black women have with it, we must confront the past and listen even when it seems to be silent.

Notes

Abbreviations

AHC   Kenan Research Center-Atlanta History Center, Atlanta, Georgia
ECSC   Elbert County Superior Courthouse, Elberton, Georgia
GA   Georgia Archives, Morrow, Georgia
LC   Library of Congress, Washington, D.C.
MSRC   Moorland-Spingarn Research Center, Washington, D.C.
NARA   National Archives and Records Administration, Washington, D.C.
SRLA   City of Savannah Research Library and Municipal Archives, Savannah, Georgia
UGA   University of Georgia, Hargrett Rare Book and Manuscript Library, Athens, Georgia

Prologue

1. Burns, *I Am a Fugitive from a Georgia Chain Gang*, 142–44. Robert Burns's memoir chronicles his arrests, escapes, recaptures, and reincarceration in Georgia's infamous chain gang system. His exposé is credited with the abolition of the chain gang system in Georgia and in the southern states.

Introduction

1. E. C. Bruffey, "Only Woman Blacksmith in America Is a Convict," *Atlanta Constitution*, August 19, 1903.

2. Ibid.

3. Ibid.

4. Acknowledging the existence of multiple New Souths, historian Howard N. Rabinowitz coined the phrase "First New South" to distinguish the initial phase of southern transformation from subsequent periods of change. In his estimation, the "First New South" marks the period between the end of the Civil War and the close of World War I. For further reading, see Rabinowitz, *The First New South*.

5. For a broader discussion of convict leasing in the southern states, see Mancini, *One Dies, Get Another*; Oshinsky, *"Worse than Slavery"*; Lichtenstein, *Twice the Work of Free Labor*; Curtin, *Black Prisoners and Their World*; Miller, *Crime, Sexual Violence, and Clemency*; Blackmon, *Slavery by Another Name*; Fierce, *Slavery Revisited*; Shapiro, *A New South Rebellion*; Ayers, *Vengeance and Justice*; Ward and Rogers, *Convicts, Coal, and the Banner Mine Tragedy*; Colvin, *Penitentiaries, Reformatories, and Chain Gangs*; Myers, *Race, Labor, and Punishment in the New South*; Ortiz, *Emancipation Betrayed*; and Miller, *Hard Labor and Hard Time*.

6. Curtin, *Black Prisoners and Their World*, 113. For additional reading on black women and convict labor in the New South, see Curtin, "The 'Human World' of Black Women"; LeFlouria, " 'The Hand That Rocks the Cradle Cuts Cordwood' "; LeFlouria, "Convict Women and Their Quest for Humanity."

7. Curtin, *Black Prisoners and Their World*, 113.

8. The U.S. Constitution, Amendment 13, section 1, states, "Neither slavery nor involuntary servitude, except as a punishment for crime whereof the party shall have been duly convicted, shall exist within the United States, or any place subject to their jurisdiction."

9. In his seminal study, *Origins of the New South*, C. Vann Woodward argues that in the years following the Civil War, the South became industrialized and situated itself as a part of the modern national economy. Although the region's departure from agrarianism was slow to occur, the Old South gradually slipped into obscurity as southern elites and northern industrialists renegotiated the region's financial future. Yet, to date, the degree of economic continuity or discontinuity that existed between the antebellum and postbellum (Old and New) Souths is still debated by historians. For a full historical treatment of this topic, see Woodward, *Origins of the New South*; Wright, *Old South, New South*; Ayers, *The Promise of the New South*.

10. Georgia General Assembly, Proceedings of the Joint Committee Appointed to Investigate the Condition of the Georgia Penitentiary, June 1870, Legislative Reports and Investigations, 122, Georgia Archives, Morrow, Ga., hereafter cited GA.

11. Information reflected in Table 1 was obtained from the Georgia Prison Commission, *Thirteenth Annual Report*, 1909–1910, Microfilm Drawer 199, box 60, GA; Registers of Convicts Received, Pardoned, Discharged, Died, or Escaped, 1871–1886, GA. The numbers of African American and white men confined at the state prison farm after 1899 are not racially disaggregated in official reports. Thus, the population totals provided in Table 1 are for all male felons, not excluding those working at the state prison farm. Based on amassed totals, an average of 135 white and black men resided annually at the state farm between 1899 and 1908. Note that the leasing of female convicts began in 1869 (see chapter 2).

12. *Thirteenth Annual Report*, 1909–1910, 16.

13. Schwartz, *Birthing a Slave*, 315. For a broader discussion of race, gender, health, and medicine in the post–Civil War South, see Savitt, *Medicine and Slavery*, *Race and Medicine*; Stowe, *Doctoring the South*; McCandless, *Slavery, Disease, and Suffering*; Fett, *Working Cures*; McGregor, *From Midwives to Medicine*; Weiner, *Sex, Sickness, and Slavery*; Roberts, *Infectious Fear*; Long, *Doctoring Freedom*; Downs, *Sick from Freedom*.

14. Camp, *Closer to Freedom*, 2.

15. Gross, "Exploring Crime and Violence," 57.

16. Hartman, "Venus in Two Acts," 3.

17. In this study, the term "Negro" is used as a historical marker, not as a literal or derogatory idiom used to typify African Americans during the postbellum period.

Chapter One

1. "Foully Murdered while Asleep in His Bed, by a Negro Woman Whom He Had Befriended," *Macon Telegraph*, March 16, 1882.

2. Ibid.

3. Ibid.

4. Ibid.

5. Ibid.

6. "Testimony of Adeline Willis," *Slave Narratives*, vol. 4, Georgia Narratives, part 4, 166, Library of Congress, Washington, D.C., hereafter cited LC.

7. "Testimony of Frances Willingham," *Slave Narratives*, vol. 4, Georgia Narratives, part 4, 159–60, LC.

8. Jones, *Labor of Love, Labor of Sorrow*, 89. For further reading, see Mann, "Slavery, Sharecropping, and Sexual Inequality." Also see Brown, "Black Women in American Agriculture."

9. On January 16, 1865, during the final months of the Civil War, Union general William Tecumseh Sherman issued Special Field Order No. 15. The edict resulted in the confiscation of approximately 400,000 acres of Confederate land stretching from Charleston, South Carolina, to the Georgia Sea Islands. The land was subsequently reallocated to newly freed black families. Unfortunately, however, the order was rescinded by President Andrew Johnson in the fall of 1865. Johnson restored the coastal property to its original owners—ex-Confederates and former slaveholders.

10. Drago, "Militancy and Black Women," 842.

11. *Atlanta Constitution*, July 10, 1869, as quoted in Foner, *Reconstruction*, 85.

12. *Macon Daily Telegraph*, April 7, 1866, as quoted in Drago, "Militancy and Black Women," 842.

13. Jones, *Labor of Love, Labor of Sorrow*, 45.

14. For a comprehensive reading on the virtual reenslavement of black sharecroppers—by means of legally binding debt-laden farmers to plantations in the postbellum South, see Daniel, *The Shadow of Slavery*.

15. "The Mississippi Black Code (1865)," cited in Foner, *Voices of Freedom*, 7–11. Mississippi was the first southern state to adopt Black Codes, a set of laws put in place to regulate and restrict the freedom of former slaves.

16. Ibid.

17. Author unknown, "The New Slavery in the South," *Independent*, February 25, 1904.

18. Ibid.

19. Ibid.

20. Ibid.

21. Ibid.

22. Ibid. While the name of the senator to whom the "Negro Peon" and his wife were subjugated was never mentioned in the sharecropper's interview, it is almost certain that ex-senator James Monroe Smith was the lessee and farmer in this case.

23. "Horrid Butchery of an Aged Negress," *Atlanta Daily Sun*, March 21, 1872.

24. Cardyn, "Sexualized Racism/Gendered Violence," 679. For further reading on the impact of racialized violence and terror on freedwomen in the postemancipation South, see Hall, "The Mind That Burns in Each Body"; Rosen, *Terror in the Heart of Freedom*; Feimster, *Southern Horrors*; Williams, *They Left Great Marks on Me*.

25. For further reading, see Clinton, "Bloody Terrain."

26. For a historical background on the evolution of sexual stereotypes against African American women, see White, *Arn't I a Woman*.

27. "Affadavit of the Wife of a Discharged Georgia Black Soldier," September 25, 1866, in Berlin, Reidy, and Rowland, *Freedom*, 807.

28. Ibid.

29. Testimony of Mary Brown, Atlanta, Georgia, October 21, 1871, *Report of the Joint Select Committee*, Georgia, vol. 6, hereafter cited KKK Hearings, 375. On April 20, 1871, the United States Congress passed the Ku Klux Klan Act, which outlawed the organization and censured its violent activities. A joint congressional committee, consisting of seven senators and fourteen representatives, was appointed and ordered to hold hearings to "inquire into the condition of the late insurrectionary States, so far as regards the execution of the laws and the safety of the lives and property of the citizens of the United States"; as cited in the Ku Klux Klan Act of 1871, ch. 22, 17 Stat. 13, U.S. Constitution. Committee members interviewed a broad range of witnesses, black and white, and compiled their testimonies in a thirteen-volume report. The investigations revealed that numerous African Americans and their white allies were brutalized, terrorized, raped, and murdered by Klansmen in the former confederate states.

30. Ibid.

31. Feimster, *Southern Horrors*, 160. For further reading, see Brundage, *Lynching in the New South*.

32. Feimster, *Southern Horrors*, 172.

33. "Five Lynched in Brooks Co.," *Columbus Ledger-Enquirer*, May 20, 1918.

34. Ibid. For further reading, see Armstrong, *Mary Turner and the Memory of Lynching*; Harrison, *Enslaved Women and the Art of Resistance*, 69.

35. "Lynched: Old Negress Cuts Mistress' Throat," *Macon Telegraph*, June 25, 1912.

36. Ibid. For a more thorough discussion of the ways in which some southern working-class black women used lethal violence as a survival and resistance strategy against race oppression, labor exploitation, and white violence, see Harris, "The Commonwealth of Virginia vs. Virginia Christian."

37. Ibid.

38. Ibid.

39. KKK Hearings, 534.

40. Hunter, *To 'Joy My Freedom*, 45. Hunter's analysis provides the most comprehensive examination of working-class black women's lives and labors in the urban South.

41. Ibid., 48–49.

42. Jones, *Labor of Love, Labor of Sorrow*, 113; Harris, "Work and the Family in Black Atlanta." For scholarship on black women and domestic service in the post–

Civil War South, see Katzman, *Seven Days a Week*; Palmer, *Domesticity and Dirt*; Clark-Lewis, *Living In, Living Out*; Harley, "For the Good of Family and Race."

43. Hunter, *To 'Joy My Freedom*, 51.

44. "Testimony of Georgia Telfair," *Slave Narratives*, vol. 4, Georgia Narratives, part 4, 4, LC.

45. Jones, *Labor of Love, Labor of Sorrow*, 128.

46. Ingersoll, "The City of Atlanta," 39, cited in Hunter, *To 'Joy My Freedom*, 57.

47. During the summer of 1881, Atlanta's washerwomen organized a massive strike. The protest drew approximately three thousand supporters who voiced their economic and political complaints: the women insisted that they be paid higher wages for their work and battled to preserve the independence of their trade. For an extensive overview of the Atlanta washerwomen's strike, see Hunter, "Domination and Resistance."

48. "More Slavery at the South," *Independent*, January 25, 1912. This essay, written by a reporter for the Atlanta-based African American newspaper the *Independent*, was transcribed from an interview with an unidentified black female domestic worker in Georgia.

49. Ibid.

50. Ibid.

51. Ibid.

52. Ibid.

53. "Her Trip Delayed by Cruel Officer," *Macon Daily Telegraph*, March 9, 1908.

54. Ibid.

55. "Negro Cook Is Charged with Theft," *Columbus Daily Enquirer*, January 28, 1910.

56. Ibid.

57. "Negro Domestic Proves a Thief," *Columbus Ledger-Enquirer*, March 7, 1905.

58. Gross, *Colored Amazons*, 4. For additional reading on black women and crime during the postemancipation era, see Butler, *Gendered Justice in the American West*; Hicks, *Talk with You Like a Woman*.

59. "More Slavery at the South," *Independent*.

60. "Ice Boxes Rifled; Cook Is Suspected," *Macon Telegraph*, January 17, 1918.

61. "Didn't Bring It Back," *Macon Telegraph*, May 4, 1910.

62. Gross, *Colored Amazons*, 42.

63. Harley, "Working for Nothing but for a Living," 56.

64. "Mrs. Flahive's Cook Settles Fine of $100," *Macon Daily Telegraph*, June 5, 1912.

65. Winter, "Prohibition in Georgia," 442.

66. Ibid., 443.

67. Ibid., 444.

68. "City Court Grinds," *Macon Telegraph*, July 21, 1912.

69. For further reading on black women and sex work at the turn of the twentieth century, see Gross, *Colored Amazons*; Hicks, *Talk with You Like a Woman*; Blair, *I've Got to Make My Livin'*.

70. "Little Locals," *Augusta Chronicle*, October 11, 1917.

71. "The Recorder's Decision in the Cases Tried before Him Thursday Morning," *Macon Telegraph*, August 29, 1886.

72. "City Court Was Busy Yesterday, Judge Hodges Used the Spurs and Everything Went along Speedily," *Macon Telegraph*, September 7, 1906.

73. Gross, *Colored Amazons*, 88–89.

74. "Dancing Negress Killed Partner," *Augusta Chronicle*, October 3, 1905.

75. Ibid.

76. "Joe Simpson Shot and Killed by Woman," *Macon Telegraph*, May 9, 1906.

77. "Killed and Burned: Negro Woman's Awful Crime in Putnam," *Macon Telegraph*, April 16, 1899.

78. Mabel Johnson's testimony was transcribed in a newspaper article entitled "Cooked Breakfast for Woman's Hubby-Fight," *Columbus Ledger-Enquirer*, August 18, 1913.

79. Ibid.

80. Ibid.

81. "A Negro Girl's Jealousy Caused Her to Kill Her Dusky Rival," *Macon Telegraph*, November 21, 1893.

82. Ibid.

83. Ibid.

84. "An African Giantess Belabors a Delicate Sister," *Daily Constitutionalist*, July 18, 1869.

85. Hine, "African American Women and Their Communities," 17.

86. "Georgia News and Telegraph," *Macon Telegraph*, April 18, 1896.

87. Green, "Infanticide and Infant Abandonment," 204.

88. Lena Fry, *Applications for Executive Clemency*, 1915, box 38, Records of the Georgia Governor's Office, GA.

89. Ibid.

90. Associated Press, *Georgia Weekly Telegraph & Messenger*, July 16, 1872.

91. Jasper County Superior Court Case Files, box 30, 2, Records of the Georgia Governor's Office, GA.

92. Ibid.

93. Ibid., 3.

94. Ibid.

95. Soet, Brack, and Dilorio, "The Prevalence and Predictors of Women's Experience," 36.

96. Ibid., 37.

97. "A Horrible Crime: Incest and Infanticide," *Columbus Daily Enquirer*, July 30, 1890.

98. Curtin, *Black Prisoners and Their World*, 117.

99. Lombroso, "Why Homicide Has Increased in the United States," 647.

100. Born in Italy in 1835, Cesare Lombroso is considered the founder of criminal anthropology. His scholarship received wide international acclaim and became a staple text in the study of modern criminology and female crime. Lombroso's most popular texts include *Criminal Woman* (1893); *Criminal Man* (1911); and *Crime: Its*

Causes and Remedies (1911). For further reading on Lombroso, see Gibson, *Born to Crime*; Rafter, *Creating Born Criminals*; Becker and Wetzell, *Criminals and Their Scientists*.

101. Lombroso, *Criminal Woman*, 182–89.

102. Ibid., 149–50.

103. McCord, *The American Negro*, 42–43.

104. Baker, *From Savage to Negro*, 14.

105. Nolen, *The Negro's Image in the South*, 19. Also see Frederickson, *The Black Image in the White Mind*.

106. For further reading, see Muhammad, *The Condemnation of Blackness*, which critically examines how social scientists combined census data with their preexisting racist hypotheses to quantify black pathology in the North.

107. Nolen, *The Negro's Image in the South*, xv.

108. Work, "Crime among the Negroes of Chicago," 222–23.

109. Hoffman's *Race Traits and Tendencies of the American Negro*, published in 1896, was the most comprehensive and influential study of race and crime to appear in the late nineteenth century. For an involved discussion on the significance of this study to the evolution of race-based criminology, see Muhammad, *The Condemnation of Blackness*.

110. Hoffman, *Race Traits and Tendencies of the American Negro*, 95.

111. L. C. Allen, "The Negro Health Problem," 203.

112. William J. Northen, "Tuberculosis among Negroes," 419, in William J. Northen Papers, box 3, folder 10, Records of the Georgia Governor's Office, GA.

113. Ibid.

114. Ibid., 415–19. For further reading on the southern response to the tuberculosis epidemic, and the racialization of tuberculosis, see Roberts, *Infectious Fear*; Hunter, *To 'Joy My Freedom*.

115. Taylor, "The Negro and His Health Problems," 515. Also see Steel, "Regarding the Prevalence of Gonorrhea in the Negro," 205.

116. Sutherland, "Health Conditions of the Negro in the South," 399.

117. Lynch, McInnes, and McInnes, "Concerning Syphilis in the American Negro," 450.

118. Turnipseed, "Hymen of the Negro Women," 194–95.

119. Author unknown, "Genital Peculiarities of the Negro," 842–43.

120. Ibid., 844. For a secondary reading on this subject, see Haller, "The Physician versus the Negro," 162.

121. For further reading, see Sommerville, *Rape & Race in the Nineteenth-Century South*; Hodes, *White Women, Black Men*.

122. Author unknown, "Genital Peculiarities of the Negro," 844.

123. Author unknown, "A Colored Woman," 2221–24, cited in Lerner, *Black Women in White America*, 166–68.

124. Harley, "Mary Church Terrell," 311.

125. Giddings, *When and Where I Enter*, 89. For further reading, see White, *Too Heavy a Load*; Shaw, "Black Club Women"; Scott, "The Most Invisible of All."

126. Williams, "Club Movement among Colored Women," 383.

127. Born in 1863 in Memphis Tennessee, Mary Eliza Church (Terrell) was the product of formerly enslaved parents, both of whom managed to rise out of poverty and acquired wealth and affluence. Terrell was one of the first African American women to attain a college degree in the United States. After she graduated from Oberlin College in 1884, she began teaching courses at Wilberforce University. Later, she taught at the Colored High School in Washington, D.C. In 1895, Terrell became the first African American and the second woman to serve on the board of education in the District of Columbia. In 1896, she became president of the NACW. For further reading on Terrell, see Jones, "Mary Church Terrell"; McCluskey, "Setting the Standard"; LeFlouria, "Mary Church Terrell."

128. Davidson, "A Speech by Olivia A. Davidson," 299.

129. Ibid.

130. Ibid., 302.

131. Ibid., 304.

132. Ibid.

133. Terrell, *The Progress of Colored Women*, 10–11.

134. Davidson, "A Speech by Olivia A. Davidson," 304; Terrell, "Lynching from a Negro's Point of View," 856.

135. Terrell, *The Progress of Colored Women*, 14–15.

136. Davidson, "A Speech by Olivia A. Davidson," 302.

137. In 1896, W. E. B. Du Bois was recruited by the University of Pennsylvania to conduct a study of Philadelphia's seventh ward and its residents. The crime problem in the district generated a heightened degree of public concern and, thereby, formed the basis of Du Bois's investigation. In 1899, Du Bois published his findings in a groundbreaking study, *The Philadelphia Negro*, which situated him as one of the founding fathers of sociological criminology. He also produced studies on the subject of black criminality in the postbellum South, and he indicted the region for its essential reenslavement of black men, women, and youth under the southern convict lease system. For further reading, see Gabbidon, *W. E. B. Du Bois on Crime and Justice*; Greene and Gabbidon, *African American Criminological Thought*. For a complete biography on Du Bois, see Lewis, *W. E. B. Du Bois*.

138. Du Bois, *The Philadelphia Negro*, 285.

139. Du Bois, "The Spawn of Slavery," 738. Also see Du Bois, *Some Notes on Negro Crime*, 4.

140. Du Bois, *Some Notes on Negro Crime*, 4.

141. Du Bois, *The Philadelphia Negro*, 241.

142. Ibid., 311–12.

143. McCord, *The American Negro*, 75.

144. Cimbala, *Under the Guardianship of the Nation*, xiv.

145. Ibid., 131.

146. Farmer-Kaiser, *Freedwomen and the Freedmen's Bureau*, 93.

147. McCord, *The American Negro*, 204.

148. *Williams & Wellborn's Pamphlet*, 17.

149. *Atlanta Constitution*, August 28, 1903.

150. "Dives Raided: Forty-Eight Negroes Arrested by the Police Last Night," *Macon Telegraph*, January 28, 1894.

151. *Williams & Wellborn's Pamphlet*, 17.

152. Nolen, *The Negro's Image in the South*, 27.

Chapter Two

1. "The News in Georgia, Gathered by Correspondence and from the Press," *Macon Telegraph*, October 25, 1884.

2. Ella Gamble, *Applications for Executive Clemency*, 1904, box 38, Records of the Georgia Governor's Office, GA.

3. Ibid.

4. Ibid.

5. Grady, *The New South*, viii. For further reading, see Davis, *Henry Grady's New South*; Nixon, *Henry W. Grady*.

6. Grady's "New South" speech was delivered on December 22, 1886, in New York City.

7. For further reading, see McLeod, *Workers and Workplace Dynamics*.

8. Maclachlan, "Women's Work," 77–81. Also see Hickey, *Hope and Danger in the New South City*. For further reading on the Fulton Mill strike of 1914, see Kuhn, *Contesting the New South Order*. For a general reading on the growth of the urban South, see Larsen, *The Rise of the Urban South*; Larsen, *The Urban South*.

9. Maclachlan, "Women's Work," 72–74.

10. Jones, *Labor of Love, Labor of Sorrow*, 135. For a comprehensive reading on the role black and white women workers in the Upper South played in the development of the region's tobacco industry after the Civil War, see Janiewski, *Sisterhood Denied*.

11. Goldin, "Female Labor Force Participation," 97.

12. Maclachlan, "Women's Work," 87. For a comprehensive examination of the ways in which black women's labor was limited and devalued in the South, see Branch, *Opportunity Denied*.

13. *Report of the Principal Keeper of the Georgia Penitentiary*, 1873, 10, GA; Bonner, *Milledgeville*, 54. Stocks and pillories were composed of heavy wooden frames with holes in which the feet, hands, or head of an offender were locked.

14. Findlay, *History of the Georgia Prison System*, 32.

15. Bonner, *Milledgeville*, 55.

16. Drobney, "Where Palm and Pine Are Blowing," 414.

17. *Report of the Principal Keeper*, 1878, 8, GA.

18. In 1870, Rufus Bullock resigned from his post as governor. His decision to leave emanated from threats of violence issued by the Ku Klux Klan and intense criticism from white southerners for his support of black enfranchisement and equality. For further reading, see Duncan, *Entrepreneur for Equality*; Duncan, "A Georgia Governor Battles Racism"; Cook, *The Governors of Georgia*.

19. Reynolds, *Iron Confederacies*, 75. Also see Summers, *Railroads, Reconstruction, and the Gospel of Prosperity*; Kolko, *Railroads and Regulation, 1877–1916*.

20. Reynolds, *Iron Confederacies*, 78.

21. Taylor, "The Convict Lease System," 9.

22. Proceedings of the Joint Committee, May 1870, 14, GA.

23. *Report of the Principal Keeper*, 1869, 9, GA.

24. Mann, "Slavery, Sharecropping, and Sexual Inequality," 779.

25. On June 16, 1870, Thornton Hightower, a convict leased to the Grant and Alexander firm, testified to the joint committee assembled to investigate the Georgia state penitentiary that female and male convicts worked together on the Air-Line Railroad and were privy to the same laboring and living conditions (Proceedings of the Joint Committee, June 1870, 122, GA).

26. Ibid., 145.

27. Proceedings of the Joint Committee, June 1870, 159, GA.

28. Ibid., 121.

29. As it pertains to administrative levels of authority within Georgia's prison camps, the overseer and whipping boss was generally the same person entrusted with the same duties—to enforce order among prisoners and dole out punishments. The terms "overseer" and "whipping boss" are used synonymously in the historical record. Also, the term "flying camp" refers to railroad camps that move along with its laborers as the work progresses.

30. Cardyn, "Sexualized Racism/Gendered Violence," 714.

31. Proceedings of the Joint Committee, June 1870, 130, GA.

32. Cited in Felton, "The Convict System," 485.

33. Proceedings of the Joint Committee, June 1870, 145, GA. James Maxwell, a former prisoner of Grant, Alexander, and Company, also told investigators that female and male prison laborers on the Macon & Brunswick Railroad were whipped for the same offenses and received an equal number of lashes.

34. Reynolds, *Iron Confederacies*, 78. According to historian Alex Lichtenstein, "between 1869 and 1871, alone, Georgia's convicts graded the roadbeds of at least 469 miles of new rail lines"; cited in *Twice the Work of Free Labor*, 46.

35. *Report of the Principal Keeper*, 1875, 4, GA.

36. Prison Commission, *Reports*, 1899–1900, 6, GA.

37. Lichtenstein, *Twice the Work of Free Labor*, 77.

38. Ibid.

39. Ibid.

40. Roberts, *Joseph E. Brown*, 91–92.

41. Mancini, *One Dies, Get Another*, 86.

42. "Beat It on Down the Line" was first recorded in 1958 by blues musician Jesse "The Lone Cat" Fuller.

43. *Georgia House Journal* (1890), 722, and (1892), 652; cited in Lewis, "African American Convicts," 265.

44. Dade County Superior Court Minutes, Grand Jury Presentments, 1893, 1894, GA; cited in Lewis, "African American Convicts," 265.

45. Mancini, *One Dies, Get Another*, 86. In 1874, Elizabeth Sciplin was, reportedly, the only white woman detained in Georgia's prison system. Although Greene

and Sciplin were both convicted of murder, Greene was given a life sentence while Sciplin was confined to the penitentiary for ten years. Racial politics played a critical role in sentencing procedures. African American prisoners, female and male, almost always received heavier penalties for similar offenses committed by whites.

46. Brown, *Senator Brown's Argument*, 5.

47. When the "water cure" was applied, a prisoner's hands were tied while a hose was turned on the victim's face. Rushing water filled the sufferer's nostrils and mouth, sometimes until the contents flowed into the lungs and out of the ears. If the sweat box was implemented, in substitution of the lash, an individual was crammed into a small wooden box and left to swelter in the blazing-hot sun.

48. "Report of Georgia Penitentiary Convicts Punished at Dade Coal Company's Works, Dade County, Georgia," State Prison Board of Inspections Reports ("Whipping Reports"), 1882, GA.

49. "The Georgia Prison Camp: Convict Labor Considered in Its Relationship to Senator Joe Brown's Millions," *St. Louis Daily Globe-Democrat*, August 19, 1887.

50. Davis, *Women, Race, & Class*, 7.

51. Hine and Thompson, *A Shining Thread of Hope*, 170.

52. The physical and sexual violence imposed on incarcerated black women left indelible somatic, psychological, and emotional injuries. Because the impact of bodily trauma on the female prisoners' psyche has been overlooked by historians, I am putting forth a preliminary scholarly attempt to interpret the psychical dimensions of abuse on female captives. Undergirding this intellectual decision is historian Deborah Gray White's charge, to pursue with rigor the violence levied against black women as a way to de-center lynching as the principal site and foremost expression of white (sexual) anxiety on the black body. For further reading, see White, *Arn't I a Woman*, 10.

53. Hartman, "Venus in Two Acts," 3, 12.

54. Cling, "Rape and Rape Trauma Syndrome," 249–50. For further reading on the impact of sexual violence on African American women, see West, *Wounds of the Spirit*. Also see Long and Ullman, "The Impact of Multiple Traumatic Victimization," 8.

55. "Testimony of Rose Williams," *Slave Narratives*, vol. 16, Texas Narratives, part 4, 178, LC. Also cited in White, *Arn't I a Woman*, 10.

56. Hine, "Rape and the Inner Lives of Black Women," 37.

57. "List of Convicts on Air-Line Railroad under Grant, Alexander & Company for the Week Ending Saturday, April 29, 1871," State Prison Commission-MISC Records 1866–1909, box 1, folder 6, GA.

58. Although, under the convict lease system, women prisoners were scarcely engaged in the practice of mining, the use of female slave labor in coal mines and iron foundries can be traced to the nineteenth-century slavery regime of the Upper South. According to Jonathan McLeod, between 1812 and 1813, enslaved men and women detained at the Oxford Iron Works in Campbell County, Virginia, participated in coal and iron production. Even though female slaves were grossly outnumbered by male captives, "at this factory, gender formed no basis for distinction in task

assignments, as slave women performed some of the most strenuous tasks at the blast furnace and on the ore banks, digging and raking as well as cleaning the ore." For further reading, see McLeod, *Workers and Workplace Dynamics*, 57.

59. *Report of the Principal Keeper*, 1875, 8, GA.

60. Correspondence, Leased Convicts to Albany and Brunswick, 1875, GA.

61. Brown, "Social Death and Political Life," 1233. Also see Patterson, *Slavery and Social Death*.

62. *Report of the Principal Keeper*, 1875, 9, GA.

63. Mancini, *One Dies, Get Another*, 90.

64. Blackmon, *Slavery by Another Name*, 343–45. For further reading, see Berry, "Free Labor He Found Unsatisfactory."

65. Berry, "Free Labor He Found Unsatisfactory," 34.

66. "Bricks: A Great Industry on the Chattahoochee," *Atlanta Constitution*, September 23, 1882.

67. Ibid. The following description of the brick-manufacturing process is partially drawn from Berry, "Free Labor He Found Unsatisfactory," 46–47.

68. Blackmon, *Slavery by Another Name*, 344–45.

69. "Bricks."

70. Ibid.

71. Ibid.

72. Berry, "Free Labor He Found Unsatisfactory," 46.

73. "Memorandum of Convicts Received by Penitentiary Co. No. 3, 1884," Registers of Convicts Received, Pardoned, Discharged, Died, or Escaped, 1871–86, GA.

74. Edwards, *Gendered Strife and Confusion*, 151.

75. Bruffey, "Only Woman Blacksmith in America Is a Convict."

76. "Whipping Report at Chattahoochee Camp," 1885, GA.

77. Ibid.

78. Camp, *Closer to Freedom*, 2.

79. Historian Alex Lichtenstein's discussion of slave theft is extremely useful in helping to explain how convict women rationalized the act of stealing from their possessors. For further reading, see Lichtenstein, "That Disposition to Theft."

80. Scott, *Domination and the Arts of Resistance*, xii.

81. Weis and Borges, "Victimology and Rape," 72.

82. Winkler, "Rape as Social Murder," 12. Also see Sheffield, "Sexual Terrorism."

83. Camp, *Closer to Freedom*, 62.

84. Enacted in 1935, the Works Progress Administration was the largest and most comprehensive New Deal agency to emerge during the period of the Great Depression. The bureau provided employment to millions of men and women, skilled and unskilled, who were displaced from the free labor marketplace. Between 1936 and 1938, a group of journalists and writers hired by the Federal Writers' Project— funded by the Works Progress Administration—conducted interviews with more than two thousand surviving ex-slaves from eighteen southern states. These oral histories were recorded, transcribed, and published.

85. "Testimony of Adeline Willis," *Slave Narratives*, vol. 4, Georgia Narratives, part 4, 162, LC.

86. Hunt, "Clothing as an Expression of History," 394–97. Also see Hunt, "The Struggle to Achieve Individual Expression."

87. White, *Arn't I a Woman*, 173.

88. Hicks, *Talk with You Like a Woman*, 57. For further reading on African American women and their relationship to "true womanhood," see Yee, *Black Women Abolitionists*. Also see Giddings, *When and Where I Enter*.

89. White, *Arn't I a Woman*, 185. The terms "Amazon" and "Sapphire" were racist misnomers used to describe African American women, who were vilified and publicly graded as masculine, physically powerful, temperamental, confrontational, disposed to criminality, and emasculating.

90. The term "Cult of True Womanhood" was coined by Barbara Welter and refers to a set of attitudes that circumscribed middle-class and upper-class white women's social identity throughout the nineteenth century. "True womanhood" was affixed to notions of purity, piety, submissiveness, and domesticity. White women were considered the moral agents of their households and the domestic anchors of their homes and families. It is important to note that the concept of "true womanhood" was not a static one. Even after the Civil War, notions of white female "virtue" were contrasted against black female "impiety." For further reading, see Welter, "The Cult of True Womanhood," 151–74.

91. "Whipping Report at Chattahoochee Camp," 1886, GA.

92. Franklin and Schweninger, *Runaway Slaves*, 2.

93. Curtin, *Black Prisoners and Their World*, 38.

94. Camp, *Closer to Freedom*, 62.

95. Curtin, *Black Prisoners and Their World*, 126.

96. A. T. Henley to R. H. Dawson, Sept. 1, 1891, Reports of Inspectors and Other Officials, Department of Corrections, Alabama Department of Archives and History, cited in Curtin, *Black Prisoners and Their World*, 126. It is unclear how incarcerated women acquired civilian clothing. However, as in slavery, persons who were hired out were sometimes allowed to keep a small portion of their wages. Because Alabama's system of convict leasing was, in many ways, akin to slavery, it is not beyond the bounds of reason to assume that this was the case.

97. Ibid.

98. Hunter, *To 'Joy My Freedom*, 172.

99. For further reading on white southerners' attempts to curb social activities among African Americans in Alabama, see Harris, "Reforms in Government Control of Negroes."

100. Ibid., 175. For further reading on the art and history of blues dancing, see Hazzard-Gordon, *Jookin'*; Stearns and Stearns, *Jazz Dance*; Malone, *Steppin' on the Blues*.

101. The conceptual framework used to describe pleasure as a form of resistance for imprisoned women is drawn from Camp, "The Pleasures of Resistance"; Hunter, *To 'Joy My Freedom*; and Hunter, "'Work That Body.'"

102. *Biennial Report of the Principal Physician of the Georgia Penitentiary*, 1884–86, 129–31, GA.

103. Information obtained from the *Biennial Report of the Principal Physician*, 1886–88, 104–15, GA; *Report of the Principal Keeper*, 1888–90, 15–17, GA.

104. Schwartz, *Birthing a Slave*, 75.

105. Ibid., 83.

106. Ibid., 88–89.

107. Greene, "Hypodermic Medication," 131–32.

108. Ibid., 143.

109. Ingraham, "Atlanta Academy of Medicine Report," 332.

110. Taliaferro, "Uterine Cloth Tents," 435.

111. *Twelfth Census of the United States, Georgia, Baldwin County, Georgia State Prison Farm, June 13, 1900*, Accessed via Internet Archive, U.S. Federal Census Collection.

112. Clarissa Olds Keeler, Untitled Manuscript (1898), Mary Church Terrell Papers, box 16, folder 285, Moorland-Spingarn Research Center, Howard University, hereafter cited MSRC.

113. Fett, *Working Cures*, 2.

114. Schwartz, "'At Noon, Oh How I Ran,'" 241.

115. Rawick, *The American Slave*, 332.

116. Schwartz, "'At Noon, Oh How I Ran,'" 242.

117. For a comprehensive reading on the degradation of black motherhood and the historical assault on black women's reproductive bodies, see Roberts, *Killing the Black Body*. For a history of the evolution of racially centered ideas regarding enslaved women's productive and reproductive roles within the Atlantic slave trade and plantation economy of early America, see Morgan, *Laboring Women*.

118. Keeler, *The American Bastiles*, 32.

119. "Hear the Other Side: You Cannot Spare the Lash in the Camps," *Augusta Chronicle*, September 27, 1887.

120. Terrell, *A Colored Woman in a White World*, 168.

121. Curtin, *Black Prisoners and Their World*, 113, 124.

122. Ibid., 122.

123. Ibid., 124.

Chapter Three

1. Keeler, Untitled Manuscript (1898), MSRC.

2. Selena Sloan Butler, *The Chain Gang System, by Mrs. Selena S. Butler, Atlanta, GA., Read before the National Association of Colored Women at Nashville, Tenn., September 16, 1897* (Tuskegee: Normal School Steam Press Print, 1897), 7, in African American Perspectives: Pamphlets from the Daniel A. P. Murray Collection, LC.

3. "Weekly Sick at Camp Heardmont," Convicts in Prison Camp Hospitals, Weekly Registers, vol. 3, 204, GA. Also cited in Keeler, Untitled Manuscript (1898), MSRC.

4. Kellor, "The Criminal Negro," 421.

5. Cable, "The Convict Lease System in the Southern States," 586.

6. Ibid.

7. Ida B. Wells was the most influential activist in the campaign against lynching. She was born a slave in Mississippi in 1862, and she had firsthand knowledge of the injustices bred by the slavery institution. Her practical approach to racial uplift

during the postemancipation era was largely influenced by her early exposure to the vices of plantation slavery. Wells's activism was equally shaped by the damaging effects of racial hatred that hastened the occurrences of mob violence in the post-bellum South. A trained teacher and journalist, Wells attacked the lynching system head-on in her writings and drew visibility to the growing violence against blacks in the South. For readings by Ida B. Wells, see Wells, *A Red Record*; Wells, *Crusade for Justice*; and Wells, *The Memphis Diary of Ida B. Wells*. For readings about Wells, see Thompson, *Ida B. Wells-Barnett*; Giddings, *Ida: A Sword among Lions*.

8. Wells, "The Convict Lease System," 23.

9. Although many of the records from the Selena Sloan Butler papers at the Auburn Avenue Research Library on African American Culture and History have been digitized, very little secondary source material is available on Butler. Beyond encyclopedia articles, no full biography exists on Butler's life. For further reading, see "Butler, Selena Sloan"; Womack, "Selena Sloan Butler."

10. Frank Weldon, "Women in Stripes: The Penitentiary Life of Georgia's Female Convicts," *Atlanta Constitution*, August 6, 1893.

11. *Atlanta Constitution*, February 18, 1890.

12. Ibid. During the nineteenth century, the handcrafting of brooms for profit was, generally, a duty reserved for the elderly and handicapped. Asylums for the deaf, blind, and orphaned also used inmate labor to produce handmade brooms to be sold on the free market. However, industrialized broom manufacturing (conducted by black female convicts) deviated from homespun broom making in the areas of mechanization, technical complexity, and volume of output.

13. Ibid.

14. *Eleventh Census of the United States, Report on Manufacturing Industries in the United States, 1890, Part I* (Washington, D.C.: Government Printing Office, 1895). In 1890, 891 female broom makers "above 15 years" were reported in the U.S. data on manufacturing industries. Prisoners were excluded from these totals.

15. "Testimony of Paul Smith," *Slave Narratives*, vol. 4, Georgia Narratives, part 3, 333, LC.

16. In post–Civil War Atlanta, negligible numbers of black women participated in the skilled and industrial free labor market. Comparatively, in the "unfree" penal-based skilled and industrial labor market, black women workers were represented in much greater numbers. The ratio of imprisoned black female industrial workers to unbound industrial laborers was more than 30 to 1.

17. In 1890, the CBC hired a man simply identified as "Cowan" to serve as whipping boss for the Bolton broom factory. At least one male guard was also hired to work at the prison camp.

18. For a detailed description of late nineteenth-century broom-making techniques, see Author unknown, *Broom-Corn and Brooms*.

19. Population Schedules of the Eighth Census of the United States, 1860, Georgia Slave Schedules, National Archives and Records Administration Microfilm Publications, M653, Roll 147, hereafter cited NARA.

20. "Testimony of Susan Matthews," *Slave Narratives*, vol. 4, Georgia Narratives, part 3, 116, LC.

21. Thomas, *History of Jefferson County*, 77.

22. Gillispie, "An Examination of an Ice House," 24.

23. Sheftall, *Ogeechee Old Town*, 41.

24. Ibid., 96.

25. Sheftall, *Ogeechee Old Town*, 125.

26. *Biennial Report of the Principal Physician*, 1886–88, 113–14, GA.

27. Northrup, *Narrative of Solomon Northrup*, 188–90.

28. Jones, "My Mother Was Much of a Woman," 239.

29. Rawick, *The American Slave*, 113. Cited in Daina Ramey, "She Do a Heap of Work," 716. For further reading, see Berry, *Swing the Sickle for the Harvest Is Ripe*.

30. This description of the cotton-planting process is partially derived from Solomon Northrup's slave narrative, which provides a detailed and familiar description of Old South agricultural production. For further reading, see *Narrative of Solomon Northrup*, 163–68.

31. Sheftall, *Ogeechee Old Town*, 143.

32. "Convict System Horrors," *Augusta Chronicle*, September 9, 1887.

33. "Hear the Other Side."

34. Ibid.

35. *Biennial Report of the Principal Physician*, 1886–88, 133, GA.

36. "Killed with the Lash: Whipping Convicts to Death in Old Town Camp," *Augusta Chronicle*, June 25, 1887.

37. "Convict System Horrors."

38. "Old Town Whipping Report," 1885, GA.

39. Ibid.

40. *Biennial Report of the Principal Physician*, 1886–88, 133, GA.

41. "Weekly Report of Sick in Hospital at Camp Oldtown," November 21, 1891, 384, GA.

42. Information culled from the *Biennial Report of the Principal Physician*, 1884–92, GA.

43. Coulter, *James Monroe Smith*, 52.

44. Ibid., 76.

45. "More about Convicts: Yesterday's Witnesses Tell What They Know," *Macon Telegraph*, July 20, 1887.

46. *Athens Weekly Banner*, September 9, 1890, as quoted in Coulter, *James Monroe Smith*, 68.

47. Ibid., 71.

48. Ibid.

49. Ibid., 75.

50. Information obtained from the *Biennial Report of the Principal Physician*, 1888–90, 104–15, GA.

51. *Biennial Report of the Principal Physician*, 1886–88, 122, GA.

52. Ibid.

53. Ibid., 123.

54. "Memorandum of Convicts Received by Penitentiary Co. No. 3, 1884," GA.

55. Although camp officials categorized cooking and other related duties as "easy" labor, in reality it was just the opposite. It is important to recognize that domestic service (cooking, cleaning, and laundering) was not a benign undertaking for female convicts. In large prison camps, kitchens essentially functioned as corporate cafeterias intended to service the appetites of more than one hundred persons daily, and washhouses hoarded enough dirty uniforms, bedcovers, and so on, to overstretch a commercial-size laundry.

56. With the exception of the Dade coal mines, gender formed no basis in determining African American women's labor roles in Georgia's prison camps.

57. "Old Town Whipping Report," 1885–86, GA.

58. Ibid.

59. *Report of the Principal Keeper*, 1875, 11, GA.

60. For further reading, see Chandler, "Death Comes to the Meanest Man in Georgia," 44–49, which provides a rare biography of William Mattox's life.

61. McIntosh, *The Official History of Elbert County*, 105.

62. Ibid., 105–6.

63. Population Schedules of the Eighth Census, 424–25, LC.

64. Ibid.

65. Chandler, "Death Comes to the Meanest Man in Georgia," 46.

66. Kane and Keeton, *Beneath These Waters*, 227.

67. Quoted in Chandler, "Death Comes to the Meanest Man in Georgia," 47.

68. Ibid.

69. Kane and Keeton, *Beneath These Waters*, 229. Also see John P. Johnson, "Pearle Cotton Mill and Dam, Elbert County Georgia," 69–71; Elbert County Superior Court Minutes, 1889–90, Elbert County Superior Courthouse, Elberton, Ga., hereafter cited ECSC.

70. Ibid.

71. *Biennial Report of the Principal Keeper*, 1890–92, 6, GA.

72. Ibid.

73. "A Queer Colony of Female Convicts," *Weekly News and Courier* (South Carolina), 1897.

74. Ibid.

75. Ibid.

76. Ibid.

77. Ibid.

78. Ibid.

79. *Biennial Report of the Principal Keeper*, 1886–88, 87, GA.

80. "Alice Will Stay at Heardmont," *Atlanta Constitution*, September 14, 1893.

81. "A Queer Colony of Female Convicts."

82. Ibid.

83. Weldon, "Women in Stripes."

84. Information culled from Weldon, "Women in Stripes"; "Nora Lea Recaptured: Colonel Mattox Has Recovered Another of His Escapes," *Atlanta Constitution*, July 28, 1893; Clarissa Olds Keeler, Untitled Manuscript (1898), MSRC.

85. Jones, *The Tribe of Black Ulysses*, 1. For a sociohistorical analysis of Georgia's lumber industry, see Armstrong, "Georgia Lumber Laborers," 435–50.

86. Weldon, "Women in Stripes."

87. Ibid.

88. "Memorandum of Convicts Received by Penitentiary Co. No. 3, 1884," GA. Although it is difficult to obtain a precise reading of Henderson's duties on the railroad, with the sparse body of evidence at hand, it is not far-fetched to assume that her experience as a "tie hack" may have informed William Mattox's decision to oblige her services in the lumber mill.

89. "Weekly Sick at Camp Heardmont," vol. 3, 200, GA.

90. Information in Table 2 was obtained from *Annual and Biennial Reports of the Principal Physician*, 1892–97, GA; Convicts in Prison Camp Hospitals, 1892–97, GA; Grand Jury Presentments, 1892–99, ECSC.

91. "Weekly Sick at Camp Heardmont," vol. 4, 263, GA.

92. "A Protest from Quitman: Against the Commutation of the Sentence of Eliza Randall," *Macon Telegraph*, February 27, 1888.

93. "Sentence Commuted: Eliza Randall Not to Be Hanged," *Macon Telegraph*, February 2, 1888.

94. Ibid.

95. Ibid.

96. "A Protest from Quitman."

97. Ibid.

98. "Whipping Report at Chattahoochee Camp," 1889, GA.

99. Gross, *Colored Amazons*, 82.

100. "Marietta Matters," *Marietta Journal*, June 4, 1891.

101. "Eloped with a Negro Convict," *Columbus Daily Enquirer*, May 21, 1891.

102. Besides Eliza Randall, two other inmates became pregnant or gave birth at Camp Heardmont—Dilly Echols and Carrie Massie. Unlike Randall, Echols and Massie were both raped. Echols reportedly suffered a "miscarriage," while Massie's offspring allegedly starved to death during her illness. Other instances of pregnancy and childbirth may have occurred at the camp but are not reflected in the official record.

103. Chandler, "Death Comes to the Meanest Man in Georgia," 46. Bud Hilley relayed the following account to Raymond E. Chandler Jr., father of the author, during the 1930s.

104. "A Queer Colony of Female Convicts."

105. "A Woman in Man's Attire: Eliza Randall as Engineer and Machinist," *Macon Telegraph*, April 25, 1898.

106. Ibid.

107. "Weekly Report of Sick at Camp Heardmont," vol. 3, 199, GA.

108. "Escaped from the Chaingang: A Mulatto Girl Walked Away in Broad Daylight," *Macon Telegraph*, May 3, 1891.

109. Weldon, "Women in Stripes."

110. Ibid.

111. Ibid.

112. Ibid.

113. Ibid.

114. "Women Convicts in Georgia," *Milwaukee Sentinel*, August 17, 1893.

115. Perrin, "Resisting Reproduction," 260–63.

116. Schwartz, *Birthing a Slave*, 315.

117. Oliphant, "Folk Remedies and Superstition," *Slave Narratives*, vol. 4, part 4, 285, LC.

118. "Weekly Report of Sick at Camp Heardmont," vol. 2, 492, GA.

119. Fett, *Working Cures*, 179. According to Fett, slave owners took a profound economic interest in the reproductive health of enslaved women, making them more attuned and responsive to bondwomen's complaints of illness. Thus, planters' pre-occupation with slave women's ability to procreate "added leverage" to their complaints of infirmity. This was not the case with incarcerated women, who held no reproductive worth.

120. "Weekly Report of Sick at Camp Heardmont," vol. 4, 260, GA; "Weekly Report of Sick at Camp Heardmont," vol. 5, 247, GA; "Weekly Report of Sick at Camp Heardmont," vol. 4, 266, GA.

121. "A Queer Colony of Female Convicts."

122. Ibid.

123. Chandler, "Death Comes to the Meanest Man in Georgia," 47.

124. "Colonel W. H. Mattox Killed: His Son in Law Was the Slayer," *Atlanta Constitution*, November 18, 1900.

Chapter Four

1. A. H. Ulm, "How Georgia Cares for Boys, Helpless Convicts and Female Prisoners; Great Work Is Now Being Accomplished by the State at Milledgeville," *Atlanta Constitution*, June 25, 1911.

2. Ibid.

3. Ibid.

4. Ibid.

5. Ibid.

6. Ibid.

7. Ibid.

8. Ibid.

9. During the late 1880s and early 1890s, reformers and advocates of organized labor insisted that Georgia felons be put to work on roads and public works projects in order to eliminate unfair competition with free laborers. The abolition of convict leasing in 1908, and the decentralization of the chain gang system during the same year, was done partway in response to the free labor problem. A deeper discussion of the demise of convict leasing, the reorganization of Georgia's chain gang system, and the debate over free and convict labor will be covered in much greater detail in chapter 5.

10. "The Colored Race in America," *Washington Bee* (Washington, D.C.), May 13, 1899.

11. "The Convict Lease System," *Colored American*, February 8, 1902.

12. Helen Pitts Douglass, "Convict Lease System" (1896), Frederick Douglass Papers, Series: Family Papers, 9, LC. While Helen Pitts Douglass's activism is sparsely documented in the historical record, her involvement in the progressive campaign against the southern convict lease system is commented on in late nineteenth-century and early twentieth-century African American newspapers and is also mentioned in rare unprocessed documents housed at the Frederick Douglass National Historic Site in Washington, D.C. For a full biographical treatment of Helen Pitts Douglass' life, see Nelson, "Have We a Cause."

13. Correspondence, *Cleveland Gazette*, May 14, 1898. The *Gazette* was a weekly newspaper published in Cleveland, Ohio, from 1883 to 1945. It was the longest-running African American weekly in the United States, and it focused on a series of controversial issues impacting African Americans throughout the nation, including lynching, convict leasing, Jim Crow segregation, and political disenfranchisement.

14. Higginbotham, "African American Women's History," 252. For further reading, see Higginbotham, *Righteous Discontent*.

15. Terrell, "Peonage in the United States," 813. For further reading, see Terrell, *A Colored Woman in a White World*.

16. Terrell, *A Colored Woman in a White World*, 167–68.

17. John H. Bracey Jr., August Meier, Anne Firor Scott, William H. Chafe, and Lillian Serece Williams, eds., Records of the National Association of Colored Women's Clubs, 1895–1992, Part I, Reel 1, Frame 32, Mary McLeod Bethune Council House Archives.

18. Rebecca Latimer Felton, "Convict Lease System," Rebecca Latimer Felton Papers, Speeches and Sermons, box 10, folder 1, University of Georgia, Hargrett Rare Book and Manuscript Library, hereafter cited UGA. The most prominent woman in Progressive Era Georgia, in 1922, eighty-seven-year-old Felton became the first woman to serve in the U.S. Senate. For a complete biographical treatment of Rebecca Latimer Felton's life, see Talmadge, *Rebecca Latimer Felton*; Staman, *Loosening Corsets*; Whites, "Rebecca Latimer Felton"; Whites, "Rebecca Latimer Felton and the Wife's Farm," 354–72.

19. Felton, "Convict Lease System,"12, UGA.

20. Whites, *Gender Matters*, 188.

21. Clarissa Olds Keeler, *The Crime of Crimes*. An insufficient amount of biographical data exists on Clarissa Olds Keeler. But, according to the records of the Congressional Cemetery (also known as the Washington Parish Burial Ground) in southeast Washington, D.C., she was born in Erie County, Pennsylvania, in June 1831, and died March 15, 1913. *The Crime of Crimes* and *The American Bastiles* are her best-known works. She was a strident activist in the social reform movement of the late nineteenth and the early twentieth centuries, and she wrote lengthily on the plight of women prisoners in the South's convict camps.

22. Cited in Wheaton, *Prisons and Prayer*, 229.

23. Ibid., 194. In her travelogue, Wheaton frequently leaves the names of the states and individuals that she references anonymous. Yet, in this passage, there are subtle, factual indications that Georgia is the place of reference.

24. Ibid., 196.

25. Ibid., 195.

26. Ibid., 9.

27. Miller, *Hard Labor and Hard Time*, 20.

28. For a comprehensive reading on the development of state-operated prison plantations in the postemancipation South, see Carleton, *Politics and Punishment*; Walker, *Penology for Profit*; Oshinsky, *"Worse Than Slavery"*; Taylor, *Down on Parchman Farm*; Perkinson, *Texas Tough*; Miller, *Hard Labor and Hard Time*.

29. Miller, *Hard Labor and Hard Time*, 9.

30. Candler and Evans, *Georgia*, 83.

31. For an in-depth reading on the history of Milledgeville, Baldwin County, and the state penitentiary at Milledgeville, see Bonner, *Milledgeville*; Beeson, *History Stories of Milledgeville and Baldwin County*; Green Cook, *History of Baldwin County*; Bonner, "The Georgia Penitentiary at Milledgeville"; Walden, "History of the Georgia Penitentiary."

32. "Georgia's Prison Farm," *Atlanta Constitution*, July 2, 1899.

33. Ibid.

34. Prison Commission, *Reports*, 1900–1901, 23, GA.

35. Ibid., 24.

36. Ibid.

37. Ibid., 23.

38. *Twelfth Census of the United States, Georgia State Prison Farm*.

39. Information reflected in Table 3 was extracted from the annual reports of the Georgia Prison Commission dating from 1899 to 1910, GA. Data from the 1902–3 report are missing from official records and are not reflected in Table 3. It is also important to make note of prison commissioners' tendency to conflate certain occupations under the general category "laborer." These vocations include laundry work, chauffeuring, housekeeping, and public works.

40. Ibid.

41. Ibid.

42. Information retrieved from the annual reports of the Georgia Prison Commission, 1900–1910, GA. The 1902–3 annual report is absent from the historical record. Also, the numbers provided for white women include felons and misdemeanants who were sent to the state farm in lieu of the chain gang.

43. "Georgia's Prison Farm," *Atlanta Constitution*, July 2, 1899.

44. Prison Commission, *Reports*, 1900–1901, 22, GA.

45. Officials of the Texas Prison System, *Annual Reports*, 1911, 16, 54; cited in Rafter, *Partial Justice*, 89.

46. Oshinsky, *"Worse Than Slavery."*

47. Fitzgerald, *Every Farm a Factory*, 3.

48. "Georgia's Prison Farm."

49. Ibid.

50. Giesen, "Cotton." For further reading on Georgia and the South's cotton economy in the post–Civil War era, see Bonner, *A History of Georgia Agriculture*; Daniel, *Breaking the Land*; Fite, *Cotton Fields No More*; Wynne, *The Continuity of*

Cotton; Aiken, *The Cotton Plantation South*; O'Donovan, *Becoming Free in the Cotton South*.

51. "State Farm Gin Open to Public: Strong Protest against Competition with Convict Labor," *Atlanta Constitution*, August 7, 1902.

52. "Georgia's Prison Farm."

53. Prison Commission, *Reports*, 1910–11, 33–34, GA.

54. Ibid.

55. Bruffey, "Only Woman Blacksmith in America Is a Convict."

56. Pink [Pinkie] Gardner, Clemency Applications, 1923, box 38, GA.

57. Ibid. For a deeper discussion of the system of domestic parole in Georgia, see Haley, "Like I Was a Man."

58. Ulm, "How Georgia Cares."

59. Ibid.

60. "Report of Convict Investigating Committee to the Extraordinary Session of the General Assembly," *Acts and Resolutions of the General Assembly of the State of Georgia, 1908* (Atlanta: Charles P. Byrd, State Printer, 1908), 1076, GA.

61. Ibid.

62. Quotes from the 1922 investigation of the Georgia state prison farm are drawn from an editorial written by *Atlanta Constitution* staff correspondent Marion Kendrick. See "Prison Probers Told of Vile Conditions at the Convict Farm," *Atlanta Constitution*, June 13, 1922.

63. Between 1930 and 1932, John. L. Spivak traveled throughout Georgia, interviewing officials from the state prison farm, county chain gang camps, and city stockades, and photographing punishment practices within the state's camps. He also collected several punishment records and used all of this information as the basis for his famous novel, *Georgia Nigger*. For additional reading on Spivak and the impact of his work, see Lichtenstein, "Chain Gangs, Communism, and the 'Negro Question.'"

64. "Georgia Penitentiary Report of Convicts Employed at the State Prison Farm Female Camp, Punishment Report," September 1931, John L. Spivak Papers, box 1, folder 1, Harry Ransom Center, the University of Texas at Austin.

65. Sarge Plunkett, "A Word to the People That Pose as 'Reformers': Are We All Hypocrites?," *Atlanta Constitution*, June 6, 1897.

66. Ibid.

67. Terrell, *The Progress of Colored Women*, 14–15.

68. For a comprehensive reading on juvenile justice in Jim Crow America and the role African American social reformers played in the "black child-savers" movement, see Ward, *The Black Child-Savers*.

69. Prison Commission, *Reports*, 1905–6, 7, GA.

70. Ibid., 1908–9, 8, GA.

71. Ibid., 1907–8, 12, GA.

72. Ibid.; ibid., 1910–11, 22, GA.

73. Ibid., 1909–10, 9, GA.

74. For further reading on the role disabled slaves played in the southern plantation economy, see Boster, *African American Slavery and Disability*; Barclay, "The Greatest Degree of Perfection."

75. "Georgia's Prison Farm."

76. Ibid.

77. Ibid.

78. Ibid.

79. Eliza Cobb, Clemency Applications, 1910, box 24, GA.

80. Ibid.

81. Ibid.

82. Ibid.

83. Sarah Dixon, Clemency Applications, 1907, box 33, GA.

84. Ibid.

85. Ibid.

86. Ibid.

Chapter Five

1. Georgia Legislature, "An Act to Provide for the Future Employment of Felony and Misdemeanor Male Convicts upon the Public Roads of the Several Counties of the State, Except Certain Classes, and to Provide for the Employment of Those Not Used upon Such Roads; to Amend Section 1039 of the Code So Far as the Same Relates to Females, and to Prevent the Hiring of Misdemeanor Convicts to Private Persons, to Make Violations of Certain Provisions of This Act Crimes and to Provide Punishment Therefore, and for Other Purposes," September 19, 1908, Acts and Resolutions of the General Assembly of the State of Georgia, 1119, GA.

2. Ibid.

3. Mattie Black, Clemency Applications, 1908, box 9, GA.

4. Prison Commission, *Reports*, 1908–9, 21, GA.

5. Mattie Black, Clemency Applications, 1908, box 9, GA.

6. Du Bois, *Some Notes on Negro Crime*, 7.

7. Lichtenstein, *Twice the Work of Free Labor*, 158. For an in-depth examination of the transition from convict leasing to the chain gang system in Georgia, and the evolution of the Good Roads Movement, see Lichtenstein's seminal article, "Good Roads and Chain Gangs in the Progressive South."

8. Mancini, "Race, Economics, and the Abandonment of Convict Leasing," 347.

9. Ibid., 348.

10. Ingram, *Dixie Highway*, 17.

11. Preston, *Dirt Roads to Dixie*, 41.

12. Ibid., 22.

13. Page, "The Necessity of Road Improvement in the South," 156–60.

14. Lichtenstein, "Good Roads and Chain Gangs in the Progressive South," 89.

15. Lichtenstein, *Twice the Work of Free Labor*, 175.

16. Lichtenstein, "Good Roads and Chain Gangs in the Progressive South," 101–2.

17. Prison Commission, *Reports*, 1899–1900, 16, GA.

18. Data from the 1902–3 and 1917–18 annual reports are missing from official records and are not included in Table 5.

19. Du Bois, *Some Notes on Negro Crime*, 49–50. Information included in Du Bois's report was drawn from the 1900 United States Census.

20. Mixon, *The Atlanta Riot*, 1–2. Also see Burns, *Rage in the Gate City*; Bauerlein, *Negrophobia*. On September 22, 1906, thousands of whites unpacked their aggressions on Atlanta's black population following claims of white women being physically and sexually assaulted by black men.

21. Du Bois, *Some Notes on Negro Crime*, 49–50. Also see Annual Reports of the Chief of Police of the City of Atlanta, Ga., Herbert T. Jenkins Papers, MSS 546, Atlanta History Center, Atlanta, G.A., hereafter cited AHC.

22. Du Bois, *Some Notes on Negro Crime*, 49–50.

23. Atlanta Police Department Court Docket, vol. 1, 1886–87, MSS 787, AHC.

24. Ibid.

25. Mixon, *The Atlanta Riot*, 42.

26. Atlanta Police Department Court Docket, vol. 1, 1886–87, 122, AHC.

27. Hunter, "The 'Brotherly Love' for which This City is Proverbial," 87.

28. Atlanta Police Department Court Docket, vol. 1, 1886–87, 139, AHC.

29. Ibid., 133.

30. Ibid., 130.

31. Hickey, "Waging War," 780. Also see Carby, "Policing the Black Woman's Body." For further reading on the gendered context of social control, see Bynum, *Unruly Women*.

32. Police Department, Jail Registers and Jail Prisoner Books, 1906–8, vol. 2, 5600PL-010, City of Savannah Research Library and Municipal Archives, Savannah, Georgia, hereafter cited SRLA. For a comprehensive reading on the black experience in post–Civil War Savannah, see Perdue, *The Negro in Savannah*.

33. Police Department, Criminal Registers, 1873–74, vol. 2, 5600PL-020, SRLA; Police Department, Criminal Register, 1877, vol. 3, 5600PL-020, SRLA.

34. Police Department, Criminal Register, 1873–74, vol. 2, SRLA.

35. Police Department, Criminal Register, 1877, vol. 3, SRLA.

36. Lizzie Boatright, Clemency Applications, 1897, box 10, GA.

37. Ibid.

38. Ibid.

39. Report of Phill. G. Byrd to Governor William Yates Atkinson, May 7, 1897, in Lizzie Boatright, Clemency Applications, 1897, box 10, GA.

40. Ibid.

41. Ibid.

42. Ibid. Also cited in "Horrors of the Chain-Gang," *Savannah Tribune*, November 13, 1897.

43. Butler, *Chain Gang System*, 5.

44. Keeler, *The Crime of Crimes*, 16.

45. Butler, *Chain Gang System*, 7.

46. Keeler, *The American Bastiles*, 40.

47. Ibid., 43.

48. Keeler, Untitled Manuscript (1898), MSRC.

49. Laura Blake, Clemency Applications, 1915, box 10, GA.

50. Lizzie Teasley, Clemency Applications, 1909, box 30, GA.

51. Ibid.

52. Ibid.

53. Annie Cuyler, Clemency Applications, 1904, box 30, GA.

54. Mamie Cason, Mattie Davis, Areta Fluker, Clemency Applications, 1922, box 21, GA.

55. Leila Blackman, Clemency Applications, 1904, box 9, GA.

56. Ibid.

57. Pearl Black, Clemency Applications, 1905, box 9, GA.

58. Minnie Black, Clemency Applications, 1904, box 9, GA.

59. Mary Dykes, Clemency Applications, 1911, box 36, GA.

60. Leila Everett, Clemency Applications, 1901, box 38, GA.

61. Ibid.

62. Lichtenstein, *Twice the Work of Free Labor*, 190.

63. Ibid., 191.

Epilogue

1. White, *Arn't I a Woman*, 23.

2. During the 1930s and 1940s, Alan Lomax, a legendary folklorist, musician, and writer, traveled throughout the southern states and collected thousands of field recordings. Many of these recordings included work songs led by black male and female prisoners.

Bibliography

Primary Sources

Manuscript Collections

Alabama Department of Archives and History, Montgomery, Alabama
  Wetumpka Prison Photographs
Auburn Avenue Research Library on African American Culture and History,
  Atlanta, Georgia
  Selena Sloan Butler Papers
City of Savannah Research Library and Municipal Archives, Savannah,
  Georgia
  Police Department, Criminal Registers, 1873–77, Vols. 2–3, Record Series:
  5600PL-020
  Police Department, Jail Registers and Jail Prisoner Books, 1906–8, Vol. 2,
  Record Series: 5600PL-010
Elbert County Superior Courthouse, Elberton, Georgia
  Grand Jury Presentments, Elbert County, 1892–99
  Superior Court Minutes, 1889–90
Georgia Archives, Jonesboro, Georgia
  Annual and Biennial Reports of the Principal Physician of the Georgia
  Penitentiary, 1890–97, RG 21-1-4
  Applications for Executive Clemency, Georgia Governor's Office, 1858–1942,
  RG 1-4-42
  Convicts in Prison Camp Hospitals, Weekly Registers, 1888–1907, RG 21-1-9
  Corporal Punishment Monthly Reports (Whipping Reports), 1884–89,
  Georgia Department of Corrections, RG 21-1-11
  Georgia General Assembly, Proceedings of the Joint Committee Appointed
  to Investigate the Condition of the Georgia Penitentiary, 1870, Legislative
  Reports and Investigations, 1866–1968, RG 37-8-4
  Georgia Legislature, Acts and Resolutions of the General Assembly of the
  State of Georgia, 1777–2013, RG 37-1-15
  Georgia Prison Commission, Georgia Prison Commission Annual Reports,
  1897–1936, Microfilm, Drawer 199, Box 60
  Georgia Prison Commission, MISC Records, 1866–1909, Box 1, Folder 6, RG
  21-1-19
  Georgia Prison Commission, Misdemeanor Chain Gangs Monthly Reports,
  1898–1901, RG 21-1-8
  Jasper County Superior Court Case Files, 1809–1922, RG 179-1-1
  Principal Keeper's Annual Reports, 1852–97, RG 21-1-1

Registers of Convicts Received, Pardoned, Discharged, Died, or Escaped, 1871–86, RG 21-1-14

Vanishing Georgia Photographic Collection

William J. Northen Papers, 1865–1929, AC 41-354M, Box 3, Folder 10

Georgia Historical Society, Savannah, Georgia

Iva Roach Benton Collection, MS1764, Box 1, Folder 1

Hargrett Rare Book and Manuscript Library, University of Georgia, Athens, Georgia

Rebecca Latimer Felton Papers, Speeches and Sermons, Box 10

Harry Ransom Center, the University of Texas at Austin, Austin, Texas

John L. Spivak Papers, RLIN Record #TXRC93-A6, Series 1, Box 1, Folder 1

Kenan Research Center–Atlanta History Center, Atlanta, Georgia

Annual Reports of the Chief of Police of the City of Atlanta, Ga., Herbert T. Jenkin Papers, MSS 546

Atlanta Police Department Court Docket, Vol. 1, 1886–87, MSS 787

Chattahoochee Brick Company Business Subject File, Folder 1

Library of Congress, Washington, D.C.

African American Perspectives: Pamphlets from the Daniel A. P. Murray Collection, 1818–1907

Born in Slavery: Slave Narratives from the Writers' Project, 1936–38 (Digital Collection)

Frederick Douglass Papers, Series: Family Papers (Digital Collection)

From Slavery to Freedom: The African American Pamphlet Collection, 1822–1909

Mary McLeod Bethune Council House Archives, Washington, D.C.

Records of the National Association of Colored Women's Clubs, 1895–1992; Part I: John H. Bracey Jr., August Meier, Anne Firor Scott, William H. Chafe, and Lillian Serece Williams, eds., Reel 1, Frame 32

Moorland-Spingarn Research Center, Howard University, Washington, D.C.

Mary Church Terrell Papers, Series H: Holograph Notes and Manuscripts by Others, Box 16, Folder 285, Manuscript Division

National Archives and Records Administration, Washington, D.C.

Population Schedules of the Eighth Census of the United States, 1860, Georgia Slave Schedules, NARA Microfilm Publications, M653, Rolls 143 and 147

Special Collections and Archives, Georgia State University Library, Atlanta, Georgia

Atlanta Journal-Constitution Photographic Archive, AJCP551-49h

State Archives of Florida, Tallahassee, Florida

Florida Memory Photographic Collection, RC05716

Published Census Records

U.S. Bureau of the Census. *Eleventh Census of the United States, Report on Manufacturing Industries in the United States, 1890, Part I.* Washington, D.C.: Government Printing Office, 1895.

———. *Twelfth Census of the United States, Georgia, Baldwin County, Georgia State Prison Farm, June 13, 1900*. Internet Archive. Retrieved November 4, 2014. https://archive.org/details/12thcensusofpopu178unit.

Published Federal Government Documents and Reports

Pearle Cotton Mill and Dam, Elbert County Georgia, Historic American Engineering Record, National Park Service, Department of the Interior. Washington, D.C., Prepared by John P. Johnson, 1980.

U.S. Congress. *Report of the Joint Select Committee Appointed to Inquire into the Condition of Affairs in the Late Insurrectionary States, so far as Regards the Execution of Laws, and the Safety of the Lives and Property of the Citizens of the United States and Testimony Taken (KKK Hearings), Georgia*. Vol. 6. Washington, D.C.: Government Printing Office, 1872.

Newspapers

Atlanta Constitution
Atlanta Daily Sun
Augusta Chronicle
Cleveland Gazette
Columbus Daily Enquirer
Columbus Ledger-Enquirer

Daily Constitutionalist
Independent
Macon Telegraph
Savannah Tribune
St. Louis Daily Globe-Democrat

Weekly News and Courier (South Carolina)
Washington Bee

Books, Pamphlets, and Articles

Allen, L. C. "The Negro Health Problem." *American Journal of Public Health* 5, no. 3 (March 1915): 194–203.

Author Unknown. *Broom-Corn and Brooms: A Treatise on Raising Broom-Corn and Making Brooms, on a Small or Large Scale*. New York: Orange Judd Company, 1876.

———. "A Colored Woman, However Respectable, Is Lower Than the White Prostitute." *Independent* 54, September 18, 1902, 2221–24.

———. "Genital Peculiarities of the Negro." *Atlanta Journal-Record of Medicine* 4 (March 1903): 842–44.

———. "More Slavery at the South by a Negro Nurse." *Independent* 72, January 25, 1912, 196–200.

———. "The New Slavery in the South: An Autobiography by a Georgia Negro Peon." *Independent* 56, February 25, 1904, 409–14.

Brown, Joseph E. *Senator Brown's Argument before the Governor in Defense of Dade Coal Company on the Convict Question*. Atlanta, 1887.

Butler, Selena S. *Chain Gang System, by Mrs. Selena S. Butler, Atlanta, Ga. Read before the National Association of Colored Women at Nashville, Tenn., September 16, 1897*. Tuskegee: Normal School Steam Press Print, 1897.

Cable, George W. "The Convict Lease System in the Southern States." *Century Illustrated Magazine* 27, no. 4 (February 1884): 582–99.

Candler, Allen P., and General Clement A. Evans, eds. *Georgia: Comprising Sketches of Counties, Towns, Events, Institutions, and Persons, Arranged in Cyclopedic Form.* Vol. 3. Atlanta: State Historical Association, 1906.

Childs, Rhoda Ann. "Affidavit of the Wife of a Discharged Georgia Black Soldier," September 25, 1866. In *The Black Military Experience.* Vol. 2 of *Freedom: A Documentary History of Emancipation, 1861–1867,* edited by Ira Berlin, Joseph Reidy, and Leslie Rowland, 807–8. Cambridge: Cambridge University Press, 1982.

Davidson, Olivia. "A Speech by Olivia A. Davidson before the Alabama State Teachers' Association, Selma, Alabama, April 21, 1886." In *The Booker T. Washington Papers: 1860–1889,* edited by Louis R. Harland, 298–305. Urbana: University of Illinois Press, 1972.

Douglass, Helen Pitts. "The Convict Lease System." Unpublished essay in the Frederick Douglass Papers at the Library of Congress, Washington D.C. Series: Family Papers (Digital Collection).

Du Bois, W. E. B. "The Damnation of Women." In *Darkwater: Voices within the Veil,* 16–86. New York: Harcourt, Brace, and Howe, 1920.

———. *The Philadelphia Negro: A Social Study.* Philadelphia: University of Pennsylvania Press, 1899.

———. *Some Notes on Negro Crime Particularly in Georgia.* Atlanta: Atlanta University Press, 1904.

———. "The Spawn of Slavery: The Convict Lease System in the South." *Missionary Review of the World* 24, no. 10 (October 1901): 737–45.

Felton, Rebecca A. "The Convict System of Georgia." *Forum* 2, no. 5 (January 1887): 484–90.

Georgia, General Assembly, Committee to Investigate the Official Conduct of Rufus B. Bullock. *Testimony Taken by Committee Appointed to Investigate the Official Conduct of Rufus B. Bullock, Late Governor of Georgia.* Atlanta: W. A. Hemphill, 1872.

Greene, W. "Hypodermic Medication." *Atlanta Medical and Surgical Journal* 9, no. 3 (June 1871): 129–46.

Hoffman, Frederick Ludwig. *Race Traits and Tendencies of the American Negro.* New York: Published for the American Economic Association by the Macmillan Company, 1896.

Ingersoll, Ernest. "The City of Atlanta." *Harper's New Monthly Magazine* 60 (December 1879): 30–43.

Ingraham, Edwin P., M. D. "Atlanta Academy of Medicine Report." *Atlanta Medical and Surgical Journal* 9, no. 3 (June 1871): 330–33.

Keeler, Clarissa Olds. *The American Bastiles.* Washington, D.C.: Carnahan Press, 1910.

———. *The Crime of Crimes; or, the Convict System Unmasked.* Washington, D.C.: Pentecostal Era Company, 1907.

———. Untitled manuscript (1898). Mary Church Terrell Papers. Moorland-Spingarn Research Center.

Kellor, Frances A. "The Criminal Negro: Advantages and Abuses of Southern Penal Systems." *Arena* 25, no. 4 (April 1901): 419–28.

Kemble, Frances Anne. *Journal of a Residence on a Georgian Plantation in 1838–1839 by Frances Anne Kemble.* Edited by John A. Scott. Athens: University of Georgia Press, 1984.

Lombroso, Cesare. *Crime: Its Causes and Remedies.* 1911. Reprint, New Jersey: Patterson Smith Publishing Corporation, 1968.

———. *Criminal Man.* 1911. Reprint, Durham, N.C.: Duke University Press, 2006.

———. *Criminal Woman, the Prostitute, and the Normal Woman.* 1893. Reprint, Durham, N.C.: Duke University Press, 2004.

———. "Why Homicide Has Increased in the United States." *North American Review* 165, no. 493 (December 1897): 641–48.

McCord, Charles H. *The American Negro as a Dependent, Defective and Delinquent.* Nashville: Benson Printing Company, 1914.

McInnes, Kenneth M. Lynch, Kater McInnes, and G. Fleming McInnes. "Concerning Syphilis in the American Negro." *Southern Medical Journal* 8, no. 6 (June 1915): 450–56.

Northrup, Solomon. *Narrative of Solomon Northrup, Twelve Years a Slave.* Auburn, N.Y.: Derby and Miller, 1853.

Olmsted, Frederick L. *Journeys and Explorations in the Cotton Kingdom.* London: S. Low, Son & Co., 1861.

Page, Logan Waller. "The Necessity of Road Improvement in the South." *South Atlantic Quarterly* 9, no. 2 (April 1910): 156–60.

Powell, J. C. *The American Siberia or Fourteen Years' Experience in a Southern Convict Camp.* Oakland, Calif.: H. J. Smith & Co, 1891.

Spivak, John. *Georgia Nigger.* New York: Brewer, Warren, and Putnam, 1932.

Steel, William A. "Regarding the Prevalence of Gonorrhea in the Negro—An Inquiry." *Southern Medical Journal* 6, no. 3 (March 1913): 205.

Sutherland, H. L. "Health Conditions of the Negro in the South: With Special Reference to Tuberculosis." *Journal of the Southern Medical Association* 6, no. 10 (October 1909): 399–407.

Taliaferro, V. H., M. D. "Uterine Cloth Tents." *Atlanta Medical and Surgical Journal* 9, no. 3 (June 1871): 431–44.

Taylor, J. Madison. "The Negro and His Health Problems." *Medical Record* 82 (September 21, 1912): 513–15.

Terrell, Mary Church. *A Colored Woman in a White World.* 1940. Reprint, Amherst: Humanity Books, 2005.

———. "Lynching from a Negro's Point of View." *North American Review* 178 (June 1904): 853–68.

———. "Peonage in the United States: The Convict Lease System and the Chain Gangs." In *The Nineteenth Century and After,* edited by James Knowles, 62. London: Spottiswoode & Co. Printers, 1907.

———. *The Progress of Colored Women.* Washington, D.C.: Smith Brothers Printers, 1898.

Thomas, Z. V. *History of Jefferson County.* Macon, Ga.: J. W. Burke Co., 1927.

Thompson, C. Mildred. *Reconstruction in Georgia, Economic, Social, Political, 1865–1872.* New York: Columbia University Press, 1915.

Turnipseed, E. B. "Hymen of the Negro Women." *Richmond and Louisville Medical Journal* 6 (1868): 194–95.

Wells, Ida B. "The Convict Lease System." In *The Reason Why the Colored American Is Not in the World's Columbian Exposition*, edited by Robert Rydell, 23–28. 1893. Reprint, Urbana: University of Illinois Press, 1999.

———. *Crusade for Justice: The Autobiography of Ida B. Wells.* Edited by Alfreda M. Duster. Chicago: University of Chicago Press, 1970.

———. *The Memphis Diary of Ida B. Wells: An Intimate Portrait of the Activist as a Young Woman.* Edited by Miriam DeCosta-Willis. Boston: Beacon Press Books, 1995.

———. *A Red Record: Tabulated Statistics and Alleged Causes of Lynchings in the United States, 1892–1893–1894.* Chicago: Donohue and Henneberry, 1895.

Wheaton, Elizabeth Ryder. *Prisons and Prayer, or A Labor of Love.* Tabor, Iowa: Chas. M. Kelley, 1906.

Williams, Fannie Barrier. "Club Movement among Colored Women of America." In *A New Negro for a New Century: An Accurate and Up-to-Date Record of the Upward Struggles of the Negro Race*, edited by Booker T. Washington, Fannie Barrier Williams, and Norman Barton Wood, 379–405. Chicago: American Publishing House, 1900.

Williams & Wellborn's Pamphlet of the Public Laws of Georgia. Milledgeville: Boughton, Nisbet, Barnes & Moore, Printers, 1866.

Winter, Rev. Lovick P. "Prohibition in Georgia." *Independent* 63, July 4, 1907, 442–44.

Work, Monroe N. "Crime among the Negroes of Chicago: A Social Study." *American Journal of Sociology* 6, no. 2 (September 1900): 204–23.

Secondary Sources

Articles and Book Chapters

Armstrong, Thomas F. "Georgia Lumber Laborers, 1880–1917: The Social Implications of Work." *Georgia Historical Quarterly* 67, no. 4 (Winter 1983): 435–50.

Barclay, Jenifer. "The Greatest Degree of Perfection: Disability and the Construction of Race in American Slave Law." *South Carolina Review* 46, no. 2 (Spring 2014): 27–43.

Bauer, Alice H., and Raymond A. Bauer. "Day to Day Resistance to Slavery." *Journal of Negro History* 27 (October 1942): 388–419.

Bonner, James C. "The Georgia Penitentiary at Milledgeville, 1817–1874." *Georgia Historical Quarterly* 55, no. 3 (Fall 1971): 303–28.

Brown, Minnie Miller. "Black Women in American Agriculture." *Agricultural History* 50, no. 1 (January 1976): 202–12.

Brown, Vincent. "Social Death and Political Life in the Study of Slavery." *American Historical Review* 114, no. 5 (December 2009): 1231–49.

Butler, Anne M. "Still in Chains: Black Women in Western Prisons, 1865–1910." In *We Specialize in the Wholly Impossible: A Reader in Black Women's History*, edited by Darlene Clark Hine, Wilma King, and Linda Reed, 321–34. Brooklyn: Carson Publishing, 1995.

"Butler, Selena Sloan." In *American National Biography*, Vol. 4, edited by John A. Garraty and Mark C. Carnes, 109–10. New York: Oxford University Press, 1999.

Camp, Stephanie. "The Pleasures of Resistance: Enslaved Women and Body Politics in the Plantation South, 1830–1861." *Journal of Southern History* 69, no. 3 (August 2002): 533–72.

Carby, Hazel V. "Policing the Black Woman's Body in an Urban Context." *Critical Inquiry* 8, no. 4 (Summer 1992): 738–55.

Cardyn, Lisa. "Sexualized Racism/Gendered Violence: Outraging the Body Politic in the Reconstruction South." *Michigan Law Review* 100, no. 4 (February 2002): 675–867.

Chandler, Raymond E., Jr. "Death Comes to the Meanest Man in Georgia." *Georgia Backroads* 10, no. 2 (Summer 2011): 44–49.

Cling, B. J. "Rape and Rape Trauma Syndrome." In *Sexualized Violence against Women and Children: A Psychology and Law Perspective*, edited by B. J. Cling, 13–40. New York: Guilford Press, 2004.

Clinton, Catherine. "Bloody Terrain: Freedwomen, Sexuality and Violence during Reconstruction." *Georgia Historical Quarterly* 76, no. 2 (Summer 1992): 313–32.

Curtin, Mary Ellen. "The 'Human World' of Black Women in Alabama Prisons, 1870–1900." In *Hidden Histories of Women in the New South*, edited by Virginia Bernhard, Betty Brandon, Elizabeth Fox-Genovese, Theda Purdue, and Elizabeth Hayes Turner, 11–30. Columbia: University of Missouri Press, 1994.

Drago, Edmund. "Militancy and Black Women in Reconstruction Georgia." *Journal of American Culture* 1, no. 4 (1978): 838–44.

Drobney, Jeffrey A. "Where Palm and Pine Are Blowing: Convict Labor in the North Florida Turpentine Industry, 1877–1923." *Florida Historical Quarterly* 72, no. 4 (1994): 411–34.

Duncan, Russell. "A Georgia Governor Battles Racism: Rufus Bullock and the Fight for Black Legislators." In *Georgia in Black and White: Explorations in the Race Relations of a Southern State, 1865–1950*, edited by John Inscoe, 38–64. Athens: University of Georgia Press, 1994.

Durling, Gregory. "Female Labor, Malingering and the Abuse of Equipment under Slavery: Evidence from the Marydale Plantation." *Southern Studies* 5, nos. 1–2 (Spring–Summer 1994): 31–49.

Giesen, James C. "Cotton." *New Georgia Encyclopedia*. May 26, 2004. Retrieved August 14, 2013. http://www.georgiaencyclopedia.org/articles/business-economy/cotton.

Goldin, Claudia. "Female Labor Force Participation: The Origin of Black and White Differences, 1870 and 1880." *Journal of Economic History* 37, no. 1 (March 1977): 87–108.

Grantham, Dewey W. "Hoke Smith: Progressive Governor of Georgia, 1907–1909." *Journal of Southern History* 15, no. 4 (November 1949): 423–40.

Green, Elna C. "Infanticide and Infant Abandonment in the New South: Richmond, Virginia, 1865–1915." *Journal of Family History* 24, no. 2 (April 1999): 187–211.

Gross, Kali N. "Exploring Crime and Violence in Early-Twentieth-Century Black Women's History." In *Contesting Archives: Finding Women in the Sources*, edited by Nupur Chadhuri, Sherry J. Katz, and Mary Elizabeth Perry, 56–74. Urbana: University of Illinois Press, 2010.

Haley, Sarah. "'Like I Was a Man': Chain Gangs, Gender, and the Domestic Carceral Sphere in Jim Crow Georgia." *Signs* 39, no. 1 (Autumn 2013): 53–77.

Hall, Jacquelyn Dowd. "The Mind That Burns in Each Body: Women, Rape, and Racial Violence." In *Powers of Desire: The Politics of Sexuality*, edited by Ann Snitow, Christine Stansell, and Sharon Thompson, 328–49. New York: Monthly Review Press, 1983.

Haller, John S. "The Physician versus the Negro: Medical and Anthropological Concepts of Race in the Late Nineteenth Century." *Bulletin of the History of Medicine* 44, no. 2 (March–April 1970): 154–67.

Harley, Sharon. "For the Good of Family and Race: Gender, Work, and Domestic Roles in the Black Community, 1880–1930." *Signs* 15, no. 2 (Winter 1990): 336–49.

———. "Mary Church Terrell: Genteel Militant." In *Black Leaders of the Nineteenth Century*, edited by Leon Litwack and August Meier, 307–22. Urbana: University of Illinois Press, 1988.

———. "When Your Work Is Not Who You Are: The Development of a Working-Class Consciousness among Afro-American Women." In *Gender, Class, Race, and Reform in the Progressive Era*, edited by Noralee Frankel and Nancy S. Dye, 42–55. Lexington: University Press of Kentucky, 1991.

———. "'Working for Nothing but for a Living': Black Women in the Underground Economy." In *Sister Circle: Black Women and Work*, edited by Sharon Harley and the Black Women and Work Collective, 48–66. New Brunswick, N.J.: Rutgers University Press, 2002.

Harris, Carl V. "Reforms in Government Control of Negroes in Birmingham, Alabama, 1890–1920." In *Black Southerners and the Law, 1865–1900*, edited by Donald G. Nieman, 105–38. New York: Garland Publishing, 1994.

Harris, LaShawn. "'The Commonwealth of Virginia vs. Virginia Christian': Southern Black Women, Crime & Punishment in Progressive Era Virginia." *Journal of Social History* 47, no. 4 (Summer 2014): 922–42.

Harris, William. "Work and the Family in Black Atlanta, 1880." *Journal of Social History* 9, no. 3 (Spring 1976): 319–30.

Hartman, Saidiya. "Venus in Two Acts." *Small Axe* 12, no. 2 (June 2008): 1–14.

Hickey, Georgina. "Waging War on 'Loose Living Hotels' and 'Cheap Soda Water Joints': The Criminalization of Working-Class Women in Atlanta's Public Space." *Georgia Historical Quarterly* 82, no. 4 (Winter 1998): 775–800.

Higginbotham, Evelyn. "African American Women's History and the Metalanguage of Race." *Signs* 17, no. 2 (Winter 1992): 251–74.

Hine, Darlene Clark. "African American Women and Their Communities in the Twentieth Century." *Black Women, Gender & Families* 1, no. 1 (Spring 2007): 1–23.

———. "Female Slave Resistance: The Economics of Sex." In *Hine Sight: Black Women and the Re-Construction of American History*, 27–36. Brooklyn: Carlson Publishing, 1994.

———. "Lifting the Veil, Shattering the Silence: Black Women's History in Slavery and Freedom." In *Hine Sight: Black Women and the Re-Construction of American History*, 3–26. Brooklyn: Carlson Publishing, 1994.

———. "Rape and the Inner Lives of Black Women: Thoughts on the Culture of Dissemblance." In *Hine Sight: Black Women and the Re-Construction of American History*, 37–47. Brooklyn: Carlson Publishing, 1994.

Hunt, Patricia. "Clothing as an Expression of History: The Dress of African American Women in Georgia, 1880–1915." In *We Specialize in the Wholly Impossible: A Reader in Black Women's History*, edited by Darlene Clark Hine, Wilma King, and Linda Reed, 393–404. Brooklyn: Carlson Publishing, 1995.

———. "The Struggle to Achieve Individual Expression through Clothing and Adornment: African American Women under and after Slavery." In *Discovering the Women in Slavery*, edited by Patricia Morton, 227–40. Athens: University of Georgia Press, 1996.

Hunter, Tera. "The 'Brotherly Love' for Which This City Is Proverbial Should Extend to All: The Everyday Lives of Working-Class Women in Philadelphia and Atlanta in the 1890s." In *The African American Urban Experience: Perspectives from the Colonial Period to the Present*, edited by Joe W. Trotter, Earl Lewis, and Tera W. Hunter, 76–98. New York: Palgrave MacMillan, 2004.

———. "Domination and Resistance: The Politics of Wage Household Labor in New South Atlanta." *Labor History* 34, nos. 2–3 (1993): 205–20.

———. "'Work That Body': African American Women, Work, and Leisure in Atlanta and the New South." In *The Black Worker: A Reader*, edited by Eric Arnesen, 72–93. Urbana: University of Illinois, 2007.

Jones, Beverly. "Mary Church Terrell and the National Association of Colored Women, 1896–1901." *Journal of Negro History* 67, no. 1 (Spring 1982): 20–33.

Jones, Jacqueline. "'My Mother Was Much of a Woman': Black Women, Work, and the Family under Slavery." *Feminist Studies* 8, no. 2 (Summer 1982): 235–69.

LeFlouria, Talitha L. "'The Hand That Rocks the Cradle Cuts Cordwood': Exploring Black Women's Lives and Labor in Georgia's Convict Camps, 1865–1917." *Labor: Studies in Working-Class History of the Americas* 8, no. 3 (Fall 2011): 47–63.

———. "Mary Church Terrell." In *Encyclopedia of African-American History*, edited by Leslie Alexander and Walter Rucker, 1048–50. Santa Barbara: ABC-CLIO, 2010.

Lewis, Ronald L. "African American Convicts in the Coal Mines of Southern Appalachia." In *Appalachians and Race: The Mountain South from Slavery to*

Segregation, edited by John Inscoe, 259–83. Lexington: University Press of Kentucky, 2001.

Lichtenstein, Alex. "Chain Gangs, Communism, and the 'Negro Question': John L. Spivak's Georgia Nigger." *Georgia Historical Quarterly* 79, no. 3 (Fall 1995): 633–58.

———. "Good Roads and Chain Gangs in the Progressive South: The Negro Convict Is a Slave." *Journal of Southern History* 59, no. 1 (February 1993): 85–110.

———. "That Disposition to Theft, with Which They Have Been Branded': Moral Economy, Slave Management, and the Law." *Journal of Social History* 21, no. 3 (Spring 1988): 413–40.

Long, LaDonna, and Sarah E. Ullman. "The Impact of Multiple Traumatic Victimization on Disclosure and Coping Mechanisms for Black Women." *Feminist Criminology* 8, no. 4 (July 2013): 295–319.

Mancini, Matthew. "Race, Economics, and the Abandonment of Convict Leasing." *Journal of Negro History* 63, no. 4 (October 1978): 339–52.

Mann, Susan. "Slavery, Sharecropping, and Sexual Inequality." *Signs* 14, no. 4 (Summer 1989): 774–98.

McCluskey, Audrey. "Setting the Standard: Mary Church Terrell's Last Campaign for Social Justice." *Black Scholar* 29, nos. 2–3 (Summer–Fall 1999): 47–53.

Perrin, Liese M. "Resisting Reproduction: Reconsidering Slave Contraception in the Old South." *Journal of American Studies* 35, no. 2 (August 2001): 255–74.

Ramey, Daina L. "'She Do a Heap of Work': Female Slave Labor on Glynn County Rice and Cotton Plantations." *Georgia Historical Quarterly* 82, no. 4 (Winter 1998): 707–34.

Schwartz, Marie Jenkins. "'At Noon, Oh How I Ran': Breastfeeding and Weaning on Plantation and Farm in Antebellum Virginia and Alabama." In *Discovering the Women in Slavery Emancipating Perspectives on the American Past*, edited by Patricia Morton, 241–59. Athens: University of Georgia Press, 1996.

Scott, Anne Firor. "The Most Invisible of All: Black Women's Voluntary Associations." *Journal of Southern History* 56, no. 1 (1990): 3–22.

Shaw, Stephanie. "Black Club Women and the Creation of the National Association of Colored Women." *Journal of Women's History* 3, no. 2 (Fall 1991): 11–25.

Sheffield, Carol J. "Sexual Terrorism: The Social Control of Women." In *Analyzing Gender: A Handbook of Social Science Research*, edited by Beth B. Hess and Myra Marx Ferree, 171–89. Newbury: Sage, 1987.

Soet, Johanna E., Gregory Brack, and Colleen Dilorio. "The Prevalence and Predictors of Women's Experience of Psychological Trauma during Childbirth." *Birth: Issues in Perinatal Care* 30, no. 1 (March 2003): 36–46.

Taylor, Elizabeth A. "The Abolition of the Convict Lease System in Georgia." *Georgia Historical Quarterly* 26 (June 1942): 273–87.

Terborg-Penn, Rosalyn. "Survival Strategies among African-American Women Workers: A Continuing Process." In *Women, Work & Protest: A Century of*

U.S. Women's Labor History, edited by Ruth Milkman, 139–55. Boston: Routledge and Kegan Paul, 1985.

Weis, Kurt, and Sandra S. Borges. "Victimology and Rape: The Case of the Legitimate Victim." *Issues in Criminology* 8, no. 2 (Fall 1973): 71–115.

Welter, Barbara. "The Cult of True Womanhood: 1820–1860." *American Quarterly* 18, no. 2 (Summer 1966): 151–74.

Whites, LeeAnn. "Rebecca Latimer Felton and the Wife's Farm: The Class and Racial Politics of Gender Reform." *Georgia Historical Quarterly* 76, no. 2 (Summer 1992): 354–72.

———. "Rebecca Latimer Felton: The Problem of Protection in the New South." In *Georgia Women: Their Lives and Times*, edited by Ann Short Chirhart and Betty Wood, 224–43. Athens: University of Georgia Press, 2009.

Winkler, Cathy. "Rape as Social Murder." *Anthropology Today* 7, no. 3 (June 1991): 12–14.

Womack, Carlise E. "Selena Sloan Butler." *New Georgia Encyclopedia*. April 15, 2005. Retrieved August 8, 2013. http://www.georgiaencyclopedia.org/articles /history-archaeology/selena-sloan-butler-ca-1872-1964.

Zimmerman, Jane. "The Penal Reform Movement in the South during the Progressive Era, 1890–1917." *Journal of Southern History* 17, no. 4 (November 1951): 462–92.

Books

Aiken, Charles S. *The Cotton Plantation South since the Civil War*. Baltimore: Johns Hopkins University Press, 1998.

Armstrong, Julie Buckner. *Mary Turner and the Memory of Lynching*. Athens: University of Georgia Press, 2011.

Ayers, Edward L. *The Promise of the New South: Life after Reconstruction*. New York: Oxford University Press, 1992.

———. *Vengeance and Justice: Crime and Punishment in the 19th-Century American South*. New York: Oxford University Press, 1984.

Baker, Lee. *From Savage to Negro: Anthropology and the Construction of Race, 1896–1954*. Berkeley: University of California Press, 1998.

Bauerlein, Mark. *Negrophobia: A Race Riot in Atlanta, 1906*. San Francisco: Encounter Books, 2001.

Becker, Peter, and Richard Wetzell, eds. *Criminals and Their Scientists: Essays on the History of Criminology*. Cambridge: Cambridge University Press, 2006.

Beeson, Leola Selman. *History Stories of Milledgeville and Baldwin County*. Macon, Ga.: J. W. Burke, 1943.

Berry, Daina Ramey. *"Swing the Sickle for the Harvest Is Ripe": Gender and Slavery in Antebellum Georgia*. Urbana: University of Illinois Press, 2007.

Blackmon, Douglas A. *Slavery by Another Name: The Re-Enslavement of Black People in America from the Civil War to World War II*. New York: Doubleday, 2008.

Blackwelder, Julia Kirk. *Now Hiring: The Feminization of Work in the United States, 1900–1995*. College Station: Texas A&M University Press, 1997.

Blair, Cynthia. *I've Got to Make My Livin': Black Women's Sex Work in Turn-of-the-Century Chicago*. Chicago: University of Chicago Press, 2010.

Bonner, James C. *A History of Georgia Agriculture, 1732–1860*. Athens: University of Georgia Press, 1964.

———. *Milledgeville: Georgia's Antebellum Capital*. Athens: University of Georgia Press, 1978.

Boster, Dea H. *African American Slavery and Disability: Bodies, Property, and Power in the Antebellum South, 1800–1860*. New York: Routledge, 2013.

Branch, Enobong Hannah. *Opportunity Denied: Limiting Black Women to Devalued Work*. New Brunswick, N.J.: Rutgers University Press, 2011.

Brundage, Fitzhugh. *Lynching in the New South: Georgia and Virginia, 1880–1930*. Urbana: University of Illinois Press, 1993.

Burns, Rebecca. *Rage in the Gate City: The History of the 1906 Atlanta Race Riot*. Cincinnati: Emmis Books, 2006.

Burns, Robert Elliot. *I Am a Fugitive from a Georgia Chain Gang*. New York: Vanguard Press, 1932.

Burns, Vincent G. *The Man Who Broke a Thousand Chains: The Story of Social Reformation of the Prisons of the South*. Washington, D.C.: Acropolis Books, 1968.

———. *Out of These Chains: Sequel to the Sensational Prison Epic: "I Am a Fugitive from a Chain Gang."* Los Angeles: New World Books, 1942.

Butler, Anne. *Gendered Justice in the American West: Women Prisoners in Men's Penitentiaries*. Urbana: University of Illinois Press, 1997.

Bynum, Victoria. *Unruly Women: The Politics of Social and Sexual Control in the Old South*. Chapel Hill: University of North Carolina Press, 1992.

Camp, Stephanie M. H. *Closer to Freedom: Enslaved Women & Everyday Resistance in the Plantation South*. Chapel Hill: University of North Carolina Press, 2004.

Carleton, Mark T. *Politics and Punishment: The History of the Louisiana State Penal System*. Baton Rouge: Louisiana State University Press, 1971.

Cimbala, Paul. *Under the Guardianship of the Nation: The Freedmen's Bureau and the Reconstruction of Georgia, 1865–1870*. Athens: University of Georgia Press, 1997.

Clark-Lewis, Elizabeth. *Living In, Living Out: African American Domestics in Washington, DC*. Washington, D.C.: Smithsonian Institution Press, 1994.

Colvin, Mark. *Penitentiaries, Reformatories, and Chain Gangs: Social Theory and the History of Punishment in Nineteenth-Century America*. New York: St. Martin's Press, 1997.

Conway, Alan. *The Reconstruction of Georgia*. Minneapolis: University of Minnesota Press, 1966.

Cook, James F. *The Governors of Georgia, 1754–2004*. 3rd ed. Macon, Ga.: Mercer University Press, 2005.

Coulter, E. Merton. *James Monroe Smith: Georgia Planter, before Death and After*. Athens: University of Georgia Press, 1961.

Curtin, Mary Ellen. *Black Prisoners and Their World: Alabama, 1865–1900*. Charlottesville: University Press of Virginia, 2000.

Daniel, Pete. *Breaking the Land: The Transformation of Cotton, Tobacco, and Rice Cultures since 1880*. Urbana: University of Illinois Press, 1985.

———. *The Shadow of Slavery: Peonage in the South, 1901–1969*. Urbana: University of Illinois Press, 1972.

Davis, Angela. *Women, Race & Class*. New York: Random House, 1981.

Davis, Harold E. *Henry Grady's New South: Atlanta a Brave and Beautiful City*. Tuscaloosa: University of Alabama Press, 1990.

Dittmer, John. *Black Georgia in the Progressive Era, 1900–1920*. Urbana: University of Illinois Press, 1977.

Downs, Jim. *Sick from Freedom: African American Illness and Suffering during the Civil War and Reconstruction*. New York: Oxford University Press, 2012.

Drago, Edmund L. *Black Politicians and Reconstruction in Georgia: A Splendid Failure*. Baton Rouge: Louisiana State University Press, 1982.

Du Bois, W. E. B. *Black Reconstruction in America*. New York: Russell & Russell, 1935.

Duncan, Russell. *Entrepreneur for Equality: Governor Rufus Bullock, Commerce, and Race in Post–Civil War Georgia*. Athens: University of Georgia Press, 1994.

Edwards, Laura. *Gendered Strife and Confusion: The Political Culture of Reconstruction*. Urbana: University of Illinois Press, 1997.

Farmer-Kaiser, Mary. *Freedwomen and the Freedmen's Bureau: Race, Gender & Public Policy in the Age of Emancipation*. New York: Fordham University Press, 2010.

Feimster, Crystal. *Southern Horrors: Women and the Politics of Lynching and Rape*. Cambridge, Mass.: Harvard University Press, 2009.

Fett, Sharla. *Working Cures: Healing, Health, and Power on Southern Slave Plantations*. Chapel Hill: University of North Carolina Press, 2002.

Fierce, Milfred. *Slavery Revisited: Blacks and the Southern Convict Lease System, 1865–1933*. New York: Africana Studies Research Center, Brooklyn College, City University of New York, 1994.

Findlay, Larry. *History of the Georgia Prison System*. Frederick, Md.: Publish America, 2007.

Fite, Gilbert. *Cotton Fields No More: Southern Agriculture, 1865–1980*. Lexington: University Press of Kentucky, 1984.

Fitzgerald, Deborah. *Every Farm a Factory: The Industrial Ideal in American Agriculture*. New Haven, Conn.: Yale University Press, 2003.

Foner, Eric. *Reconstruction: America's Unfinished Revolution, 1863–1877*. New York: Harper, 1988.

———. *Voices of Freedom: A Documentary History*. 3rd ed. New York: Norton and Company, 2010.

Franklin, John Hope, and Loren Schweninger. *Runaway Slaves: Rebels on the Plantation*. New York: Oxford University Press, 1999.

Frederickson, George M. *The Black Image in the White Mind: The Debate on Afro-American Character and Destiny, 1817–1914*. New York: Harper, 1971.

Gabbidon, Shaun L. *W. E. B. Du Bois on Crime and Justice: Laying the Foundation of Sociological Criminology*. Burlington, Vt.: Ashgate, 2007.

Gibson, Mary. *Born to Crime: Cesare Lombroso and the Origins of Biological Criminology*. Westport, Conn.: Praeger Publishers, 2002.

Giddings, Paula. *Ida: A Sword among Lions: Ida B. Wells and the Campaign against Lynching*. New York: Amistad, 2008.

———. *When and Where I Enter: The Impact of Black Women on Race and Sex in America*. New York: Bantam Books, 1984.

Grady, Henry Woodfin. *The New South: Writings and Speeches of Henry Grady*. Edited by Oliver Dyer. Savannah, Ga.: Beehive Press, 1971.

Grantham, Dewey H. *Hoke Smith and the Politics of the New South*. Baton Rouge: Louisiana State University Press, 1958.

Green Cook, Anna Maria. *History of Baldwin County, Georgia*. 1925. Reprint, Spartanburg: Reprint Co., 1992.

Greene, Helen Taylor, and Shaun Gabbidon, eds. *African American Criminological Thought*. Albany: State University of New York Press, 2000.

Gross, Kali N. *Colored Amazons: Crime, Violence, and Black Women in the City of Brotherly Love, 1880–1910*. Durham, N.C.: Duke University Press, 2006.

Hahn, Steven. *The Roots of Southern Populism: Yeoman Farmers and the Transformation of the Georgia Upcountry, 1850–1890*. New York: Oxford University Press, 1983.

Harris, Leslie M., and Daina Ramey Berry, eds. *Slavery and Freedom in Savannah*. Athens: University of Georgia Press, 2014.

Harrison, Renee K. *Enslaved Women and the Art of Resistance in Antebellum America*. New York: Palgrave MacMillan, 2009.

Hazzard-Gordon, Katrina. *Jookin': The Rise of Social Dance Formations in African American Culture*. Philadelphia: Temple University Press, 1990.

Hickey, Georgina. *Hope and Danger in the New South City: Working-Class Women and Urban Development in Atlanta, 1890–1940*. Athens: University of Georgia Press, 2003.

Hicks, Cheryl D. *Talk with You Like a Woman: African American Women, Justice, and Reform in New York, 1890–1935*. Chapel Hill: University of North Carolina Press, 2010.

Higginbotham, Evelyn. *Righteous Discontent: The Women's Movement in the Black Baptist Church, 1880–1920*. Cambridge, Mass.: Harvard University Press, 1993.

Hine, Darlene Clark. *Hine Sight: Black Women and the Re-Construction of American History*. Brooklyn: Carlson Publishing, 1994.

———. *A Shining Thread of Hope*. New York: Broadway Books, 1998.

Hine, Darlene Clark, Kathleen Thompson, Wilma King, and Linda Reed, eds. *We Specialize in the Wholly Impossible: A Reader in Black Women's History*. Brooklyn: Carson Publishing, 1995.

Hodes, Martha. *White Women, Black Men: Illicit Sex in the 19th-Century South*. New Haven, Conn.: Yale University Press, 1997.

Hunter, Tera. *To 'Joy My Freedom: Southern Black Women's Lives and Labors after the Civil War*. Cambridge, Mass.: Harvard University Press, 1997.

Ingram, Tammy. *Dixie Highway: Road Building and the Making of the Modern South*. Chapel Hill: University of North Carolina Press, 2014.

Inscoe, John. *Georgia in Black and White: Explorations in the Race Relations of a Southern State, 1865–1950.* Athens: University of Georgia Press, 1994.

Janiewski, Dolores E. *Sisterhood Denied: Race, Gender, and Class in a New South Community.* Philadelphia: Temple University Press, 1985.

Jones, Jacqueline. *Labor of Love, Labor of Sorrow: Black Women, Work, and the Family from Slavery to the Present.* New York: First Vintage Books, 1986.

Jones, William P. *The Tribe of Black Ulysses: African American Lumber Workers in the Jim Crow South.* Urbana: University of Illinois Press, 2005.

Kane, Sharyn, and Richard Keeton. *Beneath These Waters: Archeological and Historical Studies of 11,500 Years along the Savannah River.* Administered by the Interagency Archeological Services Division, National Park Service, Southeast Region, Atlanta, Ga. Washington, D.C.: National Park Service, 1993.

Katzman, David M. *Seven Days a Week: Women and Domestic Service in Industrializing America.* New York: Oxford University Press, 1978.

Kelley, Robin D. G. *Race Rebels: Culture, Politics, and the Black Working Class.* New York: Free Press, 1994.

Kessler-Harris, Alice. *Gendering Labor History.* Urbana: University of Illinois Press, 2007.

———. *Out to Work: A History of Wage-Earning Women in the United States.* New York: Oxford University Press, 1983.

———. *Women Have Always Worked: An Historical Overview.* New York: Feminist Press at CUNY, 1993.

Kirby, Jack Temple. *Darkness at Dawning: Race and Reform in the Progressive South.* Philadelphia: Lippincott, 1972.

Kolko, Gabriel. *Railroads and Regulation, 1877–1916.* Westport, Conn.: Greenwood Press, 1965.

Kuhn, Clifford M. *Contesting the New South Order: The 1914–1915 Strike at Atlanta's Fulton Mills.* Chapel Hill: University of North Carolina Press, 2001.

Larsen, Lawrence H. *The Rise of the Urban South.* Lexington: University Press of Kentucky, 1985.

———. *The Urban South: A History.* Lexington: University Press of Kentucky, 1990.

Lerner, Gerda, ed. *Black Women in White America: A Documentary History.* New York: Vintage Books, 1973.

Lewis, David Levering. *W. E. B. Du Bois: Biography of a Race, 1868–1919.* New York: Henry Holt and Company, 1993.

Lichtenstein, Alex. *Twice the Work of Free Labor: The Political Economy of Convict Labor in the New South.* New York: Verso, 1996.

Logan, Rayford W. *The Negro in American Life and Thought: The Nadir, 1877–1901.* New York: Dial Press, 1954.

Long, Gretchen. *Doctoring Freedom: The Politics of African American Medical Care in Slavery and Emancipation.* Chapel Hill: University of North Carolina Press, 2012.

Malone, Jacqui. *Steppin' on the Blues: The Visible Rhythms of African American Dance.* Urbana: University of Illinois Press, 1996.

Mancini, Matthew. *One Dies, Get Another: Convict Leasing in the American South, 1866–1928.* Columbia: University of South Carolina Press, 1996.

McCandless, Peter. *Slavery, Disease, and Suffering in the Southern Lowcountry*. New York: Cambridge University Press, 2011.

McGregor, Deborah Kuhn. *From Midwives to Medicine: The Birth of American Gynecology*. New Brunswick, N.J.: Rutgers University Press, 1998.

McGuire, Danielle. *At the Dark End of the Street: Black Women, Rape, and Resistance—A New History of the Civil Rights Movement from Rosa Parks to the Rise of Black Power*. New York: Vintage Books, 2010.

McIntosh, John H. *The Official History of Elbert County, 1790–1935*. Elberton, Ga.: Stephen Heard Chapter of the Daughters of the American Revolution, 1940.

McLennan, Rebecca M. *The Crisis of Imprisonment: Protest, Politics, and the Making of the American Penal State, 1776–1941*. Cambridge: Cambridge University Press, 2008.

McLeod, Jonathan W. *Workers and Workplace Dynamics in Reconstruction-Era Atlanta: A Case Study*. Los Angeles: Center for Afro-American Studies, University of California, 1989.

Miller, Vivien L. *Crime, Sexual Violence, and Clemency: Florida's Pardon Board and Penal System in the Progressive Era*. Gainesville: University Press of Florida, 2000.

———. *Hard Labor and Hard Time: Florida's "Sunshine Prison" and Chain Gangs*. Gainesville: University Press of Florida, 2012.

Mixon, Gregory. *The Atlanta Riot: Race, Class, and Violence in a New South City*. Gainesville: University Press of Florida, 2005.

Monkkonen, Eric H., ed. *Crime & Justice in American History: The South, Pt. 1*. New York: K. G. Saur, 1992.

———. *Crime & Justice in American History: The South, Pt. 2*. New York: K. G. Saur, 1992.

Morgan, Jennifer L. *Laboring Women: Reproduction and Gender in New World Slavery*. Philadelphia: University of Pennsylvania Press, 2004.

Muhammad, Khalil. *The Condemnation of Blackness: Race, Crime, and the Making of Modern Urban America*. Cambridge: Harvard University Press, 2010.

Myers, Martha. *Race, Labor, and Punishment in the New South*. Columbus: Ohio State University Press, 1998.

Nathans, Elizabeth Studley. *Losing the Peace: Georgia Republicans and Reconstruction, 1865–1871*. Baton Rouge: Louisiana State University Press, 1968.

Nixon, Raymond B. *Henry W. Grady, Spokesman of the New South*. New York: Knopf, 1943.

Nolen, Claude H. *The Negro's Image in the South: The Anatomy of White Supremacy*. Lexington: University Press of Kentucky, 1967.

O'Donovan, Susan Eva. *Becoming Free in the Cotton South*. Cambridge: Harvard University Press, 2007.

Ortiz, Paul. *Emancipation Betrayed: The Hidden History of Black Organizing and White Violence in Florida from Reconstruction to the Bloody Election of 1920*. Berkeley: University of California Press, 2005.

Oshinsky, David M. *"Worse Than Slavery": Parchman Farm and the Ordeal of Jim Crow Justice*. New York: Simon and Schuster, 1996.

Palmer, Phyllis M. *Domesticity and Dirt: Housewives and Domestic Servants.* Philadelphia: Temple University Press, 1989.

Patterson, Orlando. *Slavery and Social Death: A Comparative Study.* Cambridge: Cambridge University Press, 1982.

Perdue, Robert E. *The Negro in Savannah, 1865–1900.* New York: Exposition Press, 1973.

Perkinson, Robert. *Texas Tough: The Rise of America's Prison Empire.* New York: Picador, 2010.

Preston, Howard Lawrence. *Dirt Roads to Dixie: Accessibility and Modernization in the South, 1885–1935.* Knoxville: University of Tennessee Press, 1991.

Rabinowitz, Howard N. *The First New South, 1865–1920.* Arlington Heights, Ill.: Harlan Davidson, 1992.

———. *Race Relations in the Urban South, 1865–1890.* New York: Oxford University Press, 1978.

Rafter, Nicole Hahn. *Creating Born Criminals.* Urbana: University of Illinois Press, 1998.

———. *Partial Justice: Women, Prisons, and Social Control.* New Brunswick, N.J.: Transaction Publishers, 1990.

Rawick, George P., ed. *The American Slave: A Composite Autobiography.* Supplement, Series 2, Vol. 13, Georgia Narratives, Part 4. Westport, Conn.: Greenwood Press, 1977.

Reynolds, Scott. *Iron Confederacies: Southern Railways, Klan Violence, and Reconstruction.* Chapel Hill: University of North Carolina Press, 1999.

Roberts, Derrell C. *Joseph E. Brown and the Politics of Reconstruction.* Alabama: University of Alabama Press, 1973.

Roberts, Dorothy. *Killing the Black Body: Race, Reproduction, and the Meaning of Liberty.* New York: Pantheon Books, 1997.

Roberts, Samuel Kelton. *Infectious Fear: Politics, Disease, and the Health Effects of Segregation.* Chapel Hill: University of North Carolina Press, 2009.

Rosen, Hannah. *Terror in the Heart of Freedom: Citizenship, Sexual Violence, and the Meaning of Race in the Postemancipation South.* Chapel Hill: University of North Carolina Press, 2009.

Russell, James Michael. *Atlanta, 1847–1890: City Building in the Old South and the New.* Baton Rouge: Louisiana State University Press, 1988.

Savitt, Todd. *Medicine and Slavery: The Diseases and Health Care of Blacks in Antebellum Virginia.* Urbana: University of Illinois Press, 1978.

———. *Race and Medicine in Nineteenth-Century and Early Twentieth-Century America.* Kent, Ohio: Kent State University Press, 2006.

Schwartz, Marie Jenkins. *Birthing a Slave: Motherhood and Medicine in the Antebellum South.* Cambridge, Mass.: Harvard University Press, 2006.

Scott, James C. *Domination and the Arts of Resistance: Hidden Transcripts.* New Haven, Conn.: Yale University Press, 1990.

Shapiro, Karin A. *A New South Rebellion: The Battle against Convict Labor in the Tennessee Coalfields, 1871–1896.* Chapel Hill: University of North Carolina Press, 1998.

Sommerville, Diane Miller. *Rape & Race in the Nineteenth-Century South*. Chapel Hill: University of North Carolina Press, 2004.

Staman, A. Louise. *Loosening Corsets: The Heroic Life of Georgia's Feisty Mrs. Felton, First Woman Senator of the United States*. Macon, Ga.: Tiger Iron Press, 2006.

Stearns, Marshal Winslow, and Jean Stearns. *Jazz Dance: The Story of American Vernacular Dance*. New York: Da Capo Press, 1994.

Stowe, Steven. *Doctoring the South: Southern Physicians and Everyday Medicine in the Mid-Nineteenth Century*. Chapel Hill: University of North Carolina Press, 2004.

Summers, Mark W. *Railroads, Reconstruction, and the Gospel of Prosperity: Aid under the Radical Republicans, 1865–1877*. Princeton, N.J.: Princeton University Press, 1984.

Talmadge, John E. *Rebecca Latimer Felton: Nine Stormy Decades*. Athens: University of Georgia Press, 1960.

Taylor, William Banks. *Down on Parchman Farm: The Great Prison in the Mississippi Delta*. Columbus: Ohio State University Press, 1999.

Thompson, Mildred I. *Ida B. Wells-Barnett: An Exploratory Study of an American Black Woman, 1893–1930*. Brooklyn: Carlson Publishing, 1990.

Waldrep, Christopher, and Donald G. Nieman, eds. *Local Matters: Race, Crime, and Justice in the Nineteenth-Century South*. Athens: University of Georgia Press, 2001.

Walker, Donald R. *Penology for Profit: A History of the Texas Prison System, 1867–1912*. College Station: Texas A&M University Press, 1988.

Ward, Geoffrey. *The Black Child-Savers: Racial Democracy and Juvenile Justice*. Chicago: University of Chicago Press, 2012.

Ward, Robert David, and William Warren Rogers. *Convicts, Coal, and the Banner Mine Tragedy*. Tuscaloosa: University of Alabama Press, 1987.

Weiner, Marli Frances. *Sex, Sickness, and Slavery: Defining Illness in the Antebellum South*. Urbana: University of Illinois Press, 2012.

West, Traci C. *Wounds of the Spirit: Black Women, Violence, and Resistance Ethics*. New York: New York University Press, 1999.

White, Deborah Gray. *Arn't I A Woman?: Female Slaves in the Plantation South*. New York: Norton and Company, 1985.

———. *Too Heavy a Load: Black Women in Defense of Themselves, 1894–1994*. New York: Norton and Company, 1999.

Whites, LeeAnn. *Gender Matters: Civil War, Reconstruction, and the Making of the New South*. New York: Palgrave MacMillan, 2005.

Williams, Kidada E. *They Left Great Marks on Me: African American Testimonies of Racial Violence from Emancipation to World War I*. New York: New York University Press, 2012.

Williams, Rhonda Y. *The Politics of Public Housing: Black Women's Struggles against Urban Inequality*. New York: Oxford University Press, 2005.

Williamson, Joel. *The Crucible of Race: Black–White Relations in the American South since Emancipation*. New York: Oxford University Press, 1984.

Woodward, C. Vann. *Origins of the New South, 1877–1913*. Baton Rouge: Louisiana University Press, 1951.

Wright, Gavin. *Old South, New South: Revolutions in the Southern Economy since the Civil War*. New York: Basic Books, 1986.

Wynne, Lewis Nicholas. *The Continuity of Cotton: Planter Politics in Georgia, 1865–1892*. Macon, Ga.: Mercer University Press, 1986.

Yee, Shirley J. *Black Women Abolitionists: A Study in Activism, 1828–1860*. Knoxville: University of Tennessee Press, 1992.

Zieger, Robert H. *For Jobs and Freedom: Race and Labor in America since 1865*. Lexington: University Press of Kentucky, 2007.

Dissertations and Theses

Berry, David Charles. "Free Labor He Found Unsatisfactory: James W. English and Convict Lease Labor at the Chattahoochee Brick Company." Master's thesis, Georgia State University, 1991.

Gillispie, Elizabeth A. "An Examination of an Ice House at Old Town Plantation." Master's thesis, Georgia Southern University, 2006.

LeFlouria, Talitha. "Convict Women and Their Quest for Humanity: Examining Patterns of Race, Class, and Gender in Georgia's Convict Lease and Chain Gang Systems, 1865–1917." Ph.D. diss., Howard University, 2009.

Maclachlan, Gretchen Ehrmann. "Women's Work: Atlanta's Industrialization, and Urbanization, 1879–1929." Ph.D. diss., Emory University, 1992.

Nelson, Julie R. "Have We a Cause: The Life of Helen Pitts Douglass, 1838–1903." Master's thesis, Shippensburg University, 1995.

Russell, James Duncan. "Rufus Brown Bullock, Reconstruction and the 'New South,' 1834–1907: An Exploration into Race, Class, Party, and the Corruption of the American Creed." Ph.D. diss., University of Georgia, 1988.

Sheftall, John McKay. "Ogeechee Old Town: The Story of a Georgia Plantation." Master's thesis, University of Virginia, 1980.

Taylor, Elizabeth A. "The Convict Lease System in Georgia, 1866–1908." Master's thesis, University of North Carolina, 1940.

Walden, Mary Patricia. "History of the Georgia Penitentiary at Milledgeville, 1817–1868." Master's thesis, Georgia State University, 1974.

Index

Page numbers in italic type indicate illustrations. Page numbers followed by *t* indicate tables.

142–44, 173; death rate from, 55; diminished popularity of, 174; disease and, 18, 80, 94–97, 115, 128–30; economic rewards of, 74; end of, 139, 147, 171, 172, 175; farm work and, 12, 109–15, 116–19, 146, 174; as free labor competition, 173–74; Georgia limitation of, 147; Georgia origins of, 9–10, 19, 65–67; important functions of, 67; industries using, 9, 10–13, 67–82, 174; investigations of, 70–71, 80–81, 103–5; number of felons in (1869–1908), 11t; operating years of (1868–1908), 10; profitability of, 74, 141; racist basis of, 18; rationale behind, 59–60; slavery compared with, 8, 20, 55, 59–62, 98, 123, 190; sociological impact of, 81; three-tiered approach to, 12; "whipping reports" and, 16

Cooks, 32, 34, 49; convict lease system and, 61, 76, 84, 85, 91, 113, 131; prison revenge ploys by, 119

Corporal punishment. *See* Flogging; Punishment

Cotton, 156–58; black female picking skill, 112; crop diversification and, 157–58; price crash, 139; production of, 25, 109, 110, 111–15, *111*, 140, 146; textile mills, 64, 121–22; worker exploitation, 57–58

Cotton gin, 113, 133

Coulter, Ellis Merton, 117

Cowan, "Boss," 107

Cracker factories, 64

Cranial measurement, 7

Crawford, Mattie, 4, 5, 84, 88, 134; blacksmith skill of, 4, 5, 84–85, 159, 160

Crime: black uplift response to, 53–55; Georgia misdemeanor arrests and convictions, 176, 177–78t, 178–81; racialized and gendered theories of, 14, 17–18, 22–23, 37–41, 45–50, 52–54,

59–60, 69, 126, 178–79; socioeconomic pressures and, 17–18, 41–45, 54–56, 178; types of women felons' convictions, 10, 35–36, 126, 179; unfair sentencing and, 54; urban misdemeanor arrests and imprisonments, 178–81. *See also* Chain gangs; Convict leasing; Prison farms

Crime of Crimes, The (Keeler), 145

Criminal anthropology, 45–46

"Criminal class" belief, 54

Criminal Woman (Lombroso), 45

Crisp County, Ga., 30

Crittenden, Caroline, 112, 116, 127–28

Crops, diversification of, 157–58. *See also* Agricultural production; Cotton; Fieldwork

Cross-dressing (females in male clothes), 4, 5, 14, 85, 88–89, 90, 91, 93, 103, 133, 159, 160, 181–82

Crow, Will, 34

"Cult of True Womanhood," 90, 126

Cureton, Hubbard, 71

Curry, Joe, 184, 185

Cursing, 14, 86, 119, 180

Curtin, Mary Ellen, 7, 91, 101; *Black Prisoners and Their World*, 7

Cuyler, Annie, 185

Dade Coal Company, 5, 10–11, 74–75, 76, 132

Dade County, Ga., 21, 73, 75

Dance halls, 92–93

Daniel, Nora, 87, 91, 107

David, Mary, 150

Davidson, Olivia, 52–54

Davis, James R., 169–70

Davis, Mattie, 185

Davison, Chairman (of Georgia prison farm), 140–41

Death, 114, 182; Camp Heardmont prisoners, 103, 128–30, 129–30t; from childbirth, 103, 118; convict clemency incurable conditions, 168–70, 184–88; convict coal mine laborers,

76; convict leasing rate, 55; of infants, 99–100, 103, 133; tuberculosis, 94. *See also* Infant deaths; Infanticide; Murder

Debt peonage, 25–26, 52

Decatur Street (Atlanta, Ga.), 179–80

Defeminization, 14, 18–19, 76, 85, 88, 90–92, 93, 103, 105, 127–28, 133–34, 141, 146, 159, 160, 181–82

DeKalb County, Ga., 144

Depressions (economic), 139, 174, 188, 191

DeVaney, Jesse, 70–71

Deviance theory, 22–23, 59–60

Dickson, William Thomas, 74–75

Diet, 59, 80, 118, 161. *See also* Food

Disease and disabilities, 4, 18, 19, 61, 80, 94–97, 119, 128–30, 138, 182; clemency applications, 168–71, 173, 184–87; criminalization of, 46, 48–50, 59; feigning of, 137–38, 139; fieldwork and, 115–16; gynecological disorders, 95–97, 113–14, 116; infections and, 115, 116; injuries and, 95, 116, 128–30, 129–30t, 133; post-traumatic stress disorder and, 43–44; racist view of, 48–50; sexual transmission of, 49–50, 116; tuberculosis, 49, 50, 94; worked performed by prisoners with, 167–68. *See also* Doctors; Medical treatment

Disenfranchisement, 178

Disorderly conduct, 33, 178, 179, 180–81

Dissemblance, art of, 79

Dissent. *See* Resistance

Dives, 92

Dixon, Sarah, 170, 171

Doctors (prison camp), 12–13, 113, 115–16, 138, 139; annual reports of, 15, 16; clemency applications and, 168–69, 173, 184, 186; gynecological disorder treatments by, 13–14;

95–97; infant mortality and, 99–100; mediocre training of, 13; prisoner feigned illness and, 138; as sexual marauders, 113–14. *See also* Medical treatment

Dog handlers, 160

Domestic disputes, 38, 39–40

Domesticity, cult of, 143. *See also* "True Womanhood"

Domestic service, 6, 31–37; abuses by employers, 15, 33; female convict assignments, 12, 91–93, 113, 149, 150; as freedwomen's option, 14–15, 31–33, 63, 64; as master-slave relation, 32; occupational hazards of, 33; in prison farm hierarchy, 159; stealing and, 33–35, 87

Dooly County, Ga., 30, 187

Dougherty County, Ga., 24, 58, 188

Douglass, Frederick, 142

Douglass, Helen Pitts, 142–43

Dozier, Dr., 168–69

Drayton Street (Savannah, Ga.), 180

Dress. *See* Clothing

Drinking, 56, 179, 180. *See also* Liquor laws

Drinks, Fannie, 130

Dropsy (edema), 94

Du Bois, W. E. B., 22–23, 54–56; *Some Notes on Negro Crime,* 55

Durham Coal and Coke, 82

Dyer, Dallas, 27

Dykes, Mary, 187–88

Dysmenorrhea, 95, 96, 116

Ear cropping, 65

Eason, Thomas, 149, 155–56, 175

Echols, Dilly, 130, 136

Economic oppression. *See* Socioeconomic forces

Education: female prisoner levels of, 155; of juvenile prisoners, 167. *See also* Illiteracy

Edwards, Laura, 85

Edwards, Sarah, 180

Segregation (Jim Crow), 126, 165, 168, 178; Atlanta districts, 31; of juvenile offenders, 165, 166–67; legal code of, 52; southern legalization of, 52

Servants. *See* Domestic service

Sex crimes. *See* Prostitution; Rape

Sex organs, beliefs about anatomical structure of, 50–51

Sexual assault. *See* Rape; Sexualized violence

Sexual deviance, 18

Sexuality: black middle-class uplift and, 56; racist stereotypes about, 28, 49, 50–51, 52, 59, 77–78

Sexualized violence, 13, 14, 15, 50, 51, 59, 105; assaults on black female prisoners, 9, 28, 29, 61, 69, 71–72, 77–79, 113, 143, 146, 182; emotional impact of, 78–79; Ku Klux Klan and, 27–29; Old and New South and, 8. *See also* Rape

Sexually transmitted diseases, 49–50, 116

Sexual purity, 56

Sexual relations: bartering of, 132; consensual between prisoners, 100, 101; interracial, 26, 37, 50, 133, 145. *See also* Pregnancy and childbirth; Rape

Sex work. *See* Prostitution

Sharecroppers, 23–26, 25, 109

Shaw, Mrs. Edward, 34

Shelton, Mary Lou, 34

Sherman's raid, 63

Shermantown (Atlanta black neighborhood), 31

Shoe manufacture, 64

Sickness. *See* Disease and disabilities

Simpson, Joe, 38

Simpson, W. W., 73

Sims, Rosa, 179

Singing. *See* Song

Skilled work, 4, 9, 19, 64, 67, 69, 84–85, 159, 160, 168, 191, 204 (n. 84), 207 (n. 16)

Skin conditions, 94

Skin tone. *See* Colorism

Slave narratives, 137

Slavery: black women's bodies and, 89; community experience of, 124; convict labor as form of, 8–9, 20, 55, 59–60, 123, 190; cotton production and, 109, 110; as criminal punishment, 66; emancipation and, 27, 47, 67; experience in chain gang vs., 190; feminine identity and, 89; former drivers as convict whipping bosses, 114; healing rituals and, 137; "jumping the broom" wedding rite and, 106; kinship ties and, 23; legend of Mattox cruelty and, 120–21; miscegenation and, 145; nongendered work and, 69; paternalism and, 46; physical disabilities from, 116; polygenist justification for, 47; postbellum transition from, 15, 27, 32, 47, 56, 57, 67, 89 (*see also* Freedpeople; Freedwomen); property rights and, 78; rape law excluded from, 28, 78; sharecropping as vestige of, 25–26; as social death, 81; theft and, 87; women fieldworkers and, 109, 111–32; women's reproductive value and, 8, 14, 98–99, 100, 138, 190

Smith, Hampton, 30

Smith, James Milton, 72–73

Smith, James Monroe, 116–19

Smith, Paul, 106

Smith, T. J., 73

Smith, William E., 113, 114, 115

Smithsonia prison camp, 116–19

Smoky Row district (Dougherty County, Ga.), 58

Social activism, 143

Social anarchy, 17

Social control, 176–81; racist and sexist implications of, 180

Social death, 81–82

Social oppression, 23